DOUBLE
OUTSIDERS

HOW WOMEN OF COLOR CAN SUCCEED IN CORPORATE AMERICA

JESSICA FAYE CARTER, J.D., MBA

America's Career Publisher™

Double Outsiders

© 2007 by Jessica Faye Carter

Published by JIST Works, an imprint of JIST Publishing, Inc.
8902 Otis Avenue
Indianapolis, IN 46216-1033
Phone: 1-800-648-JIST   Fax: 1-800-JIST-FAX   E-mail: info@jist.com

Visit our Web site at **www.jist.com** for information on JIST, free job search tips, book chapters, and ordering instructions for our many products!

> Quantity discounts are available for JIST books. Have future editions of JIST books automatically delivered to you on publication through our convenient standing order program. Please call our Sales Department at 1-800-648-5478 for a free catalog and more information.

Trade Product Manager: Lori Cates Hand
Cover and Interior Designer: Trudy Coler
Cover Photo: Jon Feingersh/Masterfile
Page Layout: Toi Davis, Marie Kristine Parial-Leonardo
Proofreaders: Linda Seifert, Jeanne Clark
Indexer: Kelly D. Henthorne

Printed in the United States of America
12 11 10 09 08 07   9 8 7 6 5 4 3 2 1

Library of Congress Cataloging-in-Publication data is on file with the Library of Congress.

We have been careful to provide accurate information in this book, but it is possible that errors and omissions have been introduced. Please consider this in making any career plans or other important decisions. Trust your own judgment above all else and in all things.

Trademarks: All brand names and product names used in this book are trade names, service marks, trademarks, or registered trademarks of their respective owners.

ISBN 978-1-59357-386-7

About This Book

Double Outsiders: How Women of Color Can Succeed in Corporate America is a comprehensive guide to the professional and personal challenges facing women of color in today's workplace. These women of color—African-American, Latina, Asian-American, and Native American—are among the most misunderstood demographics in corporate America. Learn what their careers and lives are really like through in-depth interviews with professional women of color, senior executives, human resources and diversity professionals, professional organizational leaders, and researchers and academics.

It's for Women of Color

Women of color will learn different ways to manage the everyday challenges they face in corporate America, such as dealing with stereotypes, hypervisibility, and cultural adjustments. *Double Outsiders* provides resources and helpful advice to women of color about accessing informal networks, getting sponsors or mentors, and developing an individual, corporate-friendly personal style.

It's for Companies

Companies will learn more about one of their fastest-growing employee demographics, as well as effective strategies to recruit and retain women of color. Human resources and diversity professionals will encounter the unique perspectives of women of color on a variety of topics, and gain insights into the women's personal lives, professional experiences, and family cultures.

Dedication

To Mom, one of the loveliest people I know

Acknowledgments

The process of writing a book is labor intensive—even when you have the pleasure of writing about a subject with great meaning to you on a personal level, as I have. I can really only take credit for the writing, but the actual making of a book involves so much more. As the old adage goes, it really does "take a village" to move a book from conception to publication.

The JIST team (yay!) provided invaluable resources to me throughout this process. I would especially like to thank my editor, Lori Cates Hand, for her initial interest in the book, and for her saintly patience in working with me through the process of writing and editing the manuscript. Her insightful comments and experienced edits have made this book much better than it would otherwise have been. I would also like to extend my heartfelt thanks to Natalie Ostrom and Trudy Coler, also part of the JIST family, and to Anna Ghosh at Scovil Chichak Galen Literary Agency.

I want to extend my heartfelt thanks to all of the professional women of color who allowed me to interview them for this book. Each of you shared a part of yourself for this book, and though you will remain anonymous, your thoughtful insights, advice, and counsel will benefit professional women of color for years to come.

A number of business leaders, professionals, and academics went out of their way to be helpful in the making of this book, including Carol Evans, Carl Brooks, Camilla McGhee, Gail Glaspie, Professor Sheila Wellington, Janice Won, Dr. Jane Smith, Dr. Stacey Blake-Beard, and Dr. Erika Hayes James.

I would also like to express my appreciation for the research of Catalyst, ELC, The Center for Work-Life Policy, and HACR; and also for the research of Drs. Ella L.J. Edmondson Bell and Stella Nkomo, and Dr. Evangelina Holvino, though I was not able to interview them for this book.

I owe two of my mentors, Diane Ashley and Kim Green, a considerable debt of gratitude for providing me with much-needed advice and for believing in this project from the beginning.

And I couldn't have done any of this without the love and support that I have received from my friends and family. Thanks to Mom, Dad, and Sandra Holley (Doc); Ehrika, Blayne, David, Jeni, and Hutch; and David Holley for their love, help, and encouragement. Also, special thanks to Felecia Williams ("girrrrl"), Debra Northern, Lisa Tavares, Sekou Kaalund, Aqualyn Laury, Kelly and Michael Nieto, Anne Stewart, and Angela Davis. Finally, thanks also to the third Alex cabal—Jenny Smith ("former child star"), Penny Liles ("1¢"), Joy Klingeman ("la française"), and Katy Fitzhugh ("katysoc"). Can you believe it's finally done?

CONTENTS

PART 1 On Being a Woman of Color

CHAPTER 1 State of the Union: Women of Color Today

In November 1977, the U.S. government did something for women that it had never done before—and something it would never do again: It sponsored a national conference for women to address concerns related to gender equity in the United States.

The push to develop the conference began with a woman named Bella Abzug. Abzug, a New York congresswoman, capitalized on fortuitous timing to introduce a bill into Congress that would raise funding for a women's conference. Abzug's own background may have had much to do with her interest in the advancement of women. Born to Russian immigrants in the Bronx, Abzug showed early signs of promise, giving speeches to garner support for the Jewish National Fund at age 13 and serving as student body president at Hunter College in New York City as a young woman. Later she matriculated at and graduated from Columbia Law School (she applied to Harvard, which did not admit women at that time). After practicing law for 25 years, Abzug ran for Congress in New York, winning in 1970 and serving from 1971 to 1976.

Around the time Abzug won the congressional seat in New York, the United Nations declared 1975—and subsequently the entire decade—as the year of International Women. As one of 12 women in Congress, Abzug was in a position to make the most of the opportunity that the U.N. announcement afforded—and she did through a bill (P.L. 94-167) that raised $5 million for the event. In January 1974, President Gerald Ford signed Executive Order 11832, which authorized the creation of a National Commission on the Observance of International Women's Year. The Executive

Order also authorized conferences in states and U.S. territories and outlined a process for delegates to be selected as representatives for the national conference in Houston.[1]

Regional meetings were held to select delegates for the conference. Because Abzug's bill included "special emphasis on the representation of low-income women, members of diverse racial, ethnic, and religious groups, and women of all ages,"[2] many women of differing ethnicities were included in the planning and eventually in the meeting itself.

This conference has considerable significance, as the term "women of color" was coined there in 1977.[3] At that time, it was used as a political term, to identify women in what were viewed as the primary ethnic groups in the United States: women of African or Asian descent, as well as Latinas and Native American women. Although neither Abzug, nor the delegates, nor the participants in the conference, could have understood what the term "women of color" would come to mean, they played an important role in the forming of the demographic that is now recognized throughout the nation.

> **NOTE:** The term "women of color" is now used across industries and in the public and private sectors to describe ethnically diverse women as a demographic.

In 2007, this same National Women's Conference (NWC) celebrates its 30th anniversary. The theme "Generations of Women Moving History Forward" provides a link between the historical event and today's issues. And in the same way that the issues facing women have changed, the concept of "women of color" has changed, as well. Now, almost 30 years later, the use of this designation has expanded to include other ethnic groups, including South Asian, Pacific Islander, Native Alaskan, Middle Eastern, and multicultural women (those sharing an ethnic heritage of one or more of these ethnicities).

Who Are the Women of Color?

With an evolved nomenclature for women of color, we can now begin to examine their current status in the United States. Women of color already comprise over 15 percent of the U.S. population, and by 2008, they are expected to make up over 31 percent of the female U.S. population.[4] To get a sense of the relative size of this demographic, the combined demographic of women of color is larger than African-Americans (13 percent of the population), Hispanic Americans (almost 14 percent) or Asian-Americans (4.2 percent). Considering the amount of political clout that each of these ethnic groups possesses individually, why is this discrete group with a larger constituency barely visible in the U.S.? Before answering that question, it may be helpful to get a better sense of how the discrete groups within the women of color segment are identified.[5]

African-American (or Black) women typically trace a portion of their heritage to Africa, often through the Caribbean or South America, but many African-American women are also multiethnic, having European, Native American, South Asian, or East Asian as part of their heritage, as well. According to the 2000 census, African-American women were just under 13 percent of the U.S. female population, accounting for just over 18 million women.

Latinas are also comprised of a variety of ethnic groups, which hail from South America, Central America, Mexico, Cuba, Puerto Rico, and the Dominican Republic. Latinas were numbered at over 17 million (12.5 percent) of the U.S. female population as of 2002.

Asian-American women trace their heritage to one of many Far Eastern countries, including China, Japan, North or South Korea, Thailand, Laos, Vietnam, Malaysia, Taiwan, Indonesia, Singapore, Cambodia, or the Philippines. For census purposes, the federal government has a separate demographic for Native Hawaiian/Pacific Islanders, which includes 22 islands in the Pacific Ocean and possibly 1,000 languages. In 2000, more than 400,000 women identified themselves in this demographic, accounting for less than 1 percent of women in the United States. In business environments, Native Hawaiian/Pacific Islander women are likely to be included in the Asian-American or South Asian demographics, mostly because of their relatively small numbers.

South Asian women have recently begun to emerge as a group distinct from Far East Asian women. South Asian women typically hail from India, Bangladesh, Pakistan, Nepal, or any of the surrounding countries. Combined, Asian-American and South Asian women comprise just under 4 percent of U.S. women.

Native American/Alaska Native women belong to any one (or more) of 556 federally recognized tribes and state-recognized (or other) tribes. The largest subgroups in this demographic are Native Americans, Eskimos, and Aleuts,[6] and these women number just under 1 percent (approximately 1.2 million) of the U.S. female population.

Women of color come from such a wide variety of cultures and geographic regions that one could be surprised that they share so many commonalities. But it is important to remember that the majority of women of color are considered as "outsiders" in the various spheres of American life.

In Their Own Words

Jennifer Tucker, Vice President at the Center for Women Policy Studies in Washington, D.C., was one of the pioneers in research related to women of color. She observes that "we [women of color] have differences and similarities, but we all are treated a certain way in the U.S. because of our race and ethnicity."

Women of color, despite differences within their discrete subgroups, share similar experiences and treatment within American society. To examine the status of women of color in various arenas in American society is beyond the scope of this book, but it is important to note that in the business sector, women of color are not only outsiders—they are *double outsiders.*

"Double Outsiders"

The relative lack of statistics on corporate women of color lends support to this *double outsider* phenomenon. From a historical statistical perspective, women of color did not exist in sufficient numbers to measure their progress in corporate America. Over the past 10 to 15 years, organizations such as the Center for Women Policy Studies and Catalyst began to compile numbers for women of color in the aggregate, as well as for discrete subgroups within the demographic.

In Their Own Words

Sheila Wellington, a clinical professor of management and organizations at NYU's Stern School of Business, and the former president of Catalyst, described the challenges she faced in securing underwriting for the women of color studies that Catalyst pioneered in 1998. "The hardest study I've ever funded, or ever had to fund, was the woman of color study," she reflects, "and I think afterward it was very well received...it got a lot of attention, and I think it [the research] pushed the boulder up the mountain a bit."

Corporations and academics have argued that studying women of color is redundant, and that women need to be studied only generally, but Wellington disagrees. "I believed then, and I believe now, that when you study women in business, given the representation issues, you are essentially studying white women. If you didn't have studies aimed specifically at gathering data about women of color, you simply were not going to have statistically significant data." Tucker makes another astute observation about the manner in which statistics are compiled. "When we talk about minorities, we mean men...[instead] we do have to talk about women and men of color, so that everybody is included."

Statistics on corporate women of color have now been compiled, but the numbers do not demonstrate much progress. Although women of color account for more than 15 percent of the U.S. population and almost 50 percent of the U.S. labor force, they account for only 1.7 percent of all corporate officers in the Fortune 500 companies, where corporate officers are those who are board-elected or board appointed.[7]

In contrast, women overall make up about 51 percent of the population, about 47 percent of the U.S. labor force, and 16.4 percent of corporate officers.[8] Men of color hold 6.4 percent of corporate officer positions.[9] The percentages of women at the corporate officer level are generally rising, but women of color are still a tiny fraction of corporate officers in the Fortune 500. Even for women generally, the numbers are still very troubling: In 2005, more than 50 percent of Fortune 500 companies reported fewer than three women corporate officers.[10]

In terms of ceographics,[11] 11 Fortune 500 companies are currently led by women—two of these companies are in the Fortune 100, and one is led by a woman of color (Indra Nooyi of PepsiCo). And the future does not necessarily look more promising—129 CEO slots turned over in 2005,[12] but only a few women secured such slots; the status quo is still very much in place. Among the fastest-growing companies, the same trends continue: More than 90 percent of such CEOs are male and 85 percent of the men are white.[13]

Making Progress

Since the 1990s, women of color have made considerable strides in corporate America. One of the greatest achievements among women of color was Andrea Jung's appointment as chief executive officer of Avon (2006 Fortune 500 Rank: 281). Jung, who is Canadian-born Chinese, was certainly not a newcomer to the C-suite, having served as chief operating officer, and previously as a senior marketing executive, at Avon. Jung's appointment to the helm of Avon generated much interest in the possibilities for women of color. She holds sway at number 7 in the 2006 edition of *Fortune*'s "50 Most Powerful Women" list.

The most recent and visible appointment into the chairwoman's suite is Indra K. Nooyi, as Chairwoman and CEO of PepsiCo (2006 Fortune 500 Rank: 61). Nooyi, who is South Asian, is 50 years old and a familiar face at PepsiCo, having served as its President and CFO since 2001. Nooyi is ranked first on *Fortune*'s 2006 "50 Most Powerful Women" list.

Another woman of color who recently relinquished the Chairwoman and CEO title is Ann Fudge, who is African-American. Fudge, a Harvard Business School graduate who previously guided the helm of Young & Rubicam (Y&R), one of Madison Avenue's top advertising agencies. Y&R is a division of WPP Group plc, based out of the United Kingdom. In that role, Fudge oversaw global operations for a variety of marketing communications companies.

Aside from the chairman's office, another index of power in corporate America is the status as a top earner. This means that the employee is reported in the company's public filing as one of the five highest-paid employees. In 2005, 75 percent of Fortune 500 companies reported no women as top earners. In companies where women were reported as top earners, women accounted for only 6.4 percent of those earners; 1 percent were women of color. With respect to titles, women held less than 10 percent of "clout titles," meaning those higher than vice president (these numbers are not available for women of color). Based on these (and other) statistics, Catalyst estimates that female officers will not reach parity with male officers until 2046.

Gender Value

Gender diversity in corporations is an important source of value for the enterprise. Research demonstrates that companies with increased diversity have more innovative processes and solutions, are more competitive in talent recruitment, have improved marketing and sales capabilities, and increase their returns on equity and to shareholders. But looking at more than quantitative analyses is essential to understanding the business case for racial and gender diversity at companies. Labor force shrinkage, globalization of markets, and legal and regulatory issues all influence diversity efforts in corporate America.

The upcoming shift in the U.S. labor demographics is among the most critical facing corporations. Current estimates from the U.S. Department of Labor indicate that approximately 85 percent of new entrants into the labor force after 2010 will be women or people of color. Additionally, a significant shortage in the labor market is set to occur as the baby boom generation (people born between 1946 and 1964) begins to retire. Also in 2010, the majority of the U.S. population is expected to be over 45, causing an increase in the age of the labor force. By 2009, women are expected to comprise approximately 48 percent of the U.S. workforce, and women of color are the fastest-growing segment of this group.[14]

These statistics paint a picture that as the labor force begins to shift in age, and baby boomers begin to retire, a shortage will begin in the labor market, and the majority of the new entrants into the workforce to fill vacant positions will be women and people of color—of which women of color will be a significant component. Smart companies are preparing now for the changes on the horizon by developing an infrastructure to support the recruitment and retention of talented women of color.

What Companies Are Doing to Attract and Advance Women of Color

For the companies featured in *Working Mother*'s "2006 Best Companies for Women of Color," the preparations are already underway. These companies are ahead of the curve in the development of programs and initiatives that cultivate the abilities of professional women of color.

These companies are hiring. At AllState, more than 20 percent of new hires were women of color,[15] and at Procter & Gamble (P&G) 21 percent of new management hires are women of color. Over the past three years, P&G has increased the number of women holding the vice president/general manager title by 54 percent; many of these promotions have profit-and-loss (P&L) responsibility. PriceWaterhouseCoopers (PwC) hired significant numbers of women last year (approximately 1,200), and 49 women of color are included in PwC's top 20 percent earner's group.

What these numbers really indicate is that companies are beginning to recognize that corporate women of color are viable candidates for line management and other management roles. It is common business knowledge (and part of the capitalist model) that competition for labor should result in the best talent and economic benefits across all companies. Part of this competition involves selecting *all* the best talent—including talent in untapped or underutilized demographics. Ignoring a segment of the population that is competing for jobs is to ignore the capitalist model—not to mention that it could result in not hiring the best overall talent.

As companies position themselves to reach new client segments, and for entry into global markets, women of color become increasingly valuable to the organization. It is well documented in the U.S. that women make more than 85 percent of consumer purchases and have influence over the purchase of 95 percent of goods and services.[16] As the population of ethnic minorities increases, it seems highly likely that women of color will be the ones making the vast majority of these purchases or decisions. So hiring women of color is more than the right thing to do—they are also the target demographic for many companies.

The globalization of companies and market segments also renders employees from various geographic regions and cultures increasingly valuable to companies. Employees of color that are familiar with languages, local cultures, ways of doing business, and even colloquialisms will be well positioned to deliver valuable inside information that can help their companies get to market first, or at least faster than the competition.

Companies that understand this concept have begun investing in their employee base, providing management incentives for diversity, developing leadership programs, hosting networking events, and providing guidance to employees, sometimes with an emphasis on women of color, as well as recruiting top talent from external sources using diversity executive search firms.

Other companies are starting with management incentives or programs. P&G's CEO rewards his top 30 executives in stock options that are linked (in part) to diversity results.[17] Hewlett-Packard (HP) has developed "Women at HP" meetings to help women of color to network with senior leadership; these meetings happen between four and five times annually. At IBM, multicultural women executives meet annually to update and review their strategy for multicultural women.[18] They also hold teleconferences at which they dispense IBM career and life advice, and women of color are able to call in and listen. In 2005, more than 1,000 women of color IBMers listened in on the conversations.

Another strategy companies use to align management on diversity issues is a "diversity scorecard." At General Mills, this scorecard is administered quarterly, and evaluates the managers' performance related to "hiring, retaining, and promoting" women and ethnic minorities. This diversity scorecard is one of several factors included in determining each manager's annual compensation and bonus. MetLife has a similar strategy, but takes it further by requiring its managers to create a plan to develop a more inclusive team.[19]

Although it is important that individual managers receive incentives to develop diversity on their teams, it drives the process even further if that incentive is reinforced by a linkage to the larger diversity goals of the company—which is Verizon's methodology. Verizon has developed a Diversity Performance Incentive Program, which focuses on hiring and retention of ethnic employees. In the program, each manager's incentive pay is linked to divisional diversity goals.[20]

P&G challenges its managers to look at their individual business unit's diversity relative to internal organizational benchmarks. Also, P&G's annual diversity review charts this progress at the corporate and business unit level. Where diversity initiatives have been successful, it can result in high ratings or promotions for those at the associate director level or above.[21]

Going directly to the source is a strategy that Deloitte & Touche (Deloitte) has employed, recently holding focus groups with women of color employees to learn about their challenges and concerns. In response to the women of color focus groups, Deloitte now offers various programs to assist employees of color with their career development goals, including Leadership Education for employees of Asian/Pacific descent and the Executive Leadership Council for African-Americans.[22] Other companies also provide career-related services for their employees, including women of color. AllState and American Express provided career counseling for all multicultural women this past year,[23] while Verizon held a "personal empowerment forum" for women of color employees to assist them in understanding their career advancement needs.

Vanguard companies such as J.P. Morgan Chase (JPMC) have taken the step of developing an employee network for women of color; at JPMC, it is called Women of Color Connections. Women of color employed at JPMC now have the option of joining an employee resource group that focuses on their ethnic heritage and their gender. One incentive to join the network: It offers "fireside chats" with senior-level women executives. Groups of 10 to 20 women convene for "ask-me-anything" conversations in an executive dining room.[24]

As the numbers of women of color increase in the workplace, companies are also designing leadership or development programs for their employees, and women of color are availing themselves of those opportunities: at P&G, more than 2,000 women of color received career counseling and more than 750 were involved in leadership or management training. At American Electric Power, 10 percent of the 348 women who participated in management training programs were women of color.

Some companies are revising or improving their mentoring programs. P&G's corporate-wide mentoring program matches new employees of color (and all other employees) with managers—and there is a serious upshot: 100 percent of participants in the program agreed that it was "worth their time and effort." No small feat for a company-sponsored program.

Sophisticated leadership programs are one of the more recent recruiting tools that companies are using to recruit employees of color. HP employees of color can participate in a leadership program called the Focused Development Program. This past year, more than 40 percent of participants were women, and more than 150 employees total are alumni.[25] The program includes mentoring and individual-specific advice from a leadership coach. Women of color whom HP views as potential leaders are given the opportunity to participate in leadership institutes at UCLA's Anderson School of Business, including the Women's, African-American, or Asian Pacific institutes. HP further supports its employees' involvement by covering the program tuition (which can run as high as $8,400), as well as travel expenses.

Companies that value leadership usually also understand the importance of leadership (or succession) planning. Verizon's leadership development program helps participants learn about leading and become familiar with performance expectations. At the same time, Verizon also uses its leadership program to assist in its succession planning. In 2006, around 36 women of color were involved in the succession-planning process at Verizon.

Women of color newly employed at PwC may find themselves involved in its Minority Transition Plan, which assists new employees in finding their way around the company. PwC also arranges mentoring relationships for women of color with senior partners at the company through its Mentoring Partnerships Programs. PwC also has Minority Circles and Women's Networking Circles, through which multicultural employees can develop relationships with senior people at the firm.

Making resources available to employees of color is another strategy that companies use to attract minority candidates. At MetLife, where 60 percent of the employees are women and 11 percent are women of color, it is not surprising that the Multicultural Resources Network (MRN) is a widely used resource. Last year, more than 2,000 employees attended the MRN's networking sessions and self-development workshops. One efficient company strategy is e-learning; Deloitte now offers more than 20 diversity e-learning programs to its professionals.[26] HP has taken an innovative step in developing a specific course to assist multicultural employees "analyze obstacles and define strategies" in order to move successfully through personal development challenges.

Deloitte also offers a specialized program for its multicultural employees. Called the Breakthrough Leadership Program, it provides employees of color with three sessions with company leaders and feedback from company leaders, along with a self-assessment to assist with advancement.[27] Of course, such programs have been going on informally for years, but Deloitte is extending these opportunities formally to employees who may not have had the opportunity to gain such insights.

Finally, companies are demonstrating their interest in women of color through their philanthropic and community efforts. The American Express Foundation supports organizations, such as the Women's Venture Fund, that provide "entrepreneurial training" and micro loans to low-income and minority women.[28] IBM has developed education camps to teach math and science to seventh- and eighth-grade girls in urban schools, and pairs the girls with an IBM employee who mentors them throughout the school year. These companies are doing what it takes to create supportive environments in which women of color will not only work—they will excel.

The Bottom Line

Now that companies are actively developing programs and initiatives for women of color, a recent study by Catalyst should provide further support for companies looking to make the case for gender diversity. In 2004, Catalyst undertook a study entitled "The Bottom Line: Connecting Corporate Performance and Gender Diversity." This study found that Fortune 500 companies with the highest percentages of women corporate officers yielded, on average, a 35.1 percent higher return on equity than those with the lowest percentages of women corporate officers.[29] Although it is not statistically possible to fully equate the presence of women officers with a higher return on equity, these statistics are persuasive and indicate that, at a minimum, women corporate officers positively impact a company's bottom line.

But the profit and gender connection does not stop there. The owners of companies, or shareholders, are interested in more than corporate revenue—they are interested in the return they receive. In its 2004 study, Catalyst found that Fortune 500 companies with the highest percentage of women as corporate officers averaged a 34 percent higher total return to shareholders than those with the lowest percentages of women corporate officers. These sets of statistics point to a quantifiable benefit to having women as corporate officers. This benefit also applies if the women officers are ethnically diverse.

Finally, while companies are focused on recruiting all of the best and brightest candidates, including women of color, they should remain cognizant that a failure to demonstrate a commitment to diversity—or worse, actively discouraging diversity at work—could result in significant impacts to their bottom line. Lawyers, public relations staff, and the risk managers understand the difficulty that companies are faced with when confronted with legal or compliance issues related to employment discrimination. It is common business knowledge that employment discrimination on the basis of race, color, religion, gender, or national origin is prohibited by Title VII of the Civil Rights Act of 1964.

Companies such as Texaco ($176.1 million settlement), Coca-Cola ($192 million), Home Depot ($104 million), and State Farm Insurance Co. ($157 million) have learned the hard way that discrimination against employees does not pay—it costs. Today, many companies are employing an intelligent strategy by creating opportunities for all of their employees to progress, and by developing diversity-related initiatives.

Achievements by Notable Professional Women of Color

Although few women of color have made it into the chairman's seat, a number of them hold sway in the chairman's office. In the consumer product industry, Johnson & Johnson's (J&J) first female chairwoman, Christine Poon, who is Chinese-American, is responsible for more than 50 percent of J&J's revenues. Poon is Vice Chairman of J&J, as well as Worldwide Chairman of its Medicines & Nutritionals division. Ms. Poon is currently ranked 11th on the 2006 listing of *Fortune* magazine's "50 Most Powerful Women." Bridget Heller is Global President of Johnson's® Baby at J&J. Heller, an African-American woman, oversees a $1.7 billion division, including familiar brands such as BAND-AID® and Johnson's (the "no more tears" brand).

Women such as Zoe Cruz have made it in the rough-and-tumble culture of Wall Street. Cruz currently serves as Co-president of Morgan Stanley, the venerable Wall Street institution, overseeing the commodities, bonds, and currencies businesses. Cruz, a Latina and a 24-year veteran of Morgan Stanley, is ranked 19th on *Fortune* magazine's "50 Most Powerful Women" list (she is 10th on *Forbes*'s "World's Most Powerful Women"), and is stealthily referred to by John Mack, Morgan Stanley's CEO, as the "Cruz missile."

One of the most powerful women of color in the entertainment sector of business, and in American culture, is Oprah Winfrey. Winfrey is chairwoman of Harpo Productions. Although she is best known as the host of her eponymous talk show, Winfrey has ventured into publishing with *O Magazine* and *O at Home*, and has a channel on XM Radio called "Oprah & Friends."

Some other notable women of color at senior levels include the following:

- **Ursula Burns** is Senior Vice President of Xerox and serves as President of its Business Group Operations. Burns, an African-American woman, is ranked 27th on *Fortune* magazine's "50 Most Powerful Women," and was responsible for $14 billion of Xerox's $15.7 billion revenue stream in 2005.[30]

- **Yvonne Guajardo** is Senior Vice President at Prudential Financial, Inc. Guajardo, a Latina, originates fixed-income instruments to middle-market companies. She oversees 32 companies in her portfolio, accounting for roughly $2 billion in investments. Guajardo holds an MBA from the University of Texas at Austin.

- **Padmasree Warrior** is Executive Vice President and Chief Technology Officer for Motorola. Warrior, who is from India, oversees Motorola's research and development functions— which amount to a whopping $4 billion. Operationally, she has responsibility for Motorola's engineers (there are 26,000), Motorola's software, intellectual property (patents, trademarks, and so on), Motorola Labs, and the company's early-stage businesses.

- **Pamela Thomas-Graham** is group president at Liz Claiborne Inc., where she is responsible for the Liz Claiborne brand, overseeing 10 brands, which account for around 20 percent of the company's $4.6 billion in revenues. Thomas-Graham, an African-American, is the former chairwoman of CNBC and a former partner at consulting powerhouse McKinsey & Co. (at that time the youngest ever, of any race or gender). She is also a triple Harvard graduate (A.B., MBA, and J.D.)—all with honors.

- Gloria Santona, Esq., is Executive Vice President, General Counsel and Secretary of McDonald's Corporation. Santona, who is a Latina, is responsible for McDonald's global legal and compliance structure, including more than 100 attorneys in 20 countries worldwide. She is also secretary to McDonald's board of directors and provides counsel on corporate governance.

Summary

Because of the success of the women of color who are currently in the executive suite, and those who have pioneered the way to the top, women of color are now on the radar of corporations as potential leaders. Companies are responding to these new possibilities by developing initiatives, programs, and strategies in order to recruit, retain, and promote this previously ignored demographic.

As we continue to examine the issues surrounding women of color in corporate America, the focus now switches to the women of color themselves—to their challenges, obstacles, and creative solutions to juggling their career and family responsibilities.

Notes

[1] "The Texas Handbook Online," available at www.tsha.utexas.edu/handbook/online/articles/NN/pwngq.html.

[2] Jewish Women's Archive. "JWA Bella Abzug Biography," available at www.jwa.org/exhibits/wov/abzug/index.html (October 16, 2006).

[3] Jael Silliman, Marlene Gerber Fried, et al. *Undivided Rights: Women of Color Organize for Reproductive Justice* (Cambridge, Massachusetts: South End Press, 2004).

[4]U.S. Department of Health and Human Services. "Fact Sheet: Minority Women's Health," available at www.4woman.gov/OWH/pub/minority/index.htm (2003). *Wow! Women and Diversity Facts 2005* (Washington, D.C.: Diversity Best Practices/Business Women's Network), 69.

[5]U.S. Department of Health and Human Services. "Fact Sheet: Minority Women's Health," available at www.4woman.gov/OWH/pub/minority/index.htm (2003).

[6]Ibid.

[7]*Wow! Women and Diversity Facts 2005* (Washington, D.C.: Diversity Best Practices/Business Women's Network), 69.

[8]Catalyst Press Release. "Rate of Women's Advancement to Top Corporate Officer Positions Slow, New Catalyst Tenth Anniversary Census Reveals" (July 26, 2006).

[9]Ibid.

[10]Ibid.

[11]Burson-Marsteller. "Record-Breaking CEO Crunch in 2005," available at www.ceogo.com.

[12]Ibid.

[13]*Inc.* magazine (October 1, 2005).

[14]Olisemeka, Nkechi. "Springboard to success: organization to help underrepresented groups navigate the corporate landscape." *Black Enterprise* (December 2004).

[15]Working Mother Media. "Best Companies for Women of Color," available at www.workingmother.com.

[16]Learned, Andrea. "The Six Costliest Mistakes You Make in Marketing to Women." *Inc.* (January 2003).

[17]Working Mother Media. "Best Companies for Women of Color," available at www.workingmother.com.

[18]Ibid.

[19]Ibid.

[20]Ibid.

[21]Ibid.

[22]Ibid. This program is different than the professional business organization Executive Leadership Council, located in Washington, D.C.

[23]Ibid.

[24]Ibid.

[25]Ibid.

[26]Ibid.

[27]Ibid.

[28]Ibid.

[29]Catalyst, *The Bottom Line: Connecting Corporate Performance and Gender Diversity* (2004).

[30]Fortune's List, available at http://money.cnn.com/magazines/fortune/mostpowerfulwomen/2006 (October 16, 2006).

CHAPTER 2 Career Chutes and Ladders

Many people refer to business as a "game," and it certainly bears a strong resemblance to some of the games we play for fun. One particular children's game bears a surprising resemblance to the process of rising (or falling) through the ranks of corporate America. That game is Chutes and Ladders®

The game centers around certain squares set intermittently throughout the board. The important squares include either the beginning of a ladder or the starting point for a chute. Other squares on the board force the player to miss a turn or award an extra turn; still others are blank or show the end point of a chute or a ladder.

Corporate America has many similarities. As with the game, everyone comes "on board." Like the board squares, employees engaging in behaviors deemed "good" (from the corporation's perspective) are rewarded with advancement. Employees behaving neutrally, or in ways deemed "bad," plateau or are demoted to inferior ranks or divisions. The notions of good and bad are relative in corporate America: What is seen as ethical in one company is considered overkill in another. And what is considered unethical at one company is standard business practice at another. This is why corporate newcomers must learn the rules of the game upon joining a new company or division.

For women of color, learning the rules is a twofold process. Once they have learned these rules, women of color often find themselves subject to an additional set of rules that are not imposed on their non-minority or non-female peers. Because of this, squares that propel their peers upward could send women of color downward on the game board. Thus, women of color must determine their own rules and identify which squares will *really* help them up the ladder and which squares will get them demoted. For women of color, what should be a straightforward game becomes decidedly complex for those who choose to play.

The importance of the chutes and ladders on the game board also includes a telling detail: The chutes send the players backward in varying degrees, from one to seven levels down, which is almost back to the beginning of the game. The ladders send players forward in the same proportions. For professional woman of color, these chutes take the form of institutional hindrances to advancement or career derailers; the ladders are their critical success factors.

The Chutes and Ladders Backstory

Chutes and Ladders® is a popular game, first published by Milton Bradley in 1943, for children ages 4 to 7. The game board consists of 100 squares, sectioned into a 10 × 10 grid, with each square numbered. The game progresses by rolling a regular die (numbered 1 to 6) and moving the game piece forward in accordance with the die roll.

A player landing on a square showing the beginning of a ladder can move up that ladder to a higher-numbered square (between 1 and 7 levels up). A player landing on a square showing the beginning of a chute will move down the chute to a lower-numbered square (between 1 and 7 levels down). Players landing on the squares containing the end of a chute or ladder are not affected. The game's objective is to reach the hundredth square at the top of the game board before the other players.

You might be surprised to learn that the underlying concept of chutes and ladders did not originate in the United States. It is based on an ancient Indian game called Moksha-Patamu, or "Snakes and Ladders" (Moksha-Patamu was loosely based on the ancient Egyptian game "Dogs and Jackals").

Snakes and Ladders dates back to the second century B.C. and was often used as a tool of Hindu religious instruction for children. The squares containing the beginning of the ladder represented various types of good, such as Faith, Generosity, Knowledge, and Reliability; squares with the head of the snake included Vanity, Theft, Lying, Pride, and Lust. The thought was that good conduct (represented by the ladder) propelled the player upward into a "higher life"; evil conduct (symbolized by the snake) reduced the player into a "lower life."

Once the game was adopted into Victorian England, the virtues were renamed to suit English religious and moral tenets; in America, the religious undertones were almost entirely removed (only "naughty" and "nice" remained) and the game was made a bit easier—the ladders began to outnumber the chutes, instead of the other way around.

Obstacles to Success

Recent research on corporate women of color describes the four key barriers cited by women of color that hinder their advancement. The women largely view these barriers in terms of deficiencies in the opportunities they receive, such as a lack of influential sponsors or mentors, lack of informal networks with influential colleagues, stereotypes, a lack of company role models from the same racial/ethnic group, and a lack of high-visibility assignments.[1]

Lack of Influential Sponsors and Mentors

Mentors and sponsors play an invaluable role in the success of women of color in corporate America. Mentors provide women of color with career strategies and advice, and information and guidance on the corporate culture, structure, and key divisions or departments within the organization. In addition to providing general information, mentors also help women of color to avoid political missteps by sharing critical information with them about dead-end departments, thorny political thrush, and credit-stealing bosses. Sponsors have a different role: They understand their protégé's goals, endorse their efforts, and set the wheels in motion for them to move toward those goals. Sponsors tend to be highly influential people within organizations; although they sometimes serve as mentors, they often opt for a more limited role with their protégés.

In Their Own Words

Veronica Sims,* an African-American senior executive in a highly influential industry, views sponsorship as critically important to the career advancement of any professional woman, and certainly for women of color. "As I think back on my own career, as well as talking with others throughout my career...one of the issues is being able to establish what I would call 'sponsorship relationships'; not necessarily mentor relationships—but [definitely] sponsorship. Ideally, this [relationship] would be in...a reporting relationship, someone that really is an advocate for you within the organization.... That [sponsorship] relationship, or having that advocate—particularly at times that you're not in the room and decisions are being made on promotions, etc.—is very important."

*Name has been fictionalized.

Janice Won, founder of Inclusion Strategies & Diversity Solutions, agrees. Won frequently consults with companies on diversity issues, and has considerable experience related to issues surrounding women of color. She is one of the founders of the Women of Color Connections group and the Asian Women's Network at J.P. Morgan Chase. She is one of two co-executive vice presidents for the highly successful Asian Women Leadership Network, a network for Asian, Asian-American, and South Asian women professionals. Won's concerns for women of color include similar issues to those expressed by Sims.

She notes a "lack of sponsors, mentors, and key professional relationships," and "[a] lack of visibility and credibility." According to Won, women of color will continue to experience difficulties in corporate America if they do not build strategic networks or develop what she refers to as "social capital" among peers. Most importantly, Won makes a solid argument for the necessity of informal networks at the office. Without them, she suggests that a woman of color will not have a platform on which to create and relate her personal value proposition—because without networks, she won't know anyone that will be interested to hear or understand her value. Or if she should stumble in her career, she won't have a support network to help her learn from her mistakes.

Added Legitimacy

Women of color who land on the mentor or sponsor square are rewarded with another important benefit—one that has a considerable impact on their ability to reach the middle or senior management levels—legitimacy. Legitimacy in corporate America involves credibility or approval from people or institutions with power. An example of this legitimacy would be an MBA from Harvard Business School (HBS). HBS is a well-known, prestigious institution, and a degree from it carries an implicit recommendation as to the holder's intelligence and business savvy. A second example of transferred legitimacy could be an influential sponsor in your organization or division. Influential sponsors wield significant power over allocation of resources and promotions in their organizations.

They are also very highly regarded. As a result, their protégés receive a "conferred" legitimate status.[2]

Legitimacy can also be based on similarity. Studies show that we "like" people who resemble us in terms of physical characteristics—to the point that external characteristics are themselves an implicit recommendation to those who share them. Thus, very junior white males have legitimacy with senior white males based on the fact that they share similar external characteristics—something women of color have no hope of achieving. It makes sense that legitimacy is a huge component of success for women of color, as they share no indicia of power with their white male peers, unlike white females (who share race) and men of color (who share gender). Lacking the external indicia of those in power, women of color with influential mentors can receive the benefits of transferred legitimacy in a way that their hard work and efforts are unlikely to accomplish.

Dr. Stacey Blake-Beard, an African-American woman, is one of a handful of scholars who have researched women of color in business organizations. Blake-Beard is an associate professor on the research faculty for the Center for Gender in Organizations at Simmons School of Management in Boston, Massachusetts. Her primary research focus is organizational behavior, mentoring, and diversity.

Blake-Beard has an expert understanding of mentoring, and succinctly notes that "as you move further and further up the organizational ladder, you need people to vouch for you...it's not so much your technical competence, it's your ability to connect with other people." Blake-Beard's research has found that women of color often self-protect, which presents a major barrier to their development of healthy mentoring relationships within their organizations. This closing off from others and self-protection sometimes stems from prior unpleasant experiences in corporate settings. Kim Borges,* a Latina, is an international diversity consultant who sees something similar. She has observed women of color acting as "islands" and not having those bridges with others in the organization. "I think," she says, "that the higher a woman of color gets in an organization, the lonelier it can become [for her]."

When women of color close themselves off and self-protect, Blake-Beard believes that sponsorship and mentoring are impacted. "The people who might mentor you," she comments, "can't get close

*Name has been fictionalized.

enough to you to feel as if they know you, so [in turn] they can't vouch for you." The bottom line is that trust is a major component of sponsorship or mentoring relationships.

> **TIP:** Be conscious of the "stay away" signals that you may unwittingly present to others to keep them at bay. If you've had negative corporate experiences, take some time to work through those feelings and talk to a career or life coach, if necessary.

Advocacy

In addition to legitimacy, sponsors and mentors are often in a position to act on behalf of their protégés, by virtue of their seniority. This seniority is very helpful to women of color because they may not be present at certain meetings that impact their careers. Women of color with sponsors or mentors have someone at the meeting to champion their efforts and promote their abilities. This increases the likelihood that the women will get the green light for a "stretch" or developmental role that could springboard them to higher levels at the company. In addition, sponsors and mentors can shield them from detractors that would undermine their legitimacy.

In Their Own Words

Marisol Sinders,* a former marketing professional, described her first foray into corporate America and her positive experiences with her first mentor. "For my first job out of college, I was brought into a startup by my CEO after an internship. I was 21 years old and had just accepted a full-time offer, and all of my managers wanted to meet with me! Apparently, my CEO had gone back to his company and talked about me. He talked me up so much that I had tons of exposure long before I even got there. I didn't know anything about corporate America or corporate politics—I was a math major! It was amazing. And they all made the connection between me and the CEO. I really think that I was fast-tracked because they could check the boxes: One, I was vouched for by my CEO, check! I had a degree in math, check! And I had an engaging personality, check!" she laughs, obviously pleased with that period in her career.

*Name has been fictionalized.

But not everyone knew of her relationship with the CEO. "Now I was very careful not to misuse the CEO," Sinders explains. "I talked with him for long-term strategy, not just to 'get my way.' But during this one period, I was in a sales assistant role and there was a total slacker on my team. We called him "frat boy" because he was in the same fraternity as the VP of the department, and was always talking to him about 'fraternity this and fraternity that.' The slacker's role was similar to mine—there were three of us that were sales assistants.

The slacker never called back his sales leads and often walked around the office, just chatting, chatting, chatting! But he wound up getting promoted to account executive and then to sales executive and we were about the same age with similar experience. Of course I hadn't heard of or been told about any of the positions he wound up getting." She pauses for effect. "The whole situation prompted my decision to go to b-school, so I arranged to meet with the CEO about my future plans. The CEO was supportive, but wanted to know why I was returning to school. Eventually I disclosed that "frat boy" (but I didn't call him that) had gotten a promotion, but that I hadn't heard about any job openings."

Shortly thereafter, the VP who promoted "frat boy" asked to meet with her. "Girl, I was greener than green," she chuckles, "I didn't even realize the CEO had called [the VP], until I got into his office." After talking with the VP, she learned about a new job opportunity, and after discussing it with the CEO, she accepted the promotion. By having an influential mentor, Marisol was able to garner a promotion into a position about which she would probably never have heard otherwise. But she did go back to b-school later.

The importance of mentoring has been underscored by research done by Catalyst on women of color in the past decade: *Women of Color in Corporate Management* study (1998), and its follow-up study, *Women of Color in Corporate Management: Three Years Later* (2001). In its research, Catalyst found that the number of women of color with mentors increased more than 20 percent: from 35 percent in 1998 to 58 percent in 2001. The research also found that women of color with more mentors moved upward in their organizations. This indicates that mentoring—and sponsorship—helps women of color to get ahead in corporate America.

Cross-Cultural Sponsors and Mentors

But finding mentors and sponsors can be challenging for women of color, for a variety of reasons. Some women of color prefer that their sponsors and mentors share either their gender or ethnicity (and ideally both), because they want to be able to discuss issues that they believe they are facing due to their race or gender. But because fewer than 2 percent of corporate officers are women of color, this is an unlikely scenario. It is more probable that women of color will have mentors who share gender with them. But the most likely scenario is that their mentors will be white men, because they comprise the largest percentage of management in corporate America. The best advice for women of color is to identify potential mentors based on functional expertise, industry knowledge, influence, and communication style.

But cross-cultural and cross-gender mentoring and sponsoring relationships are fraught with challenges for both parties—starting with their comfort level. Many mentors are white males over the age of 50—born in 1957 at the latest. During most of these men's youth, racial segregation and discrimination was mainstream. Most likely, these executives have had very little exposure to women of color except as domestic servants, childcare workers, or checkout clerks. As such, the mentors are not likely to have enough exposure to or understanding of women of color as colleagues to feel comfortable with them in that role.

In Their Own Words

To develop relationships with mentors, Madison Davies* uses a strategy she learned in a leadership seminar. "During one-on-one meetings," she remarks, "mentors are not forced to behave in accordance with norms or the view of onlookers, so that kind of exposure is extremely powerful. I used to talk with executives that had a relationship to my project, asking for help. Sometimes I had to wait to get time with them, but executives that need things from you will

*Name has been fictionalized.

give you time. The first time we sat down, they would often blush—who knows what thoughts were in their mind?" she says. "But I think that [in one-on-one meetings] they provide me with the same mentoring that they give my white male counterparts with no thought to public opinion. Once I started this, I got endorsements all the way up to the CXO level; and it was not until after I developed these relationships that I was viewed outside of traditional women of color stereotypes. Women of color have to realize that often mentors don't understand us and are intimidated by the larger society. One-on-one time helps to take away their initial discomfort."

By recognizing the need and her ability to make others comfortable, Madison has been able to benefit from a broad network of mentors of varying ages, genders, and ethnicities.

Sometimes challenges arise between mentor and protégé in cross-cultural mentoring relationships. Dr. Blake-Beard often meets with mentors and protégés as part of her organizational consulting work. During some of these check-ins, she reports having met with mentors who gave her some discouraging news about some of the women of color they were trying to mentor. "When I come back to the midway check-in, I talk with the mentors," she begins, "and the mentors [will say], 'I'm really trying to extend myself to this person, but they are not returning my phone calls, they're busy.'" She continues the incredible end of the story: "The mentor is reaching out— and *they* [the women of color] are not responding."

Blake-Beard knows why these failed responses happen. Oftentimes, she says, women of color express frustration with the cross-cultural element of the mentoring: "'I don't know why I was put with this mentor,' a young professional might say. 'We don't have anything in common.' So what they [the women of color] will do sometimes," says Blake-Beard, "is they'll kind of just check out of the relationship. They will mentally dismiss the mentor." Her advice to women of color is to take every mentoring relationship seriously: "If you're going to be involved in a mentoring process in your organization, that's not a really smart thing to do. It doesn't make sense;

it's not politically savvy." According to Blake-Beard, such behavior is not the norm, although it does happen. Blake-Beard offers, "We [women of color] know that we have to be able to reach out across differences."

TIP: If you are going to sign up for a company mentoring program, take the mentoring relationship seriously. It reflects on your professionalism.

Lack of Informal Networks

In Catalyst's 2001 study, women of color cited a lack of informal networks with influential colleagues as a significant barrier to their corporate success. Informal networks are not formally organized, and provide access to critical information that can impact one's professional development or career options. This information is company-related, such as job openings in a specific department or new departments that are being formed. Employees that are part of informal networks often have the "inside scoop" on employee activities, including upcoming promotions, demotions, and behind-the-scenes relationships. Finally, these networks provide valuable insights into company norms and policies, from style of dress and appropriate mannerisms in meetings, to learning the company's "power" events, which could be anything from a picnic to a luncheon or a retreat at the corporate management center. It is easy to see why a lack of access to such networks is a detriment to women of color.

In Their Own Words

Veronica Sims views solid relationships with bosses and peers as integral to career success. In thinking about typical career derailers, she pauses and then says, "Not building strong relationships with peers or with your boss. Either one of those can derail you in the corporate environment." The second part of Sims' equation is linked to a woman of color's immediate supervisor. "Part of it is interviewing your boss," she says. "Who you work for, and the culture of the organization that you work in.... As I got more

> experience, I realized how important that corporate environment and that relationship was. I mean, to make sure that I was working for someone that I respected and valued, certainly their integrity, which is important to me—the worst thing you could end up with is a mismatch in that arena."

Professional women of color primarily use two networking strategies at work, as found by a recent study. The first strategy, "blending in," occurs when women of color have a network with high numbers of "whites, men, or colleagues from the same company." Women of color that are "sticking together" (the other strategy) tend to have others of the same ethnicity and gender in their networks, and fewer company colleagues.

The results of the study diverge along racial lines: Asian-American women generally used a "blending in" strategy, Latinas tended to use both the "blending in" and "sticking together" strategies, and African-American women generally used the "sticking together" strategy.[3] The dual strategy employed by Latinas may provide the most overall support for women of color. Because they encounter significant challenges, sticking together is helpful for emotional support. But to support their career advancement, it is necessary for women of color to also blend in.

> **TIP:** Is your networking style more "blending in" or "sticking together"? If you find yourself "sticking together," try to get to know colleagues outside of your ethnic group or gender. One easy way to do start: Invite someone to lunch.

Stereotypes

Stereotypes are a persistent hurdle that women of color encounter in corporate America, and are generally based on race, gender, or a combination of both. Typical stereotypes surrounding women of color: the angry, aggressive black woman; the hot-tempered, fiery Latina; and the quiet, even-tempered, geisha-like Asian-American woman.

Such stereotypes are usually reinforced by a lack of knowledge or exposure. Diversity consultant Kim Borges recently learned of some statistics on women's cross-cultural interactions. To Borges, the statistics indicated that "white women don't really know or understand the different life experiences of women of color." This points to a critical information gap between white women and women of color—they do not understand each other. This information gap often surfaces in conflict situations at work, where everyone's motives seem ambiguous, and everyone is trying to understand one another's motives. Based on the statistics Borges relayed, does a white woman understand an Asian woman's response to a conflict? And if they cannot understand one another, can they effectively resolve that conflict? Probably not.

Aside from misunderstandings and conflicts, stereotypes play a role in how an employee's performance is evaluated. Dr. Blake-Beard believes that stereotypes create a *deficit model* around women of color's performance. "There is actually a deficit model around women of color and their abilities," she states. "The rationale [for the model] differs depending on which group you're talking about...[and] ties into the stereotypes and the implicit assumptions and beliefs—and the unconscious biases that we see." Blake-Beard explains that women of color are viewed by others in accordance with stereotypes, and that they are not viewed as being competent professionals until they *prove* that they are. This confidence deficit that Blake-Beard describes amounts to a burden of proof that a professional woman of color has to overcome. So while other employees are presumed competent until they prove otherwise, women of color are presumed incompetent until they prove their competence. So much for a level playing field.

> **TIP:** Beware of allowing your colleagues' performance to influence yours. If they cut corners or otherwise do not take their work seriously, do not assume that you can do likewise.

A further problem with stereotypes is their reinforcement of the "distance" between women of color and their colleagues. When colleagues lump a woman of color into a group, they no longer see her as an individual. Her actions are viewed through a lens that is tinted with the racial, ethnic, and gender stereotypes accorded her people group. Behavior that would previously have seemed innocuous to a colleague now becomes proof of the very stereotypes that the colleague holds.

To further complicate the issue of stereotyping, it seems that sometimes such thinking is done unconsciously. Dr. Blake-Beard elaborates, "There is this implicit belief and assumption that women of color, or diverse women, are really not up to snuff [in terms of work performance]. It's not explicit, and I don't know that people even realize that they feel that way. It gets into some of the unconscious bias stuff...[and] we see these kind of assumptions, not just from whites and people in the organization. I think some of the women [of color] themselves feel that way." Some women of color are sufficiently disempowered at work that they even internalize others' negative thoughts about themselves.

> **TIP:** Write down a list of 10 positive things about yourself and read it everyday. Make every effort not to internalize the negative perceptions that others have about you.

There are no easy answers that will resolve the social stereotypes that women of color encounter at work. Companies can address the issue in their management and diversity training, but until senior and midlevel managers develop relationships with women of color, the managers will lack the necessary empathy to address the women's difficulties. Women of color are well-advised to pursue a strategy of educating others about who they are as individuals. But this adds yet another burden for an already busy professional woman of color.

Lack of Role Models

Another barrier cited by women of color in the Catalyst study is a lack of company role models who share the same ethnicity. This is a more entrenched barrier that will not be quickly overcome. It exists, in part, because of the relatively recent advancement of women of color into the most senior levels of corporations (for example, Chairwoman or CEO). Because women of color make up only 1.6 percent of corporate officers, it is not surprising that the women in the study[4] are not finding company role models of the same ethnicity and gender. As more women of color rise through the corporate ranks, this factor will become less of a concern.

The rationale for the importance of this factor is based on the manner in which corporate behaviors are assimilated. Generally, corporate behaviors are learned through modeling the behavior of others. This modeling occurs where an influential subject is observed in meetings, company functions, or otherwise; and positive attributes (or at least those attributes viewed as positive by the company) are observed and later imitated by lower-level employees—within the constraints of their positions.

The difficulty with this method of learning for women of color is the system by which corporate behaviors are evaluated. Behaviors are evaluated by interpersonal dynamics, which are heavily influenced by the racial and gender biases and stereotypes that are ingrained in American society. Thus, behaviors exhibited by a preponderance of those in the majority (white men) are likely to be deemed acceptable by the company, for a variety of reasons.

But this verdict of acceptability is rooted in acceptable norms for white men, and these norms do not extend to white women, or to men and women of color. As such, those engaging in behaviors similar to white men, that are not white men, will be evaluated differently—even if the behaviors are objectively identical.

Instead, the evaluation will be applied in accordance with what are considered normative behaviors for each different ethnic group, followed by a gender analysis. This is often done so quickly that people do not realize the depth of their analyses. So a woman of color who behaves in a manner similar to a Caucasian man (even if that is her normal way of acting) is likely to violate what is considered "normative" behavior for her gender and ethnicity, from the perspective of colleagues. Not only will she not be rewarded for such behavior, but she is likely to be criticized by others for engaging in it.

> **TIP:** One good way to develop a professional style is to observe several senior women who are well-respected at your company. Try to get a sense of what it is that people like about each one of them, and incorporate parts of those things into your own style.

In light of this multilayered evaluative system, women of color benefit greatly from having role models within their companies who share their gender and ethnicity. Such role models would help other women learn how to operate within acceptable behavioral limits (based on their race and gender) in a specific corporate context.

Lack of High-Visibility Assignments and Other Hindrances to Success

The lack of high-visibility assignments that women of color cited in a recent study seems to stem, in large part, from the other challenges they mentioned, including a lack of sponsors, mentors, and access to informal networks. Women of color without access to decision-makers are not likely to be considered for "plum" jobs without having developed a trusting relationship with senior managers. Janice Won astutely observes that "influential executives might consider it risky to give women of color a chance. [And] if the woman of color fails, then everyone [all women of color] fail." Personal relationships between senior managers and women of color provide a sort of "insurance" against the senior manager's uncertainty.

> **TIP:** If you aren't getting high-visibility assignments, don't work harder at work; instead, spend your efforts on developing your credibility.

Discerning the True Cause of the Obstacles

Merriam-Webster's Online Dictionary defines discernment as "the quality of being able to grasp and comprehend what is obscure." In corporate America, where there is always more than meets the eye, such an attribute is critical for successful business professionals.

In Their Own Words

Susan Davis* is a senior African-American executive at a highly influential diversified company. She spends considerable time mentoring younger women of color within her organization, and perceives that women of color often have a tough time evaluating difficult situations at work. This difficulty stems from their inability to clarify the stimulus behind a situation, she notes. "It's always challenging to discern [of a situation], is this due to race? Is it due to gender? Is it due to the fact that I am a young professional?" She acknowledges that women of color sometimes confront

*Name has been fictionalized.

what she refers to as "the 'isms' of the world." But according to her, other possibilities loom, such as timing and poor management. "I think the challenge for women of color," she continues, "is that it sometimes becomes too easy to take it to the lowest common denominator and say 'this is happening because I'm a woman of color,' which may not be true."

Davis's perspective in the corporate arena allows her to make another important observation: "Particularly as you're moving up into more senior positions in corporate America," she remarks, "there are lots of competing interests, and just general competition, and lots of reasons why decisions are made that may have nothing to do with your gender or your race. But," she says ruefully, "it might!" She concludes by reiterating discernment is a considerable challenge for women of color.

Davis mentions a few recent discussions she has had with women of color about difficult situations at work. "All too often," she begins, "they want to point to gender or skin" as the basis for their difficulties. But upon hearing the facts, Davis has sometimes been forced to conclude that gender and race have nothing at all to do with their difficulties. She humorously relates her side of a conversation with one such young woman: "and then you did what? And then you said what? And then you wrote a memo and did what?"

Davis also reminds women of color to realize that there are some "bad bosses" at companies. She points to situations where a woman of color is having difficulties with her boss, and that most of her colleagues are having those same problems. In such cases, Davis notes that "[you] may just have a bad boss." Davis' final analysis on which strategies women of color should adopt to handle difficult situations at work is this: "Figure out which lens to look through" in each situation.

Career-Limiting Gestures

A self-imposed obstacle that women of color face are what Davis refers to as *career-limiting gestures* (CLGs). Davis sees many examples of young professional women (including women of color) who forget that "after-work" events are the same as work—at least in the eyes of the company. Sometimes women forget this, and do things like wear inappropriate clothes, or guzzle beer with the guys from the office. "You're always working," Davis notes dryly, "drinks, baseball games, social gatherings—these are still work." Professional women of color are already dealing with stereotypes surrounding their performance, intelligence, background, and professionalism. Conducting oneself inappropriately at work or work-related events just lends support to stereotypical notions of women of color. It's far better to behave professionally.

At work functions, such as corporate holiday parties or other events where a guest is invited, Davis cautions women of color to choose their companion carefully, and to recognize that "people make decisions about you based on whom you're with." In the early stages of her career, Davis made the mistake of bringing a potential boyfriend to a company event. When the relationship ended, she was forced to bring a different escort to company events. Her colleagues joked with her, asking who she was going to bring next—sort of linking her dating life to her work. After that, Davis devised a rotational strategy, and began rotating two or three escorts (all friends) to her corporate events—one was in the same industry, so he benefited from attending the events; another was well-put together; the third was another friend who was fun to be around. By devising this strategy, Davis was able to deflect attention from her personal life (she was then single); she also made sure that her colleagues knew that her escorts were all just friends. In this way, Davis prevented her dating life from impacting her professional life. She advises in hindsight, "Don't bring someone you're interested in [to a work function]."

> **TIP:** Consider asking a friend who works in your same industry to be your escort to company events. Your friend will benefit by making new contacts, and you can have a steady companion at your work events. But be sure that he is professional!

The final CLG that Davis mentions relates to the sharing of personal information at work. Part of getting to know colleagues in corporate America involves the exchange of personal information. But Davis believes that there is a limit to how much you should share. "You don't share your personal life at work with your colleagues," she says. "You don't talk about the fight you had [with your spouse]…you never know how information can be used for or against you." She points out that a discussion with a colleague about stress at home or fighting with a spouse could lead to that same colleague's later doubts about your ability to handle an explosive work situation.

Davis' seniority attests to her understanding of corporate politics. So how does she square her caution with the advice of those who suggest women of color be more open with colleagues? "People need to feel like they know you," she notes. "Figure out what about your personal life you want to share." By judiciously selecting information to discuss at work, you can share some of your life with colleagues, but choose not to share information that could later prove damaging to your career.

Critical Success Factors

Of course, rising up the corporate ladder requires considerably better strategies than those employed in Milton Bradley's game. In Catalyst's follow-up study, women of color identified four factors critical to their professional advancement:

- Having an influential mentor or sponsor
- Performing over and above expectations
- Communicating well
- Having access to high-visibility assignments

Finding Influential Sponsors and Mentors

We have already discussed the difficulties that women of color have in getting a sponsor or mentor, but as Veronica Sims notes, "We have a difficult time understanding how [to] build that relationship, who it should be with, and how [to] actually establish that relationship." This section outlines some ways to begin building such relationships.

One of the easiest ways to start a mentoring relationship is to request feedback on a particular project. For varying reasons, this option is usually problematic for women of color. Dr. Blake-Beard explains that women of color are often overly self-reliant: "We [women of color] don't do well at asking for help… [asking for help] means that you don't have it all together, and every message we get [in corporate America] says that you have to have it all together. Mentors can't read your mind; they need for you to let them know what you need." One of the roles of mentors is to help with challenges—something that they cannot do if they are unaware of your difficulties.

> **TIP:** If you have difficulty accepting feedback or constructive criticism, always take a pen and notepad into your feedback meetings. That way you can write down the feedback and look at it later when you are feeling more objective. Just be careful not to doodle!

Janice Won also believes that women of color shortchange themselves by not asking for feedback, or by accepting low-quality or non-specific feedback, such as "you are doing fine," or "good job." Won notes that women of color with a clear understanding of their perceived strengths and shortcomings (which comes from feedback) are well-positioned to begin developing a career plan. But a lack of constructive feedback would hamper the planning process and possibly the supervisory relationship.

Blake-Beard further notes the hesitancy of women of color in seeking "hard, critical feedback," which she believes is developmentally good for them. In part, she believes that women of color do not seek feedback because they often feel troubled at work already, and do not want to add to their burdens. She also notes that a general request for feedback from women of color is unlikely to be acted upon by managers. This is because managers (particularly white managers) are often afraid of how a woman of color will react to their criticism; they also want to avoid being labeled as racist or and do not want to cause a commotion in their departments.

Besides seeking out constructive feedback, women of color need to become more open to different types of relationships. Women from ethnically homogenous backgrounds may not be very open to spending time with people outside of their ethnic group. Dr. Blake-Beard related one such story involving a young African-American woman, who told her: "'I had a mentor, a white male, and we were getting along fine, and he invited me over to his house and you know, I met his family and we did some work... [but] I just would not invite him to my house. I would not let this man in." Although her mentor opened his home and family to her, she could not trust him enough to reciprocate the invitation. For a while it must have appeared that her behavior went unnoticed.

"And finally he said to me one day, 'I am really insulted. I am opening myself up, I am extending myself and you are not reciprocating. I am doing all the work in this relationship.'" Blake-Beard notes the young woman's response: "She said 'You know what? He was right!'" Eventually she made some adjustments in her behavior, not because she was forced to, but because she found she wanted to explore the possibilities of letting a colleague into her personal life. Once she decided to take the next step, she invited him over to her house. Her ultimate verdict: She believed that her invitation to him demonstrated her commitment to the relationship, and that it made a difference in the quality of their relationship going forward. Dr. Blake-Beard agrees that women of color need to be prepared to reach out to others across what she calls "dimensions of difference."

Performing Above Expectations

The other success factors cited by women of color—communicating well and performing above expectations—are well-known advancement strategies for all business professionals. Performance is considered by many women of color to be the cornerstone of success in corporate America. Women of many different ethnicities often remark that they feel the need to overperform—to perform twice as well as their colleagues—to be considered as solid performers at their companies.

In Their Own Words

A number of the executives that were interviewed expressed the need to outwork peers. Veronica Sims observes that women of color "in their twenties... [may not] realize today that you still have to go above and beyond [your] peers. You have to be better...and because you're trying to manage against so many other factors...your performance has to be better," she pauses, and then emphasizes the point, "[it] has to be [better]. It's a given; you may as well accept it."

In part, because of this over-performance, many women of color unconsciously or consciously expect a return acknowledgement of their efforts from their companies; they sometimes become discouraged and cynical when this response does not occur. Won notes that Asian-American women in particular assume that working hard and keeping their heads down will get them the promotion they are seeking. Won agrees that such a strategy "may work initially." But she cautions that after one or two promotions, women of color who focus on their performance to the exclusion of self-promotion, or are "not known by decision makers or even their peers," will ultimately be hindered from rising in the organization by a lack of visibility.

> **TIP:** Working hard is important, but be sure to take time to chat with colleagues and learn what's going on around you at work.

The expectation of return for over-performance among women of color indicates that they have adopted a common misperception about the nature of performance in the larger corporate system. Performance does not function in a vacuum, but rather functions in conjunction with other factors, most notably sponsorship and visibility. So performance, by itself, is almost never sufficient to get a woman of color ahead in corporate environments. The interplay between performance, visibility, and other factors are discussed later this chapter.

Communicating Well

Communicating well is vital to a woman of color's career success. This communication involves more than just verbal dexterity; it also involves nonverbal interactions, style of communicating across organizational levels, and personal appearance or image. Verbal communication is extremely important in corporate America, and the ability to make yourself understood is crucial, particularly in difficult or unclear situations. If your native language is not English, you may find yourself disadvantaged because of an inability to communicate with the same speed or precision as your colleagues. Or you may face difficulties because your accent is difficult to understand.

Language Issues

At some companies, language issues are very important. Veronica Sims recalls a corporate culture where this was the case: "At my former employer, communications skills were very important," she reflects. "If you didn't have strong verbal communications skills, it really didn't matter much how smart you were or talented you were—you had to be able to articulate." Of course, not all employers value the same competencies—at other companies, professional image may supersede communication in importance, or getting along with others may be prized more highly than performance. The key is to research the background of your future (and current) organizations and get an understanding of what competencies are valued there.

Voice Pitch and Modulation

Voice pitch and modulation also play an unheralded role in verbal communication, and women of color who have developed their voices often find that their communication style goes unnoticed because it blends in with the corporate norms. In other cases, their colleagues express surprise at their articulateness. Conversely, women of color with louder or accented voices, or whose voices are otherwise distinctive, may be surprised to find that their communication style is scrutinized because it stands out from the norm. So women of color often find that their communication styles are scrutinized whether they are excellent or outside of what is expected.

TIP: If colleagues compliment you on being articulate, it is best to give a brief, silent head nod. This will acknowledge the remark, and not the (backhanded) compliment; it also won't antagonize your colleagues, who may genuinely not know what else to say.

A recent study sponsored by the Hidden Brain Drain of the Center for Work-Life Policy (CWLP) addressed issues surrounding women of color and communication. The study, *Invisible Lives: Celebrating and Leveraging Diversity in the Executive Suite*, found that close to one-third of executive women of color "worry that their speaking style labels them as lacking leadership potential."[5] If you share this concern, it is probably best to be proactive; you may consider consulting a speech therapist or vocal coach for professional help. Companies might consider whether they are unfairly marginalizing excellent employees because of language barriers, and consider getting a speech therapist or vocal coach on retainer for high-potential employees.

In Their Own Words

Although communication is highly regarded at some companies, each organization is unique. Sims observes that women of color should make it a point to understand the unique aspects of their organization. "Every organization," she remarks, "has a certain set of politics. Some are very clear, some are less clear. There are certain functional organizations that are held in higher esteem than others. There are certain unwritten rules within the organization. And sometimes it's difficult for us [women of color] initially when we come into an organization—and even some years afterward—to really truly understand what's going on."

Nonverbal Interactions

Nonverbal interactions play an unheralded role in perceived communication style. A landmark study suggests that at least 55 percent of communication is nonverbal.[6] Thus, smiling, hand gestures, eye contact—even being quiet—and myriad other factors play a part in how women of color are perceived by their colleagues. The CWLP study found that 23 percent of executive women of color "fear that colleagues perceived their animated hand gestures as inappropriate." This concern indicates that women of color are uncomfortable in their employment environments—but it is unclear who shoulders the responsibility for their discomfort. Companies evidently bear some responsibility, because they reinforce "normative communication styles" which resemble those of white men—and fail to make room for those who communicate differently.

The Paradox of Normative Communication

The whole notion of normative communication is paradoxical because women of color will not be rewarded for adopting precisely the same communication style as their white male peers; rather, they must develop a modified style that is viewed as acceptable in light of their race and gender.

But women of color shoulder some of the responsibility, as well. Everyone who works in corporate America is subject to the same rules, and those rules were made centuries ago by wealthy entrepreneurs. It is not likely that the rules are going to change just because someone arrives who is unfamiliar with those rules or plays by different rules in their native country. But often women of color come to corporate America expecting it to adjust to them, only to find that corporate America rarely makes adjustments. And when an adjustment is made, it is because it benefits companies to adjust, with less concern for individuals.

Ultimately, both companies and women of color have a part to play in addressing this issue, and it begins with a healthy dialogue on the subject at corporations. Pretending to be incommunicado (on either side) is not a smart business proposition.

Developing an Appropriate Communication Style

For anyone in corporate America, developing a communication style that is congruent with the organizational culture is a challenging process, and especially for women of color. Communicating across organizational functions and levels can play a large role in how women of color are perceived by their colleagues. This is largely because cross-functional communication demonstrates an employee's sophistication and understanding of the "invisible rules" that govern the company culture.

Sophisticated communication reflects the invisible hierarchy and culture that exist at all companies. However, some aspects of the culture are indicated by outwardly visible actions, such as junior employees deferring to senior employees. But less obvious communication ethics exist, such as those involving employees on the line (revenue-generating) side of the organization and those in the staff (non–revenue-generating) areas of the business. Because the line side of the business generates revenue for the company, it is more prestigious than the support areas of the company. Cross-functional communication needs to take into account the interplay between line and staff positions.

TIP: Even though blind copying (copying someone on an e-mail without their name being visible to other recipients) is available, never use it. Instead, forward a copy of the sent e-mail to the person you want to read it. Many people have negative feelings about the blind copy function; they feel like it is dishonest. Although such a view is questionable, better to err on the side of caution.

Also, certain functions within a company are more highly regarded than others, and tend to produce the company's CEOs. At Ford, this division is finance; at Kraft, it is marketing. As a result, those divisions tend to display more organizational power than others. Communications must also take these factors into consideration.

Ultimately, the politics of cross-functional communication, even down to meeting invitations or the necessary approvals for any project, are done with the line-staff and functional hierarchy as a backdrop. Those unaware of these sensitivities may unwittingly offend their non-departmental colleagues.

Access to High-Visibility Assignments

Getting high-visibility assignments is not something that is done in a vacuum. As you gain influential sponsors, perform well, and refine your professional style and image, you will gain the trust of managers and other influencers. Then you will gain access to broader exposure through important assignments.

Managing Your Career

Your corporate career requires the management of a variety of issues, including relationships with subordinates, supervisors, cross-functional partners, sponsors and mentors, your internal peer network, and the occasional professional enemy—and this is just at work! Because of the various parties and issues involved, much of the secret to getting ahead in corporate America seems to involve a sensible, well-thought-out use of strategy.

In Their Own Words

Veronica Sims* believes that young women of color starting out should chart a path to their destination and find out what it takes to get there. In terms of what women of color should do to get ahead, she suggests, "Certainly at the more junior levels...career pathing. How do you [as a woman of color] determine what are the right experiences and roles to have in order to ascend to higher levels in the organization—and then [go] about trying to get those roles. This is one of the things that my experience at a former employer helped with. They made it very clear—you manage your

*Name has been fictionalized.

own career.... It's really your responsibility to determine where you want to be and how you get there."

Sims suggests this analysis should start at the earliest possible stage of a woman of color's career—preferably before signing on with the company. But she advises women of color who find themselves being passed over for promotions, or in the midst of difficult circumstances, to self-assess: "One of the first things that you have to do when you enter into a new organization or [are] assessing the one that you're in, especially if someone is having a difficult time in the organization...[is] to self reflect, and say, 'Is there anything that I am not doing that I should be doing differently? Am I missing something, am I missing some cues here in terms of the politics, etc.?'"

For Sims, taking ownership of one's career involves more than knowing the next job or department—it means understanding the nature of the gaps between where you are and where you want to be. Certain gaps may be experiential, meaning that specific job experiences are required before moving into a particular role. Others may be technical, such as language proficiency before working in a certain geographic region. Whatever the variance, the smart woman of color knows to bridge those gaps *prior* to expressing interest in her dream job. Sims used this strategy during her career. "While it's ultimately not fully within your control, you certainly want to have a view of it if you want to be a C-level officer—you look at that population and try to determine where the gaps are relative to your own experiences and make sure that you get that experience."

But she warns of corporate traps that lurk for the woman of color who allows herself to be diverted from her goal. "Sometimes we [women of color] can get sidetracked into staff roles—if we're in a line role—or [into] other areas of the organization that really aren't relevant to... where you want to [ultimately] go. Especially if [you're offered] a promotion, and [it means] more money, and things like that, but [that promotion] can really derail you if you have your eye on a particular position down the road."

Carl Brooks, president of the Executive Leadership Council & Foundation, makes a similar observation about job tracking. "We find that corporations have tracking jobs, or jobs where you have to have gone through certain jobs in order to make it to the very top...minorities in general, and females...don't participate in those jobs early in their careers. Therefore they don't lead assignments, aren't part of committees (high-impact committees), and some of the visibility that they would have acquired as a result of these assignments is lost."

Honing Your Professional Image

One of the most heavily disputed issues about women of color is professional image. Because women of color do not share the indicia of power in corporate America, they are often hyper-visible, and as a result, everything about them—including their appearance—is viewed as if under a microscope. Variance across acceptable professional images is considerable, depending largely on the industry in which the woman is employed. For example

- In the financial services industry, darker, conservative, tailored suits are the norm.

- A woman in the fashion industry must go to work in fashionable (maybe even very colorful) clothing, along with trendy accessories.

- In the information technology (IT) division, employees tend to dress in business-casual clothing—in part because it is the industry trend, but also for practical reasons, since they might be called on to duck under a computer desk or visit the server room during their workday.

But professional image is more than utilitarian for women of color, because corporate cultural norms are usually considerably different from those they experience at home. As such, women of color often express their individuality, heritage, or other cultural subtleties in their professional style. At many business conferences, women of color express their heritages through accessories—an African-American woman may wear a kente cloth pin or sash, or a Latina may wear a piece of jewelry designed and handcrafted in her homeland. But CWLP's study found that women of color are not always made to feel comfortable with such expressions. The study indicates that almost 20 percent of professional women of color "feel that their dress is seen as too ethnic or flamboyant."[7] This indicates that women of color sense some disapproval from colleagues about expressions of their individuality. It is unclear whether the company culture discourages women of color from embracing their diversity, or whether some women of color are "dressing outside the lines" and unwittingly challenging company norms.

> **TIP:** If you want to know what style of dress is best for your company, look around and see what the managers and executives are wearing. Also look at your team. These are good benchmarks when developing your own style.

Even within the industry-driven constraints on corporate attire, women of color should feel comfortable expressing their individuality in a way that preserves their culture, while remaining in sync with (not identical to) company norms. Janice Won notes that women of color should not have to change who they are, but can learn to be flexible in their approach, and upon learning the acceptable boundaries can express their individuality within the constraints provided. "Be yourself," Won advises.

Putting It All Together: As Easy as "P.I.E."

The P.I.E. success model was developed by Harvey Coleman and was published in 1996 in *Empowering Yourself: The Organizational Game Revealed*. The P.I.E. model focuses on three key components of success: performance, image, and exposure. According to Coleman, performance counts for 10 percent, image counts for 30 percent, and exposure accounts for 60 percent of the success model. Inherent in Coleman's theory is a hierarchy: Performance is the point of entry; image should be developed prior to exposure (otherwise, the exposure resulting from solid performance could become negative); and once image is developed, broad, positive exposure should occur.

Women of color might use a modified version of Coleman's theory of success attainment, because strategies that work for non-minorities will not necessarily lead to corporate success for women of color. A modified P.I.E. formula would give additional weight to performance (since women of color generally need to work harder), while keeping the image percentage constant and lowering the emphasis placed on exposure (because women of color are already highly visible). But whether or not you support the notion of a modified version of Coleman's theory, P.I.E. provides valuable insight into what it takes to get ahead in corporate America.

Performance

Although performance accounts for a mere 10 percent of the success formula, it is the lynchpin of success in Coleman's theory. Performance is a threshold requirement and plays several important roles in your career. Good performance helps to establish your intellect, your execution skills, and your ability to garner (and retain) influence. Performance also elicits the necessary trust from those above you in the organizational hierarchy, and helps you get assigned "stretch projects" or "developmental roles," which are pivotal to professional success. This level of trust, once validated, often leads to even more important (and visible) projects in which you can continue your exceptional performance. If you do not perform well, increased success is not likely to happen.

In Their Own Words

Women of color generally agree that exceptional performance is a key success factor for professional women of color. Madison Davies* agrees. "I became a National Sales Director," she says. "And prior to that role I never performed below 100 percent of my number. One thing about sales: It has measurable objectives. I mean, I was promoted every two years into positions that people 15 years my senior had not been allowed to pursue. After I took the director role, my numbers always came out to 110–120 percent of the target." She pauses to think for a moment. "But once I moved into a staff role, I became confused. Prior to the staff position, performance was how I measured my contribution and perception in the organization. But no more. I think it was at that point when I realized that the major success factors [in corporate America] were unrelated to performance. I had the image and the exposure, but it wasn't until I was in a role where performance played a smaller role that I realized how crucial the non-performance criteria can be."

*Name has been fictionalized.

Davies made the critical observation on the difference between line and staff roles. A woman of color's performance in line roles, which impact the revenue of a company, is measured more objectively, and is often tied to meeting financial targets. Staff roles are somewhat tougher to navigate. Without objective performance criteria, subjectivity rules the day. Where women of color are concerned, sometimes subjectivity can be the kiss of death. Or so says Marisol Sinders.

In Their Own Words

Marisol Sinders* is a bit cynical about the role of performance in career success. "I don't know," she sighs. "I think performance is often used to validate previously held beliefs—meaning, that if they [your managers] like you, your performance is great, but if not, your performance is not." On a project at her former employer, Marisol faced a deadline for a deliverable that apparently could not be met. "My boss was complaining that the milestone [for the project] was late," she said.

I talked to my predecessor, who was promoted out of my role, and she said that she had never met the deadline for that deliverable. Then I talked with the woman in charge of the area responsible for final deliverance of the milestone. She said that in her 15 years with the company, the deliverable had never been made on time—and that I had met the deliverable the earliest out of anyone. According to her, the timeline was fundamentally incorrect. But my boss didn't want to hear that. He insisted that I was late, even though my predecessor had also missed the deadline and been promoted." Marisol correctly observed that while performance is insufficient to garner a promotion, any absence of it can be used against you by those who do not want to help you.

Image

A polished and professional demeanor comprises 30 percent of the P.I.E. success model. This component is particularly important for

*Name has been fictionalized.

professional women of color because it helps them combat stereotypes, many of which involve economics and sexuality. When women of color are presumed to be from economically disadvantaged environments, other more insidious assumptions follow regarding their intellect, ambition, and ability.

From a sexual perspective, women of color are sometimes assumed to be aggressive and sensual (for example, African-American women), passive and submissive (for example, Asian-American women), or as uninhibited and hot-blooded (for example, Latinas). Although these stereotypes are changing, they still dominate American culture on a large scale. Combine these stereotypes with the fact that many senior and midlevel executives have virtually no experience with women of color as professional colleagues, and you have a recipe for misunderstanding, misperception, and limited success for women of color across corporate America.

A professional image can help you combat some of these stereotypes and their underpinnings, by helping to demonstrate professionalism, the seriousness with which you take your job, as well as your expectations of advancement. Once colleagues have professional perceptions of you, it goes a long way toward dispelling their preconceived notions about your race and gender. Conversely, a lack of polish or professional attire can be a significant hindrance to your advancement, and could play into the very stereotypes you want to avoid. In industries involving significant client contact, the scrutiny on professional women of color is increased, such that even when you have an excellent professional image, you might find yourself facing stereotypes—or maybe even some competition.

In Their Own Words

Madison Davies* has faced additional scrutiny because of her polished professional image. "I think, the more polished the image, the more suspicious people are. My style is typically crisp, neat, appropriate, and somewhat muted—that's the way that I am—yet it always gets the attention of onlookers. I am not the nanny, babysitter, maid, or the woman who serves them in the restaurant. I often think they say [behind my back] 'she must be overdoing it.' This is a source of constant consternation because it [my attire]

*Name has been fictionalized.

is always commented upon." But the comments don't stop there. "I often get told that I am pretty," she notes, adding that colleagues express some surprise in the compliment. "Almost as if they are overwhelmed by an image that is not only together, but that they find attractive. That really sets me off," she finishes.

Exposure

The "E" in P.I.E. stands for exposure and accounts for a whopping 60 percent of the success model. This exposure occurs primarily through networking, which may result in high-visibility projects or assignments. Networking provides many benefits, one of which is increased access to information—something tremendously powerful in corporate settings. Women of color in the know use informal networking to learn about departmental changes, future company leaders, and even their own reputations. They learn which managers or departments have non-obvious alliances (like intra-office affairs) and which managers are on their company's "fast-track." As a result, these networked women of color generally avoid common pitfalls in the workplace by using information from others to develop a well-defined strategy for success.

In Their Own Words

Davies agrees that networking is important. "I make it a point to grab coffee, eat lunch, or have an informal conversation with someone new on a regular basis," she says. "It's a good way to get to know people and to learn about what's going on around the company." But it can be tough for women of color to gain access to these informal networks because they are perceived as "outsiders." When a woman of color interacts with a group, she is often perceived as different: Her behavior is judged through a different lens than that of others in the group and she is not able to let her guard down or speak freely. This is mostly because there is an increased likelihood that her words will be repeated or, worse yet, misconstrued. "You do have to show them [colleagues] your 'human' side," Davies notes.

"When people haven't had a lot of exposure to women of color, they tend to impersonalize their contact with you. Sort of like 'they do this' or 'they do that.' Once you sit down, joke, and talk with them, I think it 'humanizes' you to them and helps them to think of you more like a person, instead of a stereotype."

The other type of exposure in the P.I.E. model involves high-visibility projects. Such projects tend to provide participants with significant exposure to people at senior levels within the organization. But it can be difficult to get the opportunity to take on such highly visible assignments, for a variety of reasons. You might be unknown to powerful people in the organization, or people may be hesitant to involve you in a project due to stereotypes and other assumptions. Other times, people who view women of color as competition may try to prevent you from gaining exposure, recognizing that such exposure plays a vital role in your professional development.

For women of color, getting ahead in the corporate game is not as easy as landing on a "laddered square." Although performance, image, and exposure each has a significant impact on a woman of color's career, they are not—individually or collectively—sufficient to advance a woman's career past midlevel management. One key factor remains: Women of color who have vaulted past middle management into the senior ranks of organizations have a broad array of sponsors and mentors who have shown them the way.

Notes

[1] Catalyst. *Women of Color in Corporate Management: Three Years Later* (2001).

[2] Blake-Beard, Stacey. *CGO Insights No. 10: Mentoring Relationships Through the Lens of Race and Gender* (October 2001).

[3] Catalyst. *Connections that Count: The Informal Networks of Women of Color in the United States* (2006).

[4] Catalyst. *Women of Color in Corporate Management: Three Years Later* (2001).

[5] Center for Work-Life Policy. *Invisible Lives: Celebrating and Leveraging Diversity in the Executive Suite* (2006).

[6] Mehrabian, Albert. *Silent Messages: Implicit Communication of Emotions and Attitudes* (Thomson Learning College, Second Edition, 1980).

[7] Center for Work-Life Policy. *Invisible Lives: Celebrating and Leveraging Diversity in the Executive Suite* (2006).

CHAPTER 3 How Corporate Diversity Strategies Impact Women of Color

While companies tout their diversity programs as evidence of change in corporate America, for many women of color, the reality is that diversity initiatives have benefited them less than other women and minorities. Recent research confirms that women of color continue to lag behind other minorities in terms of salary and career advancement.

Sheila Wellington, clinical professor of management at NYU's Stern School of Business and the former president of Catalyst, has seen changes in diversity programs since she originated the women of color research at Catalyst almost a decade ago. "Over time these programs have been refined and have gotten more effective," she observes. Then she quotes a colleague's observation that "running everybody through a diversity program is the sheep-dip method of change," and she adds, "If you want to get beneath the surface [of diversity issues], you really have to mean it. And nothing's going to work if you don't have the...commitment from the top. And it has to be real...not just a memo."

In Their Own Words

Diversity initiatives have undoubtedly helped minorities to progress in corporate America, but there are plenty of women of color who do not feel a significant benefit from them. Lydia Perez,* a Latina in a male-dominated industry, is straightforward about her view: "No, I do not feel that the diversity initiatives and/or programs have been beneficial to me. When I worked at [my former employer], it took a class-action suit for management to consider placing women in key management positions." When employees see their company facing a class-action discrimination lawsuit, and the company has to be compelled to implement diversity strategies by negative media attention and the threat of a multimillion-dollar settlement, the employees are rightly skeptical of the organization's commitment to diversity.

What often happens to women of color is that they begin to see the same issues surrounding women of color at different employers. Perez experienced this very thing. "When I joined [her next employer], I was confronted with being the only female in a senior management position." Because of the size of the employer, Lydia looked for some evidence that diversity initiatives were working. She determined that "considering the total number of employees [in her division], it [was] embarrassing to see the total number of women in key positions and/or the total number of Hispanics throughout [the organization]." Large employers that have very little diversity—not only in the upper ranks of the organization, but throughout the entire company—are demonstrating that diversity is simply not a priority for the organization.

Nonetheless, Perez remains hopeful about the fundamental nature of diversity initiatives: "I genuinely believe that diversity discussions/initiatives are good and can be linked to the bottom line," she observes. "[But], like any important initiative, it requires senior management commitment and stick-to-itiveness. Unfortunately, when companies face difficult times, diversity is virtually forgotten."

*Name has been fictionalized.

The issue of longevity of diversity initiatives is an important one; some companies have short-term diversity strategies. But, because of the amount of time and resources it takes to develop a good manager or leader, and because of the threat of attrition, a short-term diversity strategy is tantamount to having no diversity strategy at all. Another reason for the short-term nature of some diversity strategies is company skepticism concerning the business case for diversity. "In reality," Perez says, "there appears to be an inherent disbelief that it [diversity] impacts the bottom line [of companies]." Certainly if companies really believed that diversity was best for their financial performance, they would not let the programs and initiatives wane.

Evaluating Diversity Initiatives

Today, many companies have diversity initiatives in place, such as mentoring programs, diversity task forces, and employee networks. In many cases, these initiatives do not benefit women of color as much as other women and minorities. This section is aimed at evaluating standard diversity programs and suggesting ways to make them more beneficial to professional women of color.

Formal Mentoring Programs

One of the most widely used corporate diversity strategies is mentoring programs. Many programs are sponsored at the corporate level; in larger corporations they may be sponsored at the subsidiary or division level. The obvious reason for developing a mentoring program is to address one of the most extensively perceived difficulties for women and minorities: developing relationships with mentors and sponsors.

For women of color, the program's strength directly relates to one of their key career hurdles: a lack of mentors and sponsors.[1] Such programs also assist women of color in developing relationships across racial and gender differences. If the mentoring relationship blossoms, it provides you with access to informal networks, which often result in helpful career advice, the "inside scoop" on company politics, corporate culture, and other important issues. Such networks and information are invaluable to anyone desiring to thrive and to advance in the company.

But mentoring programs encounter some difficulties, as well. The formal process of matching mentors with protégés invariably leads to some mismatches, because of several factors:

- **Managers feeling forced:** Company managers may feel compelled to participate in the program without always being interested (especially if senior management is not viewed as being committed to the issue of diversity).

- **Time constraints:** Managers may be busy with their own work and initiatives and do not have sufficient time to adequately develop a rapport with their protégés or provide them with guidance.

- **Not a "fit":** A mentor and protégé simply may not work well together—something that can occur when mentoring relationships do not develop naturally.

- **Cross-gender/Cross-cultural issues:** Managers and employees may be uncomfortable developing mentoring relationships across cultures and genders. This could lead to cynicism on the part of the manager and the employee.

- **Does not address sponsors:** Mentoring programs do not usually address the issue of sponsorship. Understanding the difference between mentors and sponsors, and having both types of colleagues in one's network, is important to career success. Sponsors are discussed in greater detail in chapter 6.

According to a recent *Harvard Business Review* article, "Leadership in Your Midst," 66 percent of ethnic and women professionals supported the development of corporate mentoring programs. However, these minority professionals were also hoping to be matched with senior managers whose "ethnic and cultural backgrounds" were similar to theirs.[2] Although this desire is understandable, women of color only make up 1.6 percent of corporate officers. It is unlikely that most women of color will be able to develop a mentoring relationship with a mentor who shares their ethnic background.

Sheila Wellington agrees that mentoring is important. "Everybody needs somebody to show them the ropes; to teach them what they don't learn in school," she says. "If you don't have access to that, it's awful hard to understand the politics of any organization, not just business organizations...[and] if you don't have somebody to clue you in, preferably more than one person...you're going to be stumbling around in the dark."

When companies or divisions undertake to develop a mentoring program, the program ideally involves more strategy than simply matching names, divisions, genders, and ethnicities. Otherwise, mentoring programs would become a glorified form of networking, and not really result in the value-add that organizations are looking for. Instead, a mentoring program may work best in conjunction with the performance evaluation process or the succession-planning needs of the organization. Although this is admittedly complex, organizations would generate better returns on the time and energy they spend administering mentoring programs if they matched employee needs and mentor expertise on a functional basis.

But even the most adeptly administered mentoring programs will fall flat on their faces if genuine support from the CEO and senior executives is not known throughout the company. It is endemic to corporate culture that the CEO and his or her direct reports (senior management) are the driving force behind much of what happens within the organization. Senior management's focus becomes the rest of the company's priority. As such, when senior management pays lip service to diversity without really making it a company priority, other employees recognize this and behave similarly. When CEOs take diversity initiatives seriously, and actively support them, employees do also.

Whether you work at a company where diversity is viewed as window dressing or at an organization where diversity is seriously regarded, participation in mentoring programs is advantageous to your career trajectory. But there is no need to view formal mentoring as the only way to develop mentoring relationships— it is only *one* way. Another way to find good mentors is to take a look at those who are highly respected within an organization and take time to get to know them.

TIP: Mentoring relationships, as with any relationship, take time to develop. It is not a good idea to ask bald questions, such as "will you be my mentor?"; such questions betray a lack of understanding about the manner in which mentoring relationships develop. One of the best ways to get a mentor is to ask for feedback on your assignments. When managers see that you want to improve your performance, they will often help you.

Formal mentoring relationships can sometimes become more real— sort of like Pinocchio becoming a real child. In other cases, an excellent employee is noticed by managers in the organization who will seek to help her career. But be aware that mentors are much more likely to want to be engaged in mentoring with an employee who already has a reputation for stellar performance. Although this may seem counterintuitive, it is helpful to think about it from the mentor's perspective: Why would a mentor want to be associated with someone who is not perceived well in the organization? It would serve only as a poor reflection on the mentor's managerial abilities. This is also part of the reason that a network of peers is so vital to your development—they can help you understand and improve how you are perceived. Remember, those who demonstrate facility with the corporate culture are rewarded with mentors who can assist them in further developing. So take every opportunity to develop mentoring relationships, as well as other informal relationships, with your colleagues.

Although most mentoring occurs after a woman of color is already an employee of the organization, some companies are starting the mentoring process much earlier in the careers of young women of color. The Chubb Group of Insurance Companies has developed the Collegiate Women of Color Leadership Development Institute. This program selects women of color from various colleges to assist them as they prepare for leadership roles in the future. Part of this year-long intensive program takes place at Chubb's Mt. Washington Conference Center in Baltimore, Maryland, and includes a variety of speakers who address leadership topics with the program participants. The participants receive mentors from Chubb and a generous stipend to assist them in undertaking a leadership project during their senior year of college. As companies like Chubb continue investing in women of color, they are increasing the pipeline of viable professional women of color down the road. This is the new wave of diversity initiatives.

Diversity Task Forces

In order to develop effective diversity strategies, many companies set up diversity task forces, comprised of cross-functional colleagues at the corporate level or senior leaders at the division level. Such task forces are usually made up of men and women from a cross-section of ethnic groups in the organization, and often provide a slate of recommendations to senior company leaders.

Diversity task forces can be very valuable to companies by gathering input across a broad spectrum of viewpoints and divisions. These viewpoints are used to assist in developing, refining, or reviewing an organization's diversity strategy. Diversity task forces also serve multiple purposes; they can be a method by which companies can gather feedback from their non-majority employees. This occurs because once the task force begins working, its members tend to develop diversity initiatives that are designed to address certain perceived inequities within the company. Many of these issues come out through the dialogue of the task force.

Joining diversity task forces is attractive to employees because it offers an opportunity to help the company develop relevant diversity initiatives while achieving some visibility within the organization. They also benefit from having a reputation of being diversity-friendly. Because of the benefits of serving on the task force—and because strategic thinking, political savvy, and expertise are necessary requirements—it is critical that companies establish objective criteria for selecting a diversity task force.

Occasionally the task force is given the task of determining its scope, but often this is predetermined by senior management. Task forces develop specific initiatives, a program, or a slate of ideas for senior management to review, and usually are not responsible for implementing the initiatives in the organization. The challenge for diversity task forces is to develop relevant, measurable diversity objectives within the constraints given them by senior management, and in a way that dovetails with the corporate culture.

While diversity task forces are developing or revisiting their strategies, they should intentionally develop initiatives targeting women of color. The task force should not assume that initiatives designed to benefit all minorities will benefit women of color, because this is often not the case. Specifically, task forces should increase (or begin) their inclusion of women of color as a distinct demographic that should be tracked statistically, along with women and minorities at the organization.

Many diversity task forces focus their energies on gaining exposure for high-potential minorities, but often neglect to educate them on the informal pipeline to the top of the organization. Each company has its own culture, and included in that culture are "feeder" positions that fast-track employees to higher-level positions after a one- or two-year stint. Because of their quick turnover and high visibility, employees in these roles are often recruited for other influential, higher-level positions in the organization.

At some companies, the feeder position is a plum job in a particular division (for example, finance), a chief of staff role, or a strategy role. One of the easiest predictors of the future leadership of an organization is to see who is holding these feeder slots. If diversity initiatives do not track whether high-potential women of color are getting into these roles—and do not help them get into such roles—there is little hope that they will rise to the top of the organization, except through community relations or human resource roles—areas that currently have the widest representation of women of color in corporate America today.

Diversity task forces should also consider broadening the notion of diversity initiatives. This broadening could take into account the different patterns of caregiving and family dynamics experienced by ethnic minorities in the workplace—in which women of color are often the responsible caregivers. This broadening also takes into account the differences in parenting dynamics faced by women of color. Broader diversity initiatives are discussed later in this chapter.

Employee Networks

Employee networks are one of the most obvious fruits of the diversity trends in corporate America. The vast majority of major corporations maintain such networks for employees of different ethnicities, women, and more recently, those with different sexual orientations. The purpose of these networks is usually to recruit, retain, and help their members with professional development. Although such networks are undoubtedly beneficial to the employees who participate, these same networks may cause some difficulties for women of color.

Structural Issues

Difficulties arise, in part, because of how the employee networks are structured. Employee networks, in similar fashion to the term "minority," were initially formed on the basis of employees having *one* attribute that differs from the two dominant indicia of power in corporate America: whiteness and maleness. Thus, developing employee networks for African-Americans, Latinos/Latinas, and other ethnic groups, as well as networks for women, seemed to address the issue squarely. But the structure of such networks inevitably fails to address the needs of those having *multiple* differentials from the power structure.

Dr. Evangelina Holvino, a faculty member at the Center for Gender in Organizations at the Simmons School of Management in Boston, has done considerable research on the subject. One of her articles, entitled "'Tired of Choosing': Working with the Simultaneity of Race, Gender, and Class in Organizations," notes that a woman of color is often forced "to choose between dimensions of her identity such as her gender and her race/ethnicity: 'I'm a woman' or 'I'm Puerto Rican" rather than 'I'm a Puerto Rican woman.'"[3] The current structure of most employee networks forces a woman of color to make precisely this choice.

Notions of identity for women of color are further complicated by classism. Women of color who might otherwise be disenfranchised from the corporate structure are often treated differently than their ethnic female peers when they come from economically advantaged backgrounds or have been educated at top-tier educational institutions. For example, a woman of color who graduates from Harvard Business School (HBS) may be perceived to have advantages over not only other women of color, but also over white men who attended less prominent business schools. Certainly, to some degree there are advantages to attending HBS.

But a woman of color who has graduated from HBS does not immediately become part of corporate America's power structure. She is still viewed differently than HBS alumni who are white males. Thus, companies find it difficult to meet her needs, and the woman of color is put squarely between two equally dangerous alternatives— as in Homer's epoch tale of Odysseus. During Odysseus' journey, he was faced with going through a strait that flowed directly between Scylla (a sea monster that was notorious for consuming sailors from ships) and Charybdis (a deadly whirlpool).

Odysseus chose his path through the strait with a view to saving his fellow sailors. Ultimately some lived, while others died. For women of color, the decision is not a life-or-death one; rather, like Odysseus, they are forced to navigate carefully through difficult alternatives. On one hand, they are identified as women of color, on the other, as prominent b-school graduates. Class considerations also force women of color to choose between various aspects of their identities.

For women of color, these multiplicities of identity present them with a complex dilemma. When attending meetings with the ethnic employee network, gender concerns are often not addressed; the expectation is that the women's network will deal with those issues. At the women's network, issues of ethnicity are not addressed because those issues seem to fit more in the ethnic employee network. As such, women of color cannot find an employee network where their unique concerns are addressed. In "Tired of Choosing," Dr. Holvino observes that "Having to make this choice creates a kind of identity schizophrenia where a woman of color has to deny a major part of her life experience. The choice of which part of her identity to privilege often varies by context, adding to the problematic dynamic."[4]

These contextual differences also account for some of the difficulty women of color encounter within ethnic or women's employee networks. In the context of an Asian employee network meeting, an Asian woman may be more sensitive to the gender issues in Asian male-female interactions, or to the interplay between various Asian cultures (for example, Japanese, Chinese, and Korean). In the context of a women's network, the Asian woman sees that her race plays more of a role in her interactions with other women.[5] Thus, a woman of color is challenged to examine different facets of her identity depending on the context of her employee network.

In Their Own Words

Jennifer Leung,* a Chinese-American finance professional, believes that it benefits her to have both women and Asian employee network groups at her company. "I am glad that I work at company that has organizations to support women and also Asian employees," she notes.

But she was not informed about the networks when she joined her employer, and found out about them on her own. "[W]ithout my own due diligence, I did not know that these groups [existed].... I do believe if I joined either of these groups that these programs would be beneficial to me."

As a busy professional, Leung has not yet had time to join the Asian or women's networks. Companies should take a lesson: Informing employees of these networks during orientation is more likely to lead to the employee's future involvement.

*Name has been fictionalized.

Networks for Women of Color

The solution? An employee network for women of color. Now before you think "another employee network?" you should know that some well-respected, forward-thinking companies such as PepsiCo. and J.P. Morgan Chase have already developed such networks for women of color. These networks allow women from a variety of ethnicities to share their experiences in a forum that allows for their individuality and similarities at the same time.

Ellen Lee,* an employee who helped form the women of color network at her employer, suggested that women of color have a lot of issues in common with women generally, but that the women of color network addresses the "additive issues" that women of color face due to the addition of ethnicity to their gender issues. The group was started as an internal task force, like many other employee network groups, and was comprised of African-American, Latina, and Asian-American women. Part of the impetus behind it was that women of color had already been dialoguing about issues that were unique to them, so when the opportunity came to pursue a networking group, they jumped at it.

In "Tired of Choosing," Dr. Holvino described her experience consulting with an emerging women of color employee network group. During this process, she raised three fundamental questions for the group, which are instructive for companies considering forming networks for women of color. The initial question centered on how to unify the entire group of women of color, while allowing for differences among the internal subgroups. Or, as Dr. Holvino wrote: "How do women of color resolve their own gender schisms?"[6] This is a difficult question, and one which Working Mother Media, publisher of *Working Mother* magazine, has some experience in addressing.

When Working Mother Media began its foray into the diversity of women's experiences, it developed a workable model that takes into account the similarities and differences among the various groups. At Working Mother's Best Companies for Women of Color Multicultural Conference, plenary sessions are held, during which all ethnic groups, including white women, meet together and discuss issues that are common to all women. Some "insta-polls" are given (where participants engage in immediate electronic polls), which result in provocative discussions among the various women. The

*Name has been fictionalized.

plenary session is followed up by breakout sessions for the different ethnic groups of women, and access to each group is limited to women of that particular group.

Carol Evans, CEO of Working Mother Media, and the visionary behind the Best Companies for Women of Color Multicultural Conference, believes that it is important for women of color to recognize their strengths, similarities, and differences. She notes that the breakout groups "allow women of color to self-identify," and to have private conversations with other women who self-identify similarly. Another benefit that Evans cites is that women of color begin to see the myriad differences within their ethnic group. This helps women of color to get a sense of how much work is required for women to work across racial lines effectively.

This strategy has been extraordinarily successful for Working Mother Media. Around 400 companies now send their women and women of color employees to the annual conference. Also through its efforts, several nonprofit organizations for women of color have developed, including the Asian Women Leadership Network and Madrinas (the Spanish word for godmothers), an organization for Latinas empowering other Latinas. For companies, Evans is quick to point out that networking groups are only part of a larger diversity strategy, noting that "recruitment comes first. If you [the company] are not recruiting a gender, racially, and culturally diverse workforce, then you're not really becoming part of the multicultural landscape," she concludes.

Looking at issues from a multicultural perspective is not new at Working Mother Media. With three million readers—many of them women of color—Working Mother Media has addressed issues related to women of color for years. More recently, in keeping with the newest Best Companies for Women of Color initiative, *Working Mother* magazine has published articles such as "What Color Is Your Rolodex?" and "Dear White Reader." The idea behind these articles is to get women of all ethnicities thinking about issues related to multiculturalism in non-threatening ways—by providing information that readers can use. Evans also sees generational issues as becoming increasingly important to companies, observing that such issues will impact issues surrounding women of color. Says Evans, "Gen X, Gen Y, and Millenials are a lot more multicultural than Baby Boomers were. So in a way, [multiculturalism] is wrapped up together in how companies perceive the next generational workforce as a whole."

Ellen Lee's women of color employee network was structured similarly to the Working Mother Media model. The group's leadership represented the three largest ethnic groups in the organization: African-American, Latina, and Asian-American. According to Lee, part of the importance of this representation was the exposure that the network leaders would have with senior management. It was important to the network to ensure that the senior management of the company understood the leadership to represent all of the group's constituents—and not as a vehicle for one of the subgroups to push its agenda through. This internal balancing among diverse demographics is part of what keeps a women of color network functioning well.

The second question Dr. Holvino asked the founders of the women of color network focused on the network's agenda. It is well known that women of color lag behind other minorities in terms of career advancement, and in many ways the discrimination with which they are confronted has historical underpinnings. Thus as a group, women of color often want to go beyond the traditional employee network functionality of helping to recruit, retain, and promote specific ethnic groups. Women of color want to take additional action: They want to advocate for change in the organization. As such, employee networks for women of color may take a binocular view—on one side they work to recruit, retain, and develop their constituents, but they also work with diversity task forces and human resources strategists to ensure that women of color are adequately represented in the more senior levels of the organization.

Ellen Lee's group also felt the need to advocate for change. The group observed early on that many women of color were "trapped" in non-exempt, clerical, and administrative roles. By looking at the different levels at which women of color were employed, the group was able to successfully advocate for change by developing partnerships with some of the company's internal development programs. This resulted in workshops for their group's constituents and the beginnings of change within their company for women of color.

Dr. Holvino's final question addressed the value proposition for the women of color network, and its interplay with other employee networks. The initial question would be whether such a network is even necessary, since there is some overlap between women of color and currently existing employee networks. But the key word is *some*. The overlap between women of color and other women is partial, and the overlap between women of color and other ethnic employees is partial. It is tempting to view a women of color network as redundant; in actuality, at the intersection of race and gender, women of color find a unique set of issues that need to be addressed—issues that are not currently being dealt with satisfactorily by most corporate diversity initiatives.

When Ellen Lee worked with other women of color to establish an employee network for women of color at her company, she found that senior managers did not understand the necessity of having a network for women of color, and they really did not understand the issues the women were facing. As an Asian-American woman, Lee encountered executives who did not understand why Asian women needed to be involved in such a network, as if Asian-Americans— sometimes referred to as "the model minority"—do not really need diversity initiatives to be successful. In this instance, some senior executive's stereotypes about Asian-American success caused them to overlook the realities of Asian-American women in corporate America: These women account for 0.4 percent of corporate officers, are 0.7 percent of top earners, and hold 0.8 percent of corporate board seats, according to Catalyst.[7] It is unfair to deny these women the benefits of diversity initiatives.

In considering the development of an employee network for women of color, companies may want to examine themselves internally to see whether there is an implicit expectation that a woman of color should be able to get her needs addressed in preexisting employee networks. Companies need to be aware that by insisting on making women of color one dimensional—by forcing them to acknowledge only one aspect of their identity—they are in effect declaring a willingness to address diversity only on a one-off basis—that is, where employees share one indicia of power with those in power at companies. Unfortunately, it seems that many companies are still unwilling to deal with the complexities of the issues that face women of color.

Diversity as a Component of Performance Metrics

It is a common business practice for companies to use managerial incentives to focus management on a particular business issue. These incentives are designed to align managers with the company's priorities, and management behaviors that reflect the company priorities are rewarded.

Once companies accept that diversity impacts their bottom line, they sometimes use managerial incentives to encourage their managers to take diversity seriously. These incentives link some portion of the manager's incentive compensation to his execution of the company's diversity initiatives. Women of color overwhelmingly support this strategy; 71 percent agree that a portion of a manager's performance review should include an evaluation of his recruitment of minority talent—and that the evaluation should be linked to compensation.[8]

Another way that companies can hold managers accountable for diversity initiatives is by using methods similar to those used in leadership development programs and succession planning. Most companies already have systems in place to ensure that future leaders are given developmental opportunities throughout the organization. Such companies also have detailed plans about those who can step into business-critical functions, should a key manager depart. So without adding any new programs, companies can draw on pre-existing structures to hold managers accountable for their diversity results.

Hewitt Associates, a leading multiservice provider of human resources consulting, developed a study: *How the Top 20 Companies Grow Great Leaders 2005*. This study examines corporate systems of accountability in developing leaders. In selecting the Top 20 companies, Hewitt researched a variety of factors at companies that impact leadership development, such as corporate culture, contact with senior leaders, compensation, and developmental interactions.

Part of Hewitt's study researched the methods used by Top 20 companies to hold their leaders accountable for the results of leadership initiatives. The results provide compelling insights about managing diversity. Among Hewitt's top 20 companies, 80 percent held senior management responsible for the success of leadership development initiatives, including "succession planning, performance management, and high-potential development" programs. This methodology makes sense because it gives incentive to all senior managers, instead of only one manager, to support leadership development programs. In this way, the company is harnessing the clout of all senior managers and bringing it to bear on the execution of the desired programs and initiatives.

If we apply this methodology to diversity initiatives, it is immediately apparent how diversity initiatives would benefit from a similar accountability structure. Broad senior-level support of diversity programs and initiatives would help diversity to gain wider organizational support, instead of being valued sporadically in departments. The clout of senior management would influence organizational culture toward diversity, and diversity would be taken seriously.

The study considers Top 20 companies to have an excellent accountability structure; non–Top 20 companies less so. At non–Top 20 companies, senior management does not have responsibility for leadership initiatives; they are human resources' responsibility. By making only one senior manager accountable for leadership, non–Top 20 companies may not develop the broad base of support they desire for their initiatives. Implicitly, by delegating leadership issues to human resources, the company is communicating to its employees that developing leadership is not the responsibility of the entire organization; it is one department's job. And functionality plays a role here, as well. Because human resources is generally a staff function, the division may have insufficient influence to drive organizational change around leadership accountability.

This has important implications for diversity programs because human resources is often the department held accountable for diversity initiatives. As a result, these initiatives do not enjoy the same broad-based support as other programs because only one area of the company has responsibility for them. In addition to marginalizing diversity efforts, companies, by making only one division responsible, are communicating that diversity is not important to everyone. This lack of prestige is further underscored because of the staff nature of HR. By making diversity the responsibility of a division with insufficient clout to initiate and implement change within the organizational context, companies are effectively ensuring that diversity programs will not be taken seriously.

Diversity Training: Shortcomings and Solutions

It is common practice for companies to hold diversity or cultural sensitivity training for their managers, either when the managers are hired, or at a specified time during the year. This training is usually designed to help managers get a better sense of the differences between racial and ethnic groups, and between men and women.

But all too often, such training makes generalizations about women ("they're collaborative") and men ("more hierarchical"), and about ethnic minorities ("from underprivileged backgrounds"), and then concludes with a generalized statement ("being different is okay"). Ultimately, participants leave the diversity training session with their original racial, ethnic, and gender stereotypes fully reinforced.

But when diversity training is done properly, it is an excellent way to break down stereotypes. This is why 72 percent of women of color support the notion of training to address stereotypes in the workplace.[9] Companies also need to realize that training managers to understand other genders and people groups as "okay" really does not address the crux of the issue. Managers will better understand diversity when the myths and realities about "minorities" are juxtaposed with facts, including a thorough discussion of women of color and the unique challenges they face in corporate America. Part of this understanding of women of color comes from recognizing how their challenges differ from those of white women and men of color.

When contrasting myths and realities about minorities, companies can begin with the whole notion of diversity. A good definition is "ensuring that the most qualified people of every race and gender are given opportunities." It also helps to clarify what diversity is not: quotas. Companies should also use statistics to illustrate facts, such as the impact of diversity on the company's bottom line. Some recalcitrant managers may change their minds about diversity once they understand the objective reasons for diversity initiatives and programs, and the overall benefit to the organization.

Facilitation of diversity training is probably best done by a mixture of insiders and outsiders. When only outside consultants are used as trainers, their credibility is lower than that of company insiders because of their unfamiliarity with the organizational culture. Having a senior leader kick off the session and having company insiders involved throughout the program helps employees to understand that diversity training is not perfunctory, but that important people at the company value these programs and initiatives, and they are expected to, as well.

Broadening Diversity Initiatives

Diversity initiatives and programs are an important component of any organization's overall diversity strategy. Companies developing these strategies can benefit from developing programs that address the unique issues faced by women of color. They can also benefit by broadening the concept of diversity strategy to include initiatives that support different notions of family. And when developing the evaluative methods that correspond to these initiatives, companies should ensure that women of color are included as a discrete demographic in order to effectively assess whether the initiatives that benefit other minorities are benefiting women of color, as well.

Tapping "Cultural Capital"

To date, the majority of diversity initiatives have focused almost exclusively on helping minorities achieve success in corporate America—meaning a lofty title and numerous perks. But most of this help has been focused on the business side of the employee's life, with little attention to how their outside lives might also play a role in supporting their professional development.

In "Leadership in Your Midst: Tapping the Hidden Strengths of Minority Executives," Sylvia Ann Hewlett, Carolyn Buck Luce, and Cornel West noted that the outside lives of minority employees were found to contain "cultural capital." Originally coined by sociologist Pierre Bourdieu, the term refers to "nonmonetary wealth and relationship capital generated outside the workplace."[10] The value of cultural capital is well known in organizations, evidenced by companies' associations with well-known nonprofits such as the United Way, Race for the Cure®, and other artistic and cultural organizations.

Women of color often possess large amounts of this "cultural capital." They develop this capital because they feel linked to their communities and have a strong desire to give back. This leads to their involvement in various charitable endeavors, from being a Big Sister to a young girl, to serving in churches or other places of worship, to helping the poor and disenfranchised through community organizations. These activities result in numerous relationships related to their community involvement.

According to "Leadership in Your Midst," employees keep much of this cultural capital hidden because they fear that their outside efforts will be viewed as a distraction from their career-related responsibilities. As a result, many companies do not benefit from employees' cultural capital, particularly that which is held by women of color.

It is also surprising to learn the extent to which minorities keep their outside lives "hidden" at work. Among those hiding their lives were 56 percent of the women of color surveyed at large corporations, 50 percent of younger women of color, and 49 percent of Asian-American women. Also, because women of color are extremely active in their communities, the researchers found that, among professional African-American women, 25 percent are leaders in their religious groups (compared to 16 percent of white men), and 41 percent help with "social outreach" (compared to 32 percent of white men). In terms of mentoring, 25 percent of professional African-American women are involved, whereas only 14 percent of white businesswomen are. The point is not to prove that women of color are more involved in community service; rather, the statistics make a strong argument that companies are missing out on much of the cultural capital that women of color possess.

> **TIP:** One of the best ways to showcase your outside involvements at work is to get involved with company-organized volunteer efforts, such as Volunteer Day. Usually you can work at the charitable organization of your choice, on company time, for one day. This allows your employer to see your outside involvement without it detracting from your work responsibilities. But be sure to check with your supervisor before participating.

In addition to developing an evaluative model that recognizes and harnesses cultural capital among women of color, companies could take it a step further and develop programs or partnerships with organizations to *assist* women of color in developing or refining this capital. An example of such a program is the United Way New York City's nonprofit board training program, known as Linkages. Linkages is an established board training and placement program, which trains business professionals (with particular attention to minorities) to serve on nonprofit boards in New York City. Participants undergo 14 hours of governance training through sessions held at the United Way offices. Although Linkages does not promise participants a board placement upon completion of the program, it does broker meaningful opportunities to meet with nonprofit organizations seeking board members. Linkages graduates go on to serve in the nonprofit sector in a variety of ways, but primarily through nonprofit board service.

In the 1990s, the United Way developed many similar programs across major cities throughout the United States, although the programs have different names in different locales. In Atlanta, the program is called United Way V.I.P. (Volunteer Involvement Program); in Dallas, the Dallas Blueprint for Leadership is offered through the Center for Nonprofit Management. Other similar programs are offered in cities throughout the U.S.

Because much of corporate America is already connected to the United Way, companies could build from that platform to provide a mechanism by which company employees could serve their communities. At the same time, the employees could develop leadership skills that benefit the organization. The challenging part is to develop a metric to gauge this outside leadership development. One option is to build outside leadership into the performance metrics that factor into an employee's incentive compensation. Then, to ensure that employees are not encouraged to neglect their current work duties, companies could adopt a heavier weight for their work-related performance.

Expanding Benefit Offerings

In addition to understanding the value of the cultural capital that women of color bring to the office from their outside lives, companies can also consider how to develop benefits packages that offer support for those outside lives. Specifically, women of color often take care of extended family members, or otherwise have additional family burdens. In many ways, the lives of women of color differ so much from those of white women that even "women-friendly" benefits packages may not go far enough to address the needs of women of color.

The Center for Work-Life Policy's (CWLP) research found that 51 percent of women of color are working mothers, as compared with 41 percent of white women. Although this disparity is significant, perhaps even more importantly, 18 percent of African-American women are single mothers, and only 7 percent of white women are.[11] Women raising children alone undoubtedly face additional outside challenges while working.

Apart from issues related to immediate family, some women of color are involved in caring for extended family members. CWLP found that 17 percent of African-American women care for "elders and extended family," and spend 12.4 hours on average per week doing so. White women spend 9.5 hours; white men, 6.6.[12] And in Hispanic and Asian cultures, the importance of one's extended family is well understood. Again, the point is not to prove that women of color care more for extended family than white women, but to demonstrate that women of color are spending considerable time outside of work caring for family.

In Their Own Words

Jennifer Leung views her company's benefit offerings as a plus. She is considering staying at her company "long-term, because of the great work-life balance they have here for all employees. And yes, diversity initiatives have had an impact on my tenure [here], but...a small impact."

While company diversity initiatives play a small role in persuading Leung to stay with her employer, the work-life balance component is of greater importance to her. Companies should realize that retaining women of color is not just a diversity issue; benefits and work-life balance do play a role.

Not surprisingly, CWLP found that 74 percent of women of color support an expansion of employee benefits. This expansion would include assistance with health insurance payments for up to two extended family members. Other initiatives that women of color support include annual leave (no more than a few days) to care for extended family or elders (supported by 72 percent of women of color), and assistance navigating state and federal services for various immediate and extended family concerns (supported by 74 percent of women of color).

A benefits package that takes women of color's caregiving lifestyle into account would be a welcome expansion of diversity initiatives in corporate America. Such initiatives could help women manage their lives outside of work—allowing them increased time to focus on their careers. Finally, such benefits do not always have to lead to large spending increases for the company; sometimes benefits providers can allow the company to make additional offerings available to its employees at a minimal cost to the organization.

Revamping Performance Evaluations

Performance evaluations are a touchy subject for companies, managers, and employees, for many reasons; these evaluations can also be a very sensitive subject for women of color. One reason for this uneasiness is the possibility that they will hear negative opinions or receive negative feedback—which managers generally do not enjoy giving, and employees certainly do not enjoy receiving. Moreover, because of the subjectivity of the overall evaluative process, women of color may be cynical about the integrity of the performance evaluation process. Or they may have previously received unfair, negative performance evaluations. It also happens that women of color sometimes face inconsistencies, such as receiving positive evaluations over time from their managers and then suddenly receiving a negative evaluation. This is particularly troubling where a manager has not given the woman of color any indication of performance problems prior to that evaluation. It is quite possible that managers have been less than totally frank with women of color about their performance for other reasons, such as fear of racial accusations. But women of color may still feel anxious about performance evaluations.

For all employees, but particularly for women of color, the backdrop of the feedback given in a manager-employee relationship is trust. Trust is a big factor in evaluations, especially because the evaluations play such a significant role in the career trajectory for women of color. Because of these factors, and because of the large role evaluations play in the retention of women of color, companies should work to ensure that the performance evaluation process is as transparent, open, and accessible as possible for women of color. It is up to women of color to be open and prepared to receive coaching and feedback from their managers, and to seek it out if it is not proffered. The other side of this equation is that managers have the responsibility to provide women of color with meaningful, direct feedback about their performance and how they can improve.

As part of a comprehensive diversity strategy, companies should conduct periodic reviews of the evaluations of minority employees, especially those of women of color. Recent studies have documented the presence of "hidden bias" at companies, observing that such biases are often hidden from the very people who hold them.[13] The manner in which these biases play themselves out is in amorphous, vague language regarding a particular woman of color. Examples include "she just isn't a fit with our team," or "I just can't put my finger on it, but something isn't right," or "she needs to loosen up." Statements such as these have derailed the careers of many women of color. But these statements have no substance to them. There are no concrete examples of poor performance, no indications of a lack of teamwork—just elusive, negative words. Often, what these vague statements translate into is that people are uncomfortable with a woman of color.

> **TIP:** Keep a running log of your projects and accomplishments so that during your performance review, you will be able to support your case for a particular performance rating or promotion.

To prevent managers from providing illusory feedback, companies may consider redesigning performance evaluations so that they require anecdotal or quantitative evidence of performance issues. Companies may also consider developing a system to investigate negative evaluations for high-performance women of color, to determine whether the evaluations are substantive, or are evidence of other internal issues, such as hidden biases.

Adjusting Evaluative Metrics

Since the 1980s, human resources departments have cited diversity statistics to demonstrate the professional advancement of minorities within their companies. These same statistics are also used to undergird company claims of commitment to diversity and to social responsibility. But upon further examination, most diversity statistics reveal that diversity has not progressed—at most companies—nearly as far as the companies would like outsiders to believe.

One of the most widely used diversity statistics is the percentage of minorities employed at a company. Although this information gives a partial snapshot of diversity in an organization, it often lacks any reference to the levels at which such minorities are employed. Thus, the statistic gives a picture of diversity that is far too general to give outsiders an accurate view of how minorities are progressing in the organization.

An Academic Perspective

Dr. Erika Hayes James is the Bank of America Associate Professor of Business Administration at the Darden School of Business (University of Virginia) in Charlottesville, Virginia. She notes that "[diversity] programs have unintentionally aided the advancement of people of color in support positions, rather than real functional, operational, line positions." This raises an important issue for companies; they must track the results of their diversity initiatives, to ensure that such programs are not used to steer women and minorities into positions that are less powerful in the corporate hierarchy.

Many companies with high general percentages of diversity have terrible diversity statistics as you reach more senior levels. These companies often hire minorities into lower-status jobs, such as mailroom employees, telephone operators, or administrative assistants. But at the more senior levels, minorities are rare. By using general diversity statistics, the company trumpets its diversity, but effectively masks the lack of minorities at its more senior levels. Some third-party publications on corporate diversity unwittingly help companies by not requiring more detailed information about the professional levels of the minority employees.

These third-party publications or diversity scorecards present other problems, as well. These scorecards calculate a company's diversity quotient using various diversity metrics. These metrics include the general diversity percentage at a company, the presence of diversity programs and initiatives, and the organization's business relationships with minority and women-owned businesses.

But the components of these scorecards are somewhat questionable. As noted earlier, the general diversity percentage is not really useful in determining the success of diversity initiatives. And the mere presence of diversity initiatives does not necessarily make them effective. Finally, the statistics on minority suppliers are not really relevant to a company's internal diversity, because the suppliers do not work for the organization. Using supplier diversity or multicultural marketing in a composite diversity score clouds our understanding of a company's internal diversity.

The result is that these scorecards paint a picture of the company as diversity friendly—and perhaps it is with respect to its outside vendors—but what about diversity at the company's middle and senior levels?

Where women of color are concerned, the typical diversity statistics yield even less information about their advancement at a particular company. This masking of information related to women of color generally occurs because of the manner in which the statistics are compiled. The majority of statistics group minorities together as women, as ethnic minorities, or as all minorities. Viewing diversity from this angle, women of color often are invisible—lumped in with women or minorities—and it is only when women of color are identified separately that one can ascertain just how far behind women of color are lagging.

A perfect example of how statistics can mask analysis is found in Fortune 1000 CEOs. Because so few women, minorities, and women of color are CEOs, these statistics provide an excellent opportunity to see how this masking occurs.

The total number of minority CEOs is approximately 52. Although this number is low percentage-wise (5.2 percent), many would agree that 52 Fortune 1000 CEOs presents a marked improvement in diverse senior leadership. But who has benefited? Looking more carefully, the statistics about Fortune 1000 CEOs echo the power indicia in corporate America—29 of the minority CEOs are men (57 percent); 20 are Caucasian women (39 percent), and 3—that's right, 3—are women of color (6 percent).

But if you looked at only the women statistics (45 percent) or the minority statistics (63 percent), you would completely miss that only 6 percent of Fortune 1000 CEOs are women of color. It is also telling that among the women and minority CEOs, fully 94 percent share at least one indicator of power (whiteness or maleness) with the corporate structure. These statistics are important because the high visibility of women of color leads many companies to believe that they are benefiting as much as other minorities from diversity initiatives. But once the statistics are broken down, it is evidently not the case.

Dr. Erika Hayes James makes a telling observation related to the advancement of black men and women: "When you look at black men relative to black women, I think what you'll see is that black women may have a faster rate of promotion—up to a point. But then they hit a glass ceiling at a level lower than the black men. And when you see people...crossing over into C-suite and other very senior levels in the organization, those people will predominantly be African-American men." Her astute observation applies not only to black Americans, but to Asian-Americans and Latinos, as well. Women of color still fare more poorly than their ethnic male counterparts at the most senior levels of organizations. But this information is not made clear by current diversity statistics.

If companies and third-party publications would begin to use different diversity metrics, we would gain a much clearer picture of how women of color, and minorities generally, are progressing at companies. Also, we would learn which companies are serious about *implementing* diversity programs and initiatives.

Accurately measuring diversity requires more meaningful statistics. These statistics could include the presence of an internal tracking system for high-potential minorities and the percentage of pivotal roles held, and the percentage of the company's high-potential candidates, each percentage broken down by gender, ethnicity, and women of color. Another meaningful statistic would include information about whether a company's policies require jobs at a particular level to have a diverse slate of interview candidates.

Refocusing Diversity Spending

U.S. companies are currently spending hundreds of millions of dollars annually on diversity initiatives. Despite this spending, many companies appear to continue searching for the best mix of diversity initiatives to get results throughout organizations—and in the meantime, companies are still encountering discrimination lawsuits. The lack of tangible results with many diversity initiatives should lead thoughtful companies to reexamine the focus of monies spent on diversity initiatives. *Cherchez l'argent,* a French phrase meaning "follow the money," should lead companies to examine their diversity spending to determine where the investment of funds will yield the best results. Companies should invest in diversity strategies that focus on talent development, such as recruitment and retention systems that track high-potential women of color employees (discussed further in chapter 5), or partnerships with programs that can help harness preexisting cultural capital among women of color for their benefit and for that of the organization.

Notes

[1] "'Tired of Choosing': Working with the Simultaneity of Race, Gender, and Class in Organizations." *CGO Insights* (March 2006).

[2] Catalyst. *Connections That Count: The Informal Networks of Women of Color in the United States* (2006).

[3] "Tired of Choosing," 2.

[4] Hewlett, Sylvia Ann, Carolyn Buck Luce, and Cornel West. "Leadership in Your Midst: Tapping the Hidden Strengths of Minority Executives." *Harvard Business Review* (November 2005).

[5] "Tired of Choosing," 2.

[6] Ibid.

[7] Catalyst. *2005 Catalyst Census of Women Board Directors of the Fortune 500* (2006).

[8] "Leadership in Your Midst," 6.

[9] Ibid., 7.

[10] Ibid., 2.

[11] Ibid., 6.

[12] Ibid.

[13] Ibid., 4,

PART 2 Bumps in the Road

CHAPTER 4

When Gender Discrimination Hits Home

As a woman of color, you will face certain difficulties in corporate America that men who share your ethnicity will not experience. Although there is no doubt that men of color suffer their fair share of racial discrimination at work, they also share one key indicator of power with those in charge: maleness. This maleness allows men of color to be more accepted in corporate leadership roles than women of color.

This chapter does not intend to minimize the difficult and demoralizing experiences that men of color experience in corporate America. Instead, its purpose is to examine how the additive factor of gender impacts corporate women of color when contrasted with their male counterparts.

Who Can Women of Color Turn to for Support?

In your community, you may find that your challenges as a professional woman of color are downplayed or minimized because of the success you have achieved. Among others with like success, you may find that you are expected to subordinate your gender concerns for the concerns of your race generally. The problem with this expectation is that it suggests that the good of the race or ethnicity can be achieved without addressing your concerns—which is simply not true. It is as important for the women of any culture to be affirmed in their identity as for the men. And as history has often shown, gender issues continue to plague women of color, even as advancements are made in race relations. Somewhere, our issues are getting lost in the struggle.

In Their Own Words

Women of color's experiences with their ethnic male counterparts vary widely. Some women of color have found support and assistance from ethnic male peers, whereas others have felt a distinct lack of support from the men. Lydia Perez,* a Latina, is firmly in the latter category. "From a professional [or] work perspective...there has never been a Latino male who has been supportive [of me]." She continues, "in the companies that I worked at, there were few Latino males and, frankly, they wanted desperately to blend with the white males and [to] survive. The individuals who mentored me early in my career and who supported me throughout were white males and women. They were individuals who respected outstanding performance and felt comfortable in exposing you to new opportunities."

Part of the difficulty Perez mentions is unique to lighter-skinned people of color, some of whom are less visible as minorities to their white colleagues. Most people of color are readily identifiable as such, and are visually distinct from their white counterparts. When people of color can blend in with the majority culture, they are typically confronted with fewer issues, and may be less sensitized to what is happening around them. But this is not always the case, and it should not be assumed that a person of color's skin tone determines their willingness to support others who share their ethnicity.

The other issue relates to corporate survival. Because of the challenges inherent in the corporate environment, men and women of color often try to keep as low a profile as possible. This is not always possible because visible minorities are just that—distinct. Professor Wellington puts it this way: "In general, for people who are different, the spotlight shines a little bit brighter." This spotlight can sometimes cause people of color to adjust their intra-racial interactions.

An obvious example of such adjusting occurs when a person of color becomes extremely careful about interactions with others of their race because they fear appearing clannish. Although it is unfair, the reality is that larger groups of ethnic minorities in the workplace draw attention to themselves.

*Name has been fictionalized.

That Perez was mentored by white colleagues is an experience common to most women of color, primarily because the pool of potential sponsors and mentors at just about any company is predominantly white men and women. It is a relatively rare occurrence to find women of color being mentored by other women of color. Madison Davies,* an African-American executive employed in a male-dominated industry, found that "the people who reached out [to me] before diversity initiatives were effected at my [current] company were white males."

Perez and Davies had different experiences with men of their own ethnicities. Davies found considerable support among her ethnic male peers at a prior employer, although they were few in number. At her current company, she found a senior-level male sponsor of her same ethnicity. For Davies, the determining factors in the support she has received from ethnic men were the size of the company and the men's education level. At smaller employers, Davies found that her ethnic peers "made assumptions about [me] based on stereotypes," sometimes even adopting a familiarity with her that they would not presume to have with someone of a different race. She also found that men of color with more education were more supportive of her, whereas those with less education were less so. But she is quick to add that there is no science to it, and that her remarks reflect only her experiences.

Perez's experiences with ethnic male colleagues have been consistently negative. At one employer she received little support or direction, in part because of her abilities: "My only experience with a Latin male was not a good one. I reported into him and he was intimidated by the fact that I spoke and wrote English better than he [because] he had been relocated from his native [country] to the U.S. He never did anything to support me because he was overwhelmed with the U.S. [and] headquarters' corporate culture. Again, he was basically trying to survive and was focused entirely on himself... work-wise, I cannot cite a time when I received support." Because Perez works in a male-dominated industry, it is possible that she would have faced some of these issues even with men outside of her ethnicity. Between Perez and Davies, a solid strategy emerges for women of color in handling relationships with ethnic men at work: Men of your ethnicity may or may not be supportive of your career. Where they support you, enjoy the benefits; where they are unsupportive, find mentors and sponsors who will look out for your best interests.

*Name has been fictionalized.

Men of Color Fare Better Than Women

One of the primary responses that men of color make when women of color raise gender issues in their respective cultures is to point out the disparate success levels achieved by women versus men of color. As their argument goes, women of color have achieved considerably more success in corporate America than the men; as a result, the men need more support.

Although this may hold true at the entry levels of corporations, current statistics thoroughly refute such notions. At the highest levels in corporate America, men of color fare better than women of color by a whopping margin. The "ceographics"[1] in the Fortune 1000 illustrate the disparity: Approximately 3.2 percent, or 32 out of the Fortune 1000 CEOs, are people of color. But of these 32 CEOs, men of color hold 29 of the positions, making them about 91 percent of all minority CEOs in the Fortune 1000.

Corporate Officers and Top Earners

Catalyst is a leading research and advisory organization that works with businesses on behalf of professional women. Its recent census of women corporate officers and top earners found that in the categories of "corporate officers" (those board-elected or appointed) and "top earners" (the five highest-paid employees), men of color account for a greater percentage of these roles than women of color. Overall, men of color account for 6.4 percent of corporate officers; women of color hold only 1.7 percent of such positions (see table 4.1).[2]

Table 4.1: Percentage of Corporate Officers by Race and Gender

Group (Men)	% of Corporate Officers	Group (Women)	% of Corporate Officers
Men of Color	6.4	Women of Color	1.7
African-American	2.6	African-American	1.1
Latino	1.7	Latina	0.4
Asian-American	1.5	Asian-American	0.4
Native American	0.2	Native American	0
Other	0.4	Other	0.1

A careful look at these statistics reveals that African-American men hold a greater percentage of corporate officer positions than *all women of color combined*, and Latino men hold a percentage of corporate officer positions equal to all of those held by women of color. So much for the presumption that women of color have all the advantages in corporate settings.

The statistics surrounding top earners in Catalyst's survey are also not very encouraging for any people of color. Overall, men of color only accounted for 4.1 percent of top earner positions; women of color, 1 percent. Again, the breakdown by ethnicity and gender reveals that men of color still fare better.

- **African-Americans.** Out of 23 top earner slots held by African-Americans, 20 are held by men (87 percent); 3 are held by women (13 percent).
- **Asian-Americans.** Among Asian-Americans, men hold 12 out of the 20 top earner positions (60 percent); women hold 8 positions (40 percent).
- **Latinos/Latinas.** Latino men hold 15 out of the 16 top earner positions (94 percent), while Latinas held 1 position (6 percent).

- **Native Americans.** Native Americans held only 2 positions, and both were held by men (100 percent); women held no positions.

- **Other ethnicities.** Other ethnicities held only 1 top earner position; it is held by a man (100 percent); no women hold any top earner positions.[3]

Because the numbers of people of color are so small, it is tempting to ignore the gender disparities within each ethnicity. Some may wonder whether our focus should be on increasing the overall representation of people of color in these roles. After all, people of color account for only 8.1 percent of corporate officers and 1.5 percent of top earners.

But there is no reason that the agenda for professional people of color has to be an either/or proposition. As people of color seek greater representation in influential corporate positions, they can simultaneously seek to ensure that women of color are not shortchanged in the process.

HACR's Study on Corporate Hispanics

The Hispanic Association on Corporate Responsibility's (HACR) Corporate Index 2004 found disparity in the corporate achievements of Hispanic men and women. Among its respondents, 33 percent of the companies surveyed had a Hispanic male executive within the top 10-ranked employees of the organization; however, none of those companies had a Hispanic woman at the same level. HACR also researched more thoroughly and requested information about the top 100-ranked employees at each company. They found that 82 percent of survey participants had a Hispanic person among their top 100 employees; but only 42 percent of them had a Hispanic woman in that category (HACR did not provide a specific breakdown between Hispanic men and women).[4]

Corporate Boards

Disparities also exist in the levels of participation achieved by men and women of color at the corporate board level. Catalyst's recent census on Fortune 500 boards reveals some troubling statistics on the composition of corporate boards in terms of gender, race, and ethnicity. Table 4.2 provides a snapshot of the statistics.

Table 4.2: Race and Gender on Corporate Boards of Directors

Group (Men)	% of Board Seats	Group (Women)	% of Board Seats
White Men	73.1	White Women	13.1
African-American	6.8	African-American	2.3
Latino	2.4	Latina	0.8
Asian-American	0.8	Asian-American	0.3
Native American	0.1	Native American	0
Other	0.3	Other	0

Overall, whites hold 86.2 percent of all board seats, and people of color hold 13.8 percent. Of the seats held by people of color, men hold 10.4 percent; women hold 3.4.[5] Again we see that men of color fare better than women of color. In fact, African-American men alone hold twice the percentage of board seats that all women of color hold.

To combat people of color's low representation on corporate boards, several institutions and organizations have developed initiatives to prepare women and minorities for corporate board membership. The initiatives also assist corporations in finding women and minority directors who meet the criteria for directorships. Women of color with appropriate professional experience and expertise can use these initiatives to market themselves for opportunities on corporate boards. (For more information about initiatives to get women of color on boards, see chapters 3 and 8, and appendix D.)

Staff vs. Line Functions: Where Is the Clout?

In addition to the under-representation of women of color at the highest levels of corporate America, statistics indicate that women of color have less "clout" than their ethnic male counterparts. Even when women of color are represented in the higher ranks of an organization, they may still have less power than a similarly situated man of color.

The best proxy to the clout factor is an employee's job function within the organization. In corporate America, where making money is the name of the game, employees with profit-and-loss (P&L) responsibility, or that work in "line" functions, generate revenue for the company and directly impact its "bottom line."

Although companies do not advertise this fact, in reality the other areas of a company provide support for the P&L functions. These are known as "staff" positions. From an accounting perspective, they are called "cost centers" because they cost the company money without directly generating any revenue. It is an undisputed fact that line positions, because of their revenue-generating capacity, have greater clout in the organizational hierarchy of any company than staff positions. Table 4.3 gives examples of line and staff divisions.

Table 4.3: Examples of Line and Staff Divisions

Line Divisions	Staff Divisions
Finance	Human Resources
Operations	Diversity
Marketing	Accounting
Product Areas	Legal

The disparities between the functional roles of men and women impact their organizational clout. According to Catalyst, only 10.6 percent of line roles are held by women; 89.4 percent are held by men. In the staff arena, women hold 21.1 percent of the roles, with men holding 78.9 percent.[6] Thus, women are overrepresented in staff roles and underrepresented in line roles. For women of color, this underrepresentation is probably even more severe.

One such subtlety occurs when companies steer high-potential women of color from line positions into staff roles. This steering is often very effective because of the manner in which most corporate careers are guided—from the top. If the "powers that be" ask a woman of color to consider a particular role, she cannot decline without ruffling some feathers. Moreover, a refusal could put her in a very difficult position, especially if she does not have a sponsor or mentor to manage the fallout.

Of course, some women of color enter the corporate world with a staff function as their main goal—and staff functions are very important to companies. But line roles impact an organization's revenue in ways that staff roles cannot. Thus, a woman of color who has been asked to move from a line role to a staff position should be very careful how she responds.

Stereotypes and Women of Color

One of the main reasons that companies steer women of color from line roles into staff roles is stereotyping. The title of Catalyst's study on stereotyping and leadership sums it up: *Women Take Care, Men Take Charge: Stereotyping of U.S. Business Leaders Exposed.*

Catalyst's survey found that stereotypes persist about women's abilities in leadership, which result in women being perceived as "taking care" rather than "taking charge." This research examined the presence of stereotypes in the workplace because more than 40 studies on leadership performed over the past 15 years have not found significant differences in men's and women's leadership abilities.[7] So what accounts for the differences in people's perceptions of male and female leaders?

This study's findings have major significance for women of color because of the multiple layers of stereotyping to which they are routinely subjected. At its core, stereotyping is an efficient way to categorize people and things, and it is a common practice. But there are some dangers in stereotyping, because of the following reasons:

- Generalizations about people are often much less accurate than other types of generalizations.

- Stereotypes are applied automatically without the recognition that they are being relied upon.

- Interaction with the stereotyped person often elicits behaviors from them that confirm previously held stereotypes.[8]

For women of color, these three areas of danger are amplified because of the influence of race or ethnic origin. The addition of race or ethnicity to gender results in subtle variations to gender stereotypes. We'll discuss each of the three dangers in turn.

Making Generalizations

Women of color are subject to more and different generalizations than their white female counterparts. Women of color are generalized because they are women, because of their race or ethnicity, and because of the combination of the two. Commonly held stereotypes about African-Americans suggest that they are all aggressive, outspoken, or threatening. Latinas are stereotyped as all acting feisty, temperamental, and passionate. Asian-American women are stereotyped as quiet, unassuming, and submissive.

In addition to these racio-ethnic stereotypes, women of color are often subjected to colorism, which is discrimination on the basis of skin tone. This colorism sometimes results in confusion as to a woman of color's race or ethnicity. Black Latinas, or *latinegras,* are often mistaken for African-American women because they closely resemble them in skin tone and hair texture. This results in Latinas being stereotyped as African-American women. Some multi-ethnic women with a partial African heritage or other fairer-skinned African-American women are thought to be Latinas because of their skin tone. So African-American women may be stereotyped as Latinas.

In some Asian and South Asian countries, colorism exists implicitly—people with fairer skin are thought to be more attractive by society. Colorism also exists explicitly in cultures, such as in the caste system, where skin color generally indicates a person's status in the system.

Ultimately, stereotypes are amorphous for women of color, but what can safely be said is that stereotypes related to them are directly linked to the *perceived* racial or ethnic group of the woman of color.

Using Stereotypes as a Basis for Knowledge of an Individual

One of the difficulties with stereotyping women of color is that people use the stereotypes as a basis for knowledge about the woman. The stereotypes faced by white women center less on their individual identity and more around their capabilities. Women of color face stereotypes about their identity first, and those stereotypes, in turn, predetermine their *perceived* abilities.

An example of this occurs when women of color encounter co-workers (or clients) who use certain slang, language, or pseudo-cultural references around them, to show that they identify with them. This is more than stereotyping; it is an act that identifies the woman of color with what are often negative stereotypes. For many women of color, such interactions are frustrating because the women are not allowed to share their identity with the colleague, but are forced into one based on preexisting cultural perceptions. And these perceptions often fail to describe who she really is. Every woman wants a chance to be known and accepted for who she is. But this is not even a remote possibility where colleagues have already predetermined your identity.

Professor Sheila Wellington notes that with stereotypes, others are often waiting for you to conform, and "if you do, you're conforming to a stereotype—[the] stereotype may not be flattering, but at least you're conforming to a stereotype. If you don't conform to a stereotype, then it's bad because you're not only lacking what you're supposed to be, but you're [not] what you're not supposed to be. It's tough."

> **TIP:** When you respond to being stereotyped at work, be careful to avoid appearing defensive. Even though stereotypes are offensive, how you handle them is what will be remembered.

The Inaccuracy of Stereotypes

The second concern with stereotypes is more obvious: They are often inaccurate, and are based on vivid or memorable experiences that a person has had with someone in a particular racial or ethnic group. The trouble with ascribing one person's conduct to another person of the same ethnicity is that even within the same racial or ethnic group, people differ considerably in their thoughts, perceptions, attitudes, and work ethics. Socio-economic class, education, geographic origin, family size, and other factors also affect each person's individuality. Using stereotypes robs people of their individual identities and substitutes actions that they have never taken and behaviors that they have never exhibited. Doesn't sound very fair, does it?

Obscuring Performance with Stereotypes

The final concern with stereotypes surrounding women of color is that they often obscure the woman of color's performance at the company. Dr. Jane Smith, executive director of the Center for Leadership and Civic Engagement at Spelman College, oversees its annual Women of Color Conference, now going into its fourth year. Dr. Smith recognizes the role that stereotypes play in the careers of women of color and wisely observes that "competence is recognized, but race and gender will hide it...[people] are blinded by the fact that you are a woman or of color."

In many cases, instead of stereotypes creating a filter through which women of color are viewed, they become *selective* filters, hiding aspects of women of color's performance that do not jibe with relevant stereotypes. Because of their insidiousness, the only way to address stereotypes is to expose them and replace them with actual knowledge of individuals. Only when colleagues and managers take the time to get to know women of color will these stereotypes dissipate.

TIP: Keep a log of your work accomplishments so that when performance evaluations come around, you will have excellent documentation of your progress and experience.

Automatically Applying Stereotypes

The second danger in stereotyping is that most people automatically apply them without thinking; they accept that the stereotypes are true representations of the other person. As a result, these invisible stereotypes, which may be completely false and inaccurate, will influence one person's perceptions and judgments of another. This danger acutely affects women of color, because they are likely to be perceived by others in a way that is heavily influenced by stereotypes. If stereotypes take root in their colleagues' and manager's perceptions of them, women of color probably won't be evaluated fairly in terms of their performance. Instead, they will find themselves confronted with stereotypical descriptions of their behaviors.

When high-potential women of color are asked to move from a line position to a staff role, it could reflect an unconscious company stereotype that women of color are best at staff roles. Consider this:

If a woman of color has excellent performance and is already in a line function (which generates money for the company), why move her to a non–revenue-generating area of the business? In such a case, the company is hurting itself, and is operating automatically on what it perceives to be the strength of the woman of color. But the company is not really seeing her strengths at all; rather, they are seeing what they believe her strengths *should* be, based on her ethnicity and gender.

Eliciting Behaviors That Confirm Stereotypes

Stereotypes present a third danger that is more subtle than the other two dangers we've discussed. It occurs when people behave toward others in ways that elicit a response confirming their initial stereotypes. This behavior surfaces regularly in relationships where one person evaluates another, as with managers and their direct reports.

Some managers have a philosophy that "smart people 'get it' without needing to be told," and behave as though the best employees understand their expectations without having to ask. But such a philosophy is disingenuous because these same managers are careful to tell certain employees about their expectations, while leaving others in the dark. So in effect, the managers create a situation where certain employees perform up to expectations, while others do not.

Another example of such behavior might occur in this scenario: A woman of color finds that her manager provides very little guidance or input on a report she is preparing, even when she asks him for advice. Later the manager complains that the report is not what he is looking for. At the same time, the woman's white male colleague has gotten significant input from the manager (unbeknownst to her) and he turns in a solid report. The evaluation: The woman of color is not performing at a level equal to her white male counterpart. But this disparate performance is not because she is any less competent, or because she did not ask for help. Rather, it is because she has been given considerably less information than her colleague.

> **TIP:** One way to ensure that you get necessary information from your manager at work is to end your discussions with a catch-all question, such as "is there anything else you think I should know to complete this project?"

For this manager to properly compare his direct reports, he should give them the same information and then observe how each performs. By giving one of his employees an advantage, the manager has ensured that he will get his desired outcome. In the same way, invisible stereotypes make it very difficult for companies and managers to properly evaluate the leadership abilities of women of color.

Taking Care or Taking Charge

Despite more than 15 years and 40 studies on leadership, Catalyst found that stereotypes persist that women leaders "take care." Women are consistently rated better at behaviors linked to caretaking, such as supporting, mentoring, and rewarding employees.[9] For women of color, the notion of "taking care" has unique implications because of the socio-historical nature of women of color's employment in the U.S. These implications are especially evident for African-American women and Latinas, who have historically worked as caretakers for white men and women.

Many whites in corporate America have very little interaction with women of color outside of work. As one academician put it: "[in terms of] white women... [white] guys have their mothers, their spouses, their sisters, their daughters [in their lives]. What white guy has had a woman of color in his life that he can relate to easily, casually?" Because of this lack of interaction, whites at companies often form views of women of color based on stereotypical roles. African-American women are sometimes thought of as nannies or nurses, and Latina women as housekeepers. Once people have these stereotypes in the backs of their minds, it can be very difficult for them to see women of color as colleagues, peers, and professionals. And they place undue emphasis on these women as "caretakers" more than they do with women of other ethnicities.

The "Living Room/Locker Room" Syndrome

A recent article in the American Bar Association's *Perspectives* magazine contains a term coined by Kimberle Crenshaw, a law professor at Columbia and UCLA. This term describes the situation between women of color and white men perfectly—she calls it the "living room/locker room syndrome." The term illustrates the notion that white men interact with white women in the living room, and with men of color in the locker room, but that no place exists where white men interact with women of color outside of the office.[10]

Conforming to Stereotypes

Another implication of "taking care" and "taking charge" is that men and women are expected to lead in ways that conform to stereotypical notions of masculinity and femininity. Catalyst found that women are considered better at leadership traits associated with femininity, and that men are considered better at leadership traits associated with masculinity. But the degree to which women or men were considered better at leadership traits varied depending on the trait at issue.

The most polarized views on women's and men's leadership occurred in relation to traits that fit closely with stereotypical masculine or feminine leadership styles. Thus, a woman leading in a way that others view as better suited to men is judged as a less effective leader than if she led in a way that is considered to be better suited to women.[11] Women of color, because of the addition of racial stereotypes, will be judged differently in terms of their leadership abilities than their white female counterparts. Also, African-Americans and Latinas are even more likely than other women to be viewed as most effective when they lead using behaviors associated with femininity because they are sometimes subconsciously viewed as "caretakers."

Acceptable Behavior

Another difficulty faced by women of color is the disparity between the acceptability of behaviors in their home cultures and in corporate culture. A woman of color's home culture may allow her to exercise traits that are stereotypically masculine, or may require her to exercise traits that are stereotypically feminine. But whether she acts in congruity or out of congruity with her culture in corporate America, she will find that people perceive her very differently than in her home culture.

For example, African-American culture is comfortable with direct discussions and straightforward language; corporate culture prizes aggressive, self-confident behavior in men, but views such behavior in an African-American woman as inappropriate and threatening. And much of this threat comes from her departure from the stereotypical notion of who the company thinks she should be. Ultimately, behaviors that are acceptable in her culture probably will contribute to the perception that an African-American is a less effective leader.

An Asian-American woman may find that her culture prefers indirect communication and prizes her self-effacing behavior. But if she behaves in accordance with her home culture at work, she may be viewed as an effective leader in terms of feminine leadership styles, but will probably also be viewed as a less effective leader than the men in her organization.

But what would happen if these two women reversed their home culture behavior at work? Would it make any difference in how they were perceived as leaders? Probably not. An African-American woman exhibiting stereotypical women's traits might be viewed as a more effective leader generally, but she, like other women, would still be subjected to stereotypes regarding women's leadership abilities. Moreover, because of the traditional view of African-American women as caretakers, her leadership effectiveness may be further diminished when she engaged in a feminine style of leadership.

The Asian-American woman who acts in a manner different than her home culture, and demonstrates more "masculine" behaviors, would probably find that her leadership abilities would also be viewed as less effective than those of her male colleagues. And her leadership would probably be viewed even more negatively because of her use of behaviors considered "masculine" in the workplace.

Thus, for many women of color this is a lose-lose scenario. If they act in accordance with their home cultures, whether those cultures encourage them to be aggressive or more docile, they will inevitably be viewed as less effective leaders than their male counterparts. If they act out of conformity with their home cultures, they risk feeling inauthentic, and will still be viewed as less effective leaders than their male counterparts. Moreover, if their ethnic group is generally viewed as lacking in leadership, their abilities will be called into question no matter how they behave.

Status Incongruence

The final hindrance to the acceptance of women of color as leaders is related to stereotypes, but manifests itself in an unusual manner. Status incongruence, a sociological phenomenon, occurs where a person holds a position within a hierarchy that others view as incongruent with their social status. The initial status marker tends to be gender; globally, across cultures, men are perceived as higher or as more important on the social scale than women. Ethnic groups also have a hierarchy of social status, and within a race or ethnicity, various people groups have a higher or lower social status.

In the United States, because of its history, whites hold the highest social status. After whites, there does not appear to be a general consensus as to where the different racial and ethnic groups fit within the social strata. And socioeconomic class also plays a role in the evaluation. But the fact remains that managers and employees in corporate America overwhelmingly favor white men in positions of authority, partially because they believe that their status merits such authority.

Next in the status hierarchy are white women and men of color, followed by women of color. Current statistics reflect this hierarchy in terms of Fortune 1000 CEOs, corporate officers, clout titles, and corporate board seats. But it also has historical underpinnings, as well. When the right to vote was initially enacted in the U.S., it was available only to white men—no women or minorities could vote. The first amendment to that law allowed black males to vote, followed by white and black women.

It is also important to recognize the role that status incongruence plays in others' perceived "comfort level" with leaders. When a new leader fits the status expectation of a particular role, people feel "comfortable" with that person, often believing that the person is a good "fit" with a particular team. But such language is really more of a subtext, which means that the new leader fits with their notions of a particular status, role, or functionality, and that the employee is comfortable with the social status of the new person in charge.

It is easy to see, then, why employees are less comfortable with women of color as leaders. A woman of color, no matter how competent, is viewed as having less social status than anyone else in the organization. It would be impossible for senior managers, managers, and employees not to feel some level of discomfort with her in a leadership role. No matter what she does, she will never "fit" into their preconceived notions of a particular role.

TIP: If you receive feedback that others are "uncomfortable" with your leadership, don't get annoyed. Instead, ask them what specific behavior is making them uneasy. If they give you specifics, consider making some adjustments in your actions. If they "can't put their finger on it," or don't really know why they are uncomfortable, recognize that this is probably their issue.

Where women of color are most likely to see status incongruence manifested is in their supervision of employees—whether white or of color, because such employees are often unaccustomed to reporting to a woman of color. The white employees may view the woman of color's social status as beneath theirs, and cannot respect her authority, while the employees of color may have no experience with a woman, or another person of color as supervisor, and also find her authority threatening.

For women of color, the challenges still exist. Stereotyping, misperceptions of ability, and critiques of your leadership style will not disappear. The best action you can take is to educate others about who they are individually, and choose your battles selectively.

Notes

[1] Ceographics is a term coined by the Ideas and Insights Group at Burson-Marsteller's Web site on CEOs, available at www.ceogo.com. Burson-Marsteller is part of Young & Rubicam Inc., and WPP Group plc.

[2] Catalyst. *2005 Catalyst Census of Women Corporate Officers and Top Earners of the Fortune 500* (2005), 19.

[3] Ibid., 20.

[4] Hispanic Association on Corporate Responsibility. *Corporate Index 2004.*

[5] Catalyst. *2005 Catalyst Census of Women Board Directors of the Fortune 500* (2005).

[6] Catalyst. *Women Take Care, Men Take Charge: Stereotyping of U.S. Business Leaders Exposed* (2005), 12.

[7] Ibid., 5–6.

[8] Ibid.

[9] Ibid.

[10] Hayes, Hannah. "Women of Color: Why They Are Finding the Door Instead of the Glass Ceiling—CWP Women of Color Research Initiative Prepares Preliminary Report." *Perspectives* (American Bar Association), Volume 15, No. 1 (Summer 2006), 6.

[11] Catalyst. *Women Take Care, Men Take Charge: Stereotyping of U.S. Business Leaders Exposed* (2005), 7–17.

CHAPTER 5 Getting Out = Getting Ahead: Changing Employers to Advance Your Career

The increased interest in professional women of color has yielded much in the way of useful information on ways that such women can advance their careers. One unexpected method of advancement is when a woman of color leaves her current employer and accepts a comparable or higher-level position at a different company.[1] Current statistics indicate that this strategy has been highly successful for women of color—with important implications for companies and for the women themselves.

Initial and follow-up studies on women of color found that they were employing a "get out-get ahead" strategy to advance their careers. According to the study, women of color who left their employers received promotions, earned higher salaries, and did not report as many career barriers as the other women of color who remained at their initial employers.[2] But it is questionable whether these results point to a viable strategy for women of color to advance their careers. It also raises questions as to why a company change should bring about significant advancement for professional women of color.

The Coming Labor Shortage

A "perfect storm" is brewing in U.S. labor markets, and companies are preparing to weather the coming changes. Among these changes are upcoming retirements, trends in employee company changes, and a competitive labor market.

The retirement aspect of this storm is major: Roughly 75 million baby boomers are retiring, and only about 45 million people in the next generation (Generation X) will be available to fill their roles. For many companies, this will result in the loss of senior managers and other high-potential employees. A 2005 survey by RHR International (RHR), a search consulting firm, found that half of the companies surveyed expected to lose 50 percent or more of their senior managers in the next four years. Moreover, 15 percent of surveyed companies expected to lose 75 percent or more of their senior management within the same time period.[3] Companies faced with the need to fill business-critical functions will either have internal talent ready to fill those roles, or will need to hire external candidates.

In 2004, the Bureau of Labor Statistics found that American workers (including wage and salary employees) spend a median of four years on their current jobs. This length of time points to a trend among American employees of changing jobs multiple times throughout one's career. But it is not clear why American employees change jobs so often.

NOTE: Catalyst's study found that 26 percent of African-American women, 24 percent of Latinas, and 21 percent of Asian-American women surveyed left their employers for better opportunities.[4]

The third factor in the "perfect storm" is a competitive labor market. Companies are always looking for excellent employees, some of whom are already employed and considered high-potential at other companies. When RHR asked companies whether they had enough high-potential employees to meet their future needs, only 25 percent of companies were "highly confident" that they did.

So it comes as no surprise that RHR found that almost three-quarters of companies expect to hire 25 percent or more of their future leaders from outside. Furthermore, almost 20 percent of the companies were expecting to hire more than half their leaders from outside their organization.[5] Companies that have taken the time to develop their employees should expect that their best talent will be targeted by their competitors. To the extent that this talent includes women of color, it naturally follows that the competition will take advantage of the opportunity to hire a well-qualified diverse candidate and fill their management pipeline at the same time.

Besides the competitive impact of losing talent in a shrinking labor market, companies are facing the cost of voluntary attrition of women of color. Among women of color, close to 25 percent are employing a strategy of "leaving to advance," and this number is consistent across the various subgroups that comprise women of color. Companies may spend considerable resources developing diversity programs, but unless they develop the complementary retention components, they will continue to lose talented women of color. And because the benefits of diversity programs often do not always reach women of color, retention strategies are helpful in offsetting that imbalance. Instead of focusing on new programs, companies would be well-advised to strategically use company resources to ensure that part of the diversity programming budget is used to develop tracking and retention programs for high-potential employees, especially women of color.

Tracking the Visible Minority Woman

Women of color face unique experiences in corporate America because of their paradoxical visibility and invisibility at their companies. Because they are "visible minorities," their presence at companies is obvious; but where career advancement is concerned, they often remain invisible. For some reason, organizations are surprisingly unaware of having talented women of color who are at pivotal decision points in their careers. As a result, such companies may lose these women to other companies that are sometimes their competitors.

Fragmented Recruiting and Retention Strategies

Part of the reason that some organizations are "unaware" of talented women of color in their midst is their fragmented recruitment and retention strategies. Although many companies make a concerted effort to recruit women of color, they do very little in the way of retaining the women or tracking their career development once they are on board. Of course, it is not to be expected that companies would track only women of color's careers; a system could be developed that would track the careers of all company employees.

Employee retention programs can take many different forms, and are not always explicitly labeled as such. At American Express, women of color can participate in career counseling or in a company-sponsored diversity mentoring program focused on women and ethnic minorities. These programs provide women of color with opportunities to progress and to get help with their careers; this may encourage them to remain with their employer. Each new manager at Procter & Gamble is given a mentor, with particular attention paid to managers who are women of color.[6] These mentoring programs also provide another way that companies can ensure some of their managers are tracking the career progress and concerns of women of color.

No Initiatives for Visibility

Another reason that companies are unaware of talented women of color is due to a lack of corporate initiatives through which women of color can gain professional visibility. At some companies, the prevailing logic is that programs directed at minorities, such as employee resource groups, are adequate recruitment strategies. But this view does not take into account the unique experiences of women of color, or that women of color have not necessarily benefited from diversity initiatives as much as other minority groups. Many companies do not even offer an employee resource group for women of color.

Deloitte & Touche's Breakthrough Leadership Program is an example of a retention strategy that benefits all minorities, and women of color as well. This program provides multicultural employees with three sessions with company executives. It follows up with one-on-one coaching for the employees from senior officers of the organization.[7] The strength of this program is that it allows talented multicultural employees to gain visibility at the senior levels of the organization, and to get invaluable coaching and feedback. Women of color with such opportunities might think twice before leaving the company.

No Tracking of High-Potential Women of Color

Another reason that companies let talented women of color get away is that their human resources capabilities do not have a mechanism that tracks the progress and departure of high-potential employees. As a result, when high-potential women of color decide to leave a company, it may go relatively unnoticed.

For companies that are interested in retaining their top performers, a tracking system is critical. Such a system would consist of human resource software that keeps track of a company's high-potential employees in a searchable database. This database allows departments and human resources to search employee information by selected criteria, such as compensation level, title, performance evaluations, demographic information, geographic mobility, and career plan information.

Thus, when companies develop a "short list" for internal or newly created positions, they will have immediate access to all employees meeting their criteria, including those who are women of color. Because women of color are often excluded from consideration for influential roles, this tracking system would benefit them greatly by putting them "on the radar" for new opportunities.

The tracking of employee departures through exit interviews is commonplace at most companies. During an exit interview with a high-potential woman of color, companies should have a process in place to elicit candid feedback from her regarding her reasons for leaving. This information might be useful, and may help develop programs to prevent future departures by women of color.

Why Women of Color Leave

Women of color leave their companies for a variety of reasons; some are work-related, and others concern their home lives. Following is a discussion of some of the major reasons women of color are leaving their employers.

Salary

A recent survey by Catalyst found that women of color cited salary most often as their reason for changing jobs (39 percent). These women who left their employers experienced a $17,000 average increase in salary above the women who remained with their employers. This disparity widened even further when the salary change occurred in conjunction with a promotion. Women of color who left their employers and received a promotion made approximately $30,000 more than those who remained with their employers and were promoted.[8] Thus, women of color who leave their companies often experience not only an increase in compensation, but also a greater salary increase than they would have received had they remained with their employers—even if they were promoted!

It is difficult to understand the reasons for these disparities, but there are a couple of possibilities worth considering. Firstly, it is possible that the original employer had no mechanism to track the progress of women of color at the company. This means that either the women of color were not considered high-potential (and therefore were not tracked in the organization) or were considered high-potential and were not tracked because no system was in place to track high-potentials. Either situation is problematic for companies because they are losing women of color who are often able to get better jobs, with higher salaries, at different companies. This is talent that the initial employers could have used for their own benefit.

But salary isn't the only thing that increases for women of color who leave their companies: 23 percent of the women who left experienced multiple upward moves, compared with 16 percent of their counterparts who stayed with their employers. Sixty-five percent of the women who changed employers rose at least one job level, whereas only 34 percent of women who stayed with their employers did.[9] This leaves us with the question of why these women of color, who were not considered high-potential at their original companies, were able to move to a different company, receive a salary increase, and in some cases receive a promotion—and an even larger salary increase.

Missing High-Potentials

One possible explanation for this disparity is that these women of color were not identified as high-potential by their managers, possibly due to hidden bias. The Center for Work-Life Policy's (CWLP) 2005 survey of minority professionals found that 19 percent of women of color sensed hidden biases that concerned them enough to consider leaving their companies.[10] One effect of these hidden biases is an erosion of trust between minority professionals and their employers. So it is significant that at companies with 1,000 or more employees, CWLP found that 52 percent of women of color did not trust their employers.[11] This indicates that more women of color perceive hidden biases at large companies than is reported.

Another aspect of hidden bias relates to style considerations, such as communication style and professional image. Women of color are often concerned that their mannerisms are misunderstood and may have a negative impact on their career advancement. CWLP found that among women of color, 32 percent are concerned that being soft-spoken may be viewed as evidence that they lack "leadership potential." Twenty-three percent are apprehensive that their use of hand gestures is considered unsuitable for the workplace. In particular, 34 percent of African-American women hold the belief that promotions are based more on appearance than ability.[12] Whether or not all of these women of color are on target with their assessments, it makes sense for companies to develop a mechanism to get such concerns out in the open. An ombudsman function or other "safe harbor" would probably be conducive to better understanding these concerns.

By developing an anonymous concerns hot line for employees, women of color win and companies win. A hot line would allow women of color (and other employees) to express their concerns and grievances, and would alert the company to possible hidden bias issues or other recurring concerns about managers. CWLP found that the majority of minority professionals support such programs, including 75 percent of Latinas and more than half of African-American women, African American men, and white women.[13] Companies could use follow-up internal investigations to address the complaints, determine their validity, and address the underlying issues.

Catalyst's survey found a surprising benefit reported by women of color who left their employers: a reduction in barriers to advancement at their new companies. These barriers to advancement include the lack of an influential mentor or sponsor, lack of company role models of the same ethnic group, lack of high-visibility assignments, and family commitments.[14] Other barrier reductions occurred among women who left their employers (see table 5.1).[15]

Table 5.1: Advancement Barriers Reported by Women of Color

Barrier	% of Women Reporting Who Left	% of Women Reporting Who Stayed
Not having an influential mentor or sponsor	33	53
Lack of company role models of the same racial/ethnic group	16	38
Lack of high-visibility assignments	14	33
Family commitments	4	16

Although it hardly seems possible that changing companies should result in the removal of so many career barriers, the survey results suggest that for women of color, this is, in fact, the case. The survey even took the additional step of factoring in the so-called "honeymoon period" that new employees experience—the data reflects the responses of women of color who were employed at their new companies for six months or more.

Other Factors

Other reasons why women of color reported leaving their employers were to gain a promotion (38 percent), and because of difficult managers (30 percent).[16] Managers play an integral part in women of color's experiences in corporate America—they have a direct impact on the women's salary, advancement, and related work opportunities. It is generally understood that companies invest considerable resources into managerial development, but little evidence exists that managers receive training specifically related to women of color. This specific training is necessary because women of color have experiences that are quite distinct from their ethnic male and white female counterparts. So to make managerial diversity training more effective, it should include components specifically targeted to assist managers in addressing the unique concerns related to women of color.

Another reason women of color left their employers was to find an environment that provided more support to women of their ethnicity (23 percent).[17] But this support may not necessarily take the form of a program for women of a particular ethnicity, but may consist of programs and initiatives related to women of color generally, or to employees of a particular ethnic group. The presence of such programs and initiatives are signals that a company takes diversity seriously, which is one of the underlying concerns for women of color.

Signals of Diversity

Another signal that women of color might look for in new employers is a commitment to diversity from senior management. This commitment is often evidenced by the reporting relationship of the chief diversity officer (CDO)—whether the CDO reports to the company's Chairman and CEO, or to the head of human resources. If the CDO reports to the former, then diversity plays an important role in the organization's operations. If the CDO reports to the latter, diversity is probably not viewed as integral to the company's success. Another signal of senior-level commitment would be the CEO acting as chair of the company's diversity committee.

Other signals that women of color may look for at companies are links between diversity and incentive compensation, or the presence of programs that focus specifically on women of color. Verizon Communications has developed a comprehensive diversity hiring and retention strategy through its Diversity Performance Incentive Program. Through the program, managers are held accountable for their diversity results by linking a portion of their incentive pay to those results. Such a program sends an important signal to everyone about the importance of diversity at Verizon.

In terms of programs specific to women of color, J.P. Morgan Chase (JPMC) has an employee resource group called Women of Color Connections. The group sponsors events to assist women of color with their professional development, including "fireside chats" with senior executive women of color.[18] Such programs encourage women of color considering positions at JPMC that the company is aware of their unique issues and is willing to make efforts to support their advancement.

Finally, when companies support charitable organizations that provide services to women of color and their communities, they are providing visible support for women of color. American Express and its foundation have supported nonprofit programs, including the Women's Venture Fund, that assist low-income and minority women with training to launch their own businesses, and micro-loans for their start-up costs. PriceWaterhouseCoopers recently demonstrated its support for Asian-American women through its founding sponsorship of the nascent National Asian American Society of Accountants.[19]

When companies develop programs and initiatives that demonstrate support for women of color, it sends a message to the women that their contributions are valued.

Strategies for Developing and Retaining Women of Color

Although some companies use specific programs to develop and retain women of color, companies can also make use of preexisting initiatives, such as high-potential and leadership development programs to develop and retain these women.

In 2005, Hewitt Associates researched how the best leadership companies differentiate their high-potential employees from other employees. Of the Top 20 companies for leadership development, 95 percent have a formal method by which they identify high-potential employees, and 68 percent of them inform high-potential employees of their status.[20] This strategy is effective in retaining employees because employees who are being developed as future leaders of their company have a stronger incentive to remain at the company. Part of this incentive comes from the company's obvious commitment to help them grow professionally. This same logic also applies to high-potential women of color.

Another strategy companies may consider is to develop high-potential forums for future leaders in the organization. Such a forum would allow high-potential employees to gain much-needed exposure to other high-potentials, as well as senior managers. For women of color, this strategy is especially effective because in addition to identifying them as potential leaders, it helps them to expand their informal networks, which is one of their critical success factors. For more information on linking high-potential initiatives to women of color, see chapter 3.

Studies have shown that African-American women and Latinas often have a higher commitment to organizations when they have more colleagues in their informal networks. For Asian women, their organizational commitment was not affected by the number of colleagues in their informal networks; their commitment to organizations was slightly more positive based on the number of men in their networks.[21]

But it helps companies little to develop and invest in women of color if the women leave the company and go to another organization—or worse yet, a competitor. So it is not surprising that Hewitt found that 72 percent of its Top 20 companies have a system to track the turnover of high-potential employees. One of the Top 20 companies treats high-potential resignations so seriously that the CEO must be notified if a high-potential resigns, and then a counteroffer must be made to that employee within 24 hours of the resignation. This notification and counteroffer must be made no matter what the level of the high-potential employee. Of course, making a counteroffer to an employee may not seem to be the soundest business practice (since the counteroffer could be abused), but this company finds it important not to let its best employees go without a fight. At the same company, leaders must retain 90 percent of their departmental high-potentials, or they will forfeit some portion of their incentive compensation.[22]

That one Top 20 company has taken what seem to be extreme measures in retaining its high-potential employees. But in industries where specific expertise is very valuable, and companies invest heavily in their high-potential employees (by salary, training, or otherwise), or where companies develop their high-potentials in conjunction with succession planning (all of the Top 20 companies do), losing a high-potential is a *real* loss rather than just an unfortunate cost of business.

Managers and Microinequities

Managers play a large role in the development and retention of professional women of color. But when the relationship has difficulties, some women of color may opt to leave their department or company. Examining the challenges women of color face in their manager relationships gives insight into some of the reasons that women of color leave their employers. One possible reason for a difficult relationship between a manager and a woman of color is hidden bias, as discussed earlier. But one little-understood reason women of color are leaving relates to the everyday interactions the women have with their managers and peers at work. Oftentimes, these interactions leave the women of color feeling devalued, unappreciated, and unimportant to the company; in short, the women feel microinequitized.

The word "microinequitized" is the verbal form of the word microinequities, a term coined in the early 1970s by Mary Rowe. Rowe is currently an adjunct professor of negotiation and conflict management at MIT's Sloan School of Management. In recent years, the term has been used by Stephen Young in seminars specifically focused on microinequities. The seminar is entitled: "MicroInequities: The Power of Small™."

Young is the founder of Insight Education Systems of Montclair, New Jersey, a management consulting firm focusing on leadership development and diversity. He is an expert in the power of microinequities in the workplace, and has considerable experience with diversity. He was previously Senior Vice President and Chief Diversity Officer for J.P. Morgan Chase. His current work on microinequities has been featured in the *Wall Street Journal, Time* magazine, and *O—The Oprah Magazine.*

Young defines microinequities (also called micromessages) as "subtle, semiconscious messages that are universally understood...in every country and in every culture. They have to do with looks, gestures, tone, nuance, inflection...syntax, and range from a subtle head nod that says 'yes' to a head turn that says 'I couldn't care less,' a smile of engagement, a blank look of indifference, a dismissive response, [or] a wink of understanding."

But according to Young, the focus is not merely on the outward actions. Instead, the key to micromessages is that "the message does get sent, gets received, gets acted on—and in most cases the sender is not consciously aware of sending the message differently [to different people], and the receiver is not even conscious...of what's happening that's different....[Micromessages] influence how a person actually performs in the organization, based on the subtlety of the message."

The "Conditional Apology"

The first example that Young gives of a micromessage is what he calls the "conditional apology." He briefly relates a story based on his teenage daughter, Alex, and a discussion they had about one of her friends, which ended with Alex asking Young to apologize for his remarks about her friend. Young sighed deeply, and then proffered his daughter the conditional apology—something to the effect of: "If I've offended you, I am sorry."

Listening to the story, you can immediately sense that Young's apology was not completely authentic, although you are not entirely sure why. Young pauses to explain that deep sighing that precedes an apology does not usually signify contrition; quite the reverse, it often signifies annoyance. Also, by using the word "if," the apology becomes conditional; it is not a direct apology, it is an apology only if you were offended. Young questions whether such an apology is authentic, because in settings where we *know* we have offended another party, we offer very different apologies, such as if, for example, we spill coffee on a colleague's presentation right before a big meeting. You can scarcely imagine offering this apology to your colleague whose presentation has been ruined: "If I caused you any difficulty, I apologize." Young makes his point.

Unequal Introductions

A common micromessage occurs when a manager introduces a few of his team members to others. Often, a manager's introduction will make it clear that the manager favors one of his employees more over the others. Although all the introductions may sound similar to the casual observer, Young cautions us to consider the gestures offered by the manager to differentiate between the introductions. He suggests we observe when the manager speaks in a monotone, or with inflection in his or her voice; or the manager's facial expression, word choice, and whether or not he looked at the person being introduced.

Initially these considerations may seem insignificant, or even petty, but Young argues that they provide the key to how the other party perceives the introductions, and to what the employees take away from the meeting. The other party will walk away from the introduction with a favorable impression of one employee and a less favorable impression of the other. The employee who is highly regarded feels good about the experience, but the other does not and is often not sure why. Young says, "no one ever says to themselves, 'Ah! He looked at [the other employee], but he didn't look at me...you don't know to look for [the micromessage], [but] you walk away feeling the effect. So you feel the effect, but you don't know how to define it."

By using this example, Young is getting to the heart of the micromessage: the subtle and often unwitting signal that the manager uses to convey his or her feelings to those privy to the conversation. The manager lets everyone know who he or she likes, and who is more or less important, but none of this has been spoken openly.

This is important information for women of color, who often experience troubling feelings at work, but cannot completely understand why. Young explains, "a woman...or a person of color will walk away from an experience and will say to themselves, [that person] didn't like me. I know [that person] doesn't like me, but I can't put my finger on it." Then Young describes what women and people of color often do, because they don't understand the situation—they chalk it up to their imagination, or overreaction. Young says, "You convince yourself that maybe it's just not there because [you] can't describe it. But it is there."

Attempts to Rectify Microinequities

Next, Young describes the experience a woman of color might have in trying to rectify microinequities. He queries: "Can you imagine a woman going up to her manager and talking to her manager about all of her experiences? Just picture a woman walking up to her boss and saying, 'I want to talk to you about something really important. It's the way you introduce me...you didn't look at me. You didn't smile. Your hand gestures weren't the same...your tone of voice didn't have the same inflection...' can you imagine what the manager's reaction would be?"

It is easy to see that Young is right. Managers on the receiving end of such a discussion would likely view the woman as petty or overly concerned; others might try to apologize to her—but maybe with a "conditional" apology. Originally, the woman may have sensed the manager's dislike of her, but when the manager apologizes— even though the apology is conditional—she really cannot address the concern any further. After all, the manager just apologized! But from Young's earlier example, it is clear that what the manager has proffered is not really an apology at all. So the woman leaves the meeting, and she *still* does not feel right about what happened, either in the introduction or in the meeting with her manager. Later in this chapter, we will discuss how to handle these microinequities at work.

Different Treatment for Favored Employees

Young describes another characteristic of micromessaging, which is that "we send more messages to the people we like and agree with than the people we dislike and disagree with." He gives the example of a staff meeting where a manager treats his team members differently using micromessages. A liked employee is treated in a friendly manner, and his ideas are discussed at length; other employees receive rebuffs or are given unwelcoming signals when they attempt to enter the conversation.

A woman of color may experience this when she raises an issue and the manager says "that's really important, but we need to stay focused on the agenda." Young observes that the manager says all the right words, but that the corresponding micromessage made it clear that the woman's contribution was *not* important. Also, the word choice "that's important" sounds patronizing. These are all things that the woman of color senses, but cannot put her finger on. Would anyone be surprised that she leaves the meeting feeling frustrated, and that after a year or so of such interactions looks elsewhere for a job?

Now when the woman of color's colleague raises an issue (that is also not on the agenda), the boss wants to explore it further because he likes the employee. Of course the woman of color cannot say, 'Wait a minute, his idea isn't on the agenda,' because you can't talk about that aspect of the manager's behavior. Despite the disparity in the manager's behavior, the real key to this story is the fact that the manager is often completely unaware that he is responding in such different ways to different employees. For women of color who feel left out by their managers or colleagues at meetings, Young puts it this way: "Sometimes the absence of a message is a message."

The Frequency of Micromessages

Part of the challenge of dealing with micromessages is the frequency with which they occur, and the fact that they are contextual. According to Young, in a one-on-one conversation, somewhere between 40 and 150 micromessages are sent and received in a 10-minute period between the two parties to the conversation. In a midsize meeting of 5 to 15 people, there is less one-on-one interaction, so the number of individual micromessages lessens to 20 to 40 per 10-minute period—but this number is for each person, so it is actually multiplied by the number of people in the room. If there are five people in the meeting, then around 100 to 200 micromessages are sent every 10 minutes; with 15 people, the number of micromessages escalates to 300 to 600 every 10 minutes.

Identifying Micromessages

Although micromessages affect everyone at work, Young has found that the frequency of micromessages notwithstanding, women and people of color "tend to be...much more skilled at identifying micromessages...when these things happen to you with more frequency, you become tuned in to them." Women of color face considerable challenges related to stereotyping at work, and Young has found that people have a certain set of assumptions about women of color and that the women of color "are being filtered against [a] template. When women of color engage in any behavior that fits into the template, even "the slightest bit," according to Young, they are viewed as having confirmed that they *are* the template.

One of Young's seminar activities addresses this issue. He uses the standard brain teaser containing several lines of the same length, each with arrows pointing inward and outward. But, unknown to his audience, he also makes one of the lines longer than the others. When he brings out the illustration and asks which one of the lines is longer, everyone raises their hand and says that the lines are all the same length. Young notes that they often do this without really examining the chart. He uses this opportunity to demonstrate how managers can believe that they are being fair and objective, when in actuality they are not. The managers in his seminar see something that they think they have seen before (not knowing he has altered it), thus they see it as they expect to see it—and in this instance, they are always wrong.

Addressing Microinequities

Microinequities are very difficult to address. As mentioned earlier, attempts by employees to address them directly often result in the employee appearing overly concerned about petty issues. Moreover, because managers are often unaware that they are generating these micromessages, the most effective way to address the issue is at the organizational level: Managers need to be trained to understand how micromessages affect them and their employees. Young uses an interactive technique to help managers understand how being "microinequitized" can change their performance on the spot.

At the Organizational Level

During his seminars, Young has selected managerial participants (including CEOs) to undergo a microinequity experience with him. He asks them to set up two columns and in the first column to provide general information about their length of time at the company, current responsibilities, and a sentence about a project in which they are currently involved. He then asks for a virtually identical set of information from them for the second column, except it is about a previous employer, and includes a challenge they faced in that organization instead of a current project. Young then asks the participant to tell him the information from each column. During the first column, he is very attentive and affirming of everything that the participant shares. He gives them full eye contact, nods, and appears undistracted. The participants speak fluently and talk with ease.

But when the participant begins to read from the second column—which contains information very similar to the first—Young begins the process of microinequitizing. He begins to look around, checks his Blackberry and cell phone, and even the most eloquent participants begin babbling and stumbling over their words. Sometimes Young moves over to a nearby flip chart, tears off a piece of paper, crumples it up, and tosses it into the trash can. Meanwhile, participants pause, and he reassures them, saying things like "I am listening to you," "No, really, I'm listening. Keep talking." Still struggling to communicate, the participants stammer out their answers, as Young taps on the table or his leg, as if impatient. Eventually many of the participants just stop talking, feeling frustrated.

Through this exercise, Young shows managers that how we treat people doesn't just affect their feelings, but has a direct effect on how they perform: microinequities impair employee performance. All of the participants performed well when they felt valued and affirmed, and all of them performed poorly when they felt undervalued or belittled. It had nothing to do with race or gender. Also of note is that in both instances, the columns contain information that is well known to the participant, demonstrating that their missteps during microinequitizing had nothing to do with their knowledge of the material at issue.

Young's message is effective. Twelve Fortune 500 CEOs have personally brought him in to work through the concept of micromessages with their leadership teams. In addition, three major companies now include micromessaging as part of their 360-degree managerial performance appraisal process. In the interpersonal section of the appraisal, the companies have criteria related to how a manager's employees perceive the micromessages sent between them and their managers.

At the Individual Level

At the individual level, women of color can learn to address micromessages with others while remaining cognizant of those they are sending out. Young believes that women of color sometimes anticipate micromessages: "Women of color may anticipate a message coming, [and] then...sometimes react with that anticipation." Young quickly adds that it may be necessary for women of color to respond this way, and that they may be correct in their assertions.

One way that women of color can use micromessages in a positive fashion is to use them to identify colleagues with whom they are out of sync. Once they have identified those colleagues, women of color need to spend time with those colleagues, learn to validate them (without necessarily agreeing with them), and address their concerns in a positive and supportive fashion. By saying "help me understand what you think and why," women of color allow others to express their opinions, and may receive important information about others and themselves. Often, even the most difficult colleagues can become allies (or at least neutral) when they have had an opportunity to be heard.

> **TIP:** Use micromessages to identify relationships that need reinforcement or repair.

Young is also a proponent of operating contextually. He firmly believes that women of color need to speak and communicate in a manner that fits their corporate context. He gives an insightful example: "When you're in France, are you French? No. Do you try to speak the language if you can? Yes." He expresses the necessity of conforming to certain structures and emphasizes conforming in ways that do not violate one's personal values.

Young makes a valid point that people adjust all the time—women visiting Middle Eastern countries cover their arms. Non-Jewish men entering synagogues cover their heads. In our everyday life, we conform to social norms—we generally wear black to funerals, bring presents to birthday parties, and wear exercise clothes at the gym. We address people older than us differently than those who are younger. Being contextual does not mean we cannot bring our authentic selves to the office; it means that we do so within certain constraints—which are also placed on others at the office, as well.

In operating contextually, Young cautions that women of color need to be careful of acting in ways that are subordinating—acting like people of low status and power in organizations. If you have ever seen an employee acting overly submissive to others, through excessive smiling, or just by being overly deferential, you know what Young is referring to.

Young observes that some of the issues faced by women of color in corporate America are more about perceived power and socioeconomic class than directly about gender. He notes that because women have not traditionally held power in organizations, they are viewed as having lower power—thus, issues faced by women are gender issues, but they are driven by the historical lack of power experienced by women in corporate America. Women of color experience this lack of power even more forcefully.

> **TIP:** Although it is important to be friendly at work, this does not necessarily mean you need to be cheery all of the time. A pleasant demeanor is more powerful.

Young elaborates by mentioning that women coming from contexts where women are viewed as powerful do not receive microinequities the same way, because they have established themselves as people who control their environment. Young advises women of color to consider the behavior of CEOs—when they walk into meetings, they do not smile at everyone. In fact, they are often stern and serious. Young is not suggesting that women of color adopt a sour demeanor, but one of serious business confidence. He concludes that women of color with subservient attitudes are telling others that this is how they perceive themselves. In light of this, Young suggests to women of color to be careful how you smile and gesture—which can send micromessages of low status and low power. Instead, Young advises women of color to send micromessages that say "I have power, authority, good ideas, and I expect to be respected." These micromessages are communicated in how women of color carry themselves at work.

Micromessages and Retention

Currently, hard data linking the effects of microinequities on retention of employees is not yet available. But Young comments that anecdotal evidence found in his work demonstrates that microinequities have an effect on retention. Although the data does not exist for companies to develop retention programs related specifically to micromessages, some companies have already seen the value of using micromessages as a recruitment tool. As part of their recruitment process, some companies explain micromessages to potential candidates, along with their organization's method for dealing with them—which is often open communication. Young mentions that companies have informed him that most of the questions asked by potential employers are about the micromessages.

Women of color facing microinequities have some difficult decisions—should you stay with your manager and try to improve the relationship? Or is it better for you to cut your losses and move to a new, more supportive environment? Whatever your choice, the micromessages will continue to be there. How you use them is up to you.

Should You Change Jobs to Advance Your Career?

If you are a woman of color who is seriously considering changing jobs to advance your career, there is good news: You will probably succced. But despite the monetary (and career) advantages of changing companies, it might not be a strategy that you'll want to employ for the rest of your career. In light of this, it is worth briefly revisiting the pros and cons of making such a change, and key career considerations if you decide to go the advancement-by-departure route. As for the personal concerns of women of color changing careers, they will vary too widely to give them full consideration here.

One good thing about changing careers: The stigma that used to exist for those who frequently changed companies has all but disappeared in the U.S. But the difficulty in changing companies often involves a loss of informal networks, which for women of color means gaining access to new ones. It also means building new relationships with managers, sponsors, and mentors. Such a move may also require the development of new skill sets or competencies, which are necessary for your new role. You may view these difficulties as part of the cost of changing your role—just be prepared to build entirely new networks and to adjust your current ones.

In terms of perception, if you leave to advance, you need to understand that to many companies, your most recent position *is* who you are as far as they are concerned. As one executive mentor put it: Very few companies know how to draft the athlete. This means that most companies cannot look at a resume, consider the jobs you have had, and from those jobs develop an idea of what your role could be. Instead, most companies look at your most recent position and build from there; they often lack the vision to "see" you in a different function without some touchstones on your resume to link your present position to your desired role.

TIP: If you want to change functions, consider taking outside courses to supplement your resume. This might help potential employers to "see" you in a new role.

But if you have taken these and other factors into account, and still want to change companies, the out-and-up strategy is still effective for career advancement. Just don't forget its drawbacks and benefits. Ultimately, whether you rise through the ranks of your current company or change companies to move ahead, you will begin to face new and different challenges as you rise toward the upper echelons of corporate America. We discuss these challenges in chapter 6.

Notes

[1]Catalyst. *Women of Color in Corporate Management: Three Years Later* (2001), 19–23.

[2]Ibid., 19, 21.

[3]Ibid.

[4]Ibid.

[5]RHR International Co. *Filling the Executive Bench: How Companies are Growing Future Leaders* (2005), 3.

[6]Working Mother Media. *The Best Companies for Women of Color,* available at www.workingmother.com.

[7]Ibid.

[8]Catalyst. *Women of Color in Corporate Management: Three Years Later* (2001), 20.

[9]Ibid., 21.

[10]Hewlett, Sylvia Ann, Carolyn Buck Luce, and Cornel West. "Leadership in Your Midst: Tapping the Hidden Strengths of Minority Executives." *Harvard Business Review* (November 2005), 4.

[11]Ibid.

[12]Ibid.

[13]Hewlett, Sylvia Ann, Carolyn Buck Luce, and Cornel West. "Leadership in Your Midst: Tapping the Hidden Strengths of Minority Executives." *Harvard Business Review* (November 2005), 6.

[14]Catalyst. *Women of Color in Corporate Management: Three Years Later* (2001), 22.

[15]Ibid.

[16]Ibid.

[17]Ibid.

[18]Working Mother Media. *The Best Companies for Women of Color*, available at www.workingmother.com.

[19]Ibid.

[20]Hewitt Associates. *How the Top 20 Companies Grow Great Leaders* (2005), 3.

[21]Catalyst. *Women of Color in Corporate Management: Three Years Later* (2001), 20.

[22]Hewitt Associates. *How the Top 20 Companies Grow Great Leaders* (2005), 3.

CHAPTER 6 No Woman's Land: Challenges in the Upper Echelons of Management

Arriving into the executive ranks of a company is often a bittersweet experience for a woman of color. After years of hard work, promotions, and juggling her home life and career, she has made it to the pinnacle of the organization. At this level, she reports to the CEO of the company directly, or she reports to one of the CEO's direct reports. Or in complex organizations with separate operating divisions, she may be the head of a division or a C-level officer, and likely holds one of the following corporate titles: chairman, president, executive vice president, or senior vice president.

There is no question that women of color who reach the highest levels of corporate America have some serious perks: lofty titles; high salaries; large, luxuriously furnished offices on the executive floor; one or two assistants; and all the respect and prestige that accompany a high-level corporate role. But even in the upper echelons of corporate America, they continue to face considerable challenges at work and at home. Among the more prevalent challenges at work are the following:

- Ambiguity in responsibilities and relationships
- Isolation
- Managing demands on time
- Hypervisibility or overexposure
- Changes in personal friendships

Other issues include self-care, business travel, and changing relationships with peers.

Ambiguity

One of the first things that newly senior women of color may notice in their new roles is the level of ambiguity that exists. In junior or midlevel roles, responsibilities are more clearly delineated, reporting relationships are more clearly defined, and those with the most power are easily identified. Not so at the most senior levels within an organization. Executives have to develop their own responsibilities, and dotted-line reporting relationships can make reporting relationships even more confusing. Thus, it is important for newly senior women of color to develop the skills to minimize this ambiguity, where it is possible to do so.

In Their Own Words

Nancy Hess* encountered ambiguity as she moved up through the corporate ranks: "…I will tell you in my own experience, the higher you go the more ambiguous it gets. It's not like when you're right out of school and your boss gives you a roadmap and you just execute A, B, C, D, and E. At this level, it's a blank sheet of paper and you sort of develop it and then execute it. So thinking about being clear, crisp about what you are trying to do, what the outcome is going to be, [and] how you're going to do it is even more critical at the more senior level."

Senior levels of companies are replete with ambiguity, and the greater the ambiguity of the environment, the more adept senior women of color need to be at "reading the tea leaves." But what exactly is meant by that? Historically, reading tea leaves was a fortune-telling practice. A fortuneteller, by looking at the tea leaves remaining in the bottom of a person's cup, could predict their future or foretell some future event in their life. What Hess means by "reading the tea leaves" is that it is critically important for senior women of color to get a sense of what is happening around them without necessarily having explicit information or factual knowledge.

*Name has been fictionalized.

In Their Own Words

Hess continues, "And reading the tea leaves becomes a lot more critical at the more senior levels. That's an area I think we women of color could use [an] increasing focus [on] to think about how we do it...[such as determining] where people [are] aligned on an issue."

Hess also believes that women of color can do more than just read the tea leaves; they can help to shape them. "One of the things we certainly could do better is what I call 'pre-wiring' an initiative," she says thoughtfully. "[When] you're driving an initiative, what will happen often is, you go into a meeting, [as] a woman of color, present your idea, and you just get beat up. You just have 20 questions from 20 people, 'well what about this?' 'how are you going to do that?' And you're like 'Oh my God.' Your counterpart, generally a majority male, may present an idea, and people are all nodding and [he] may get one or two questions, and that's it. Now often, a woman of color will internalize that, and will say 'my God, it was about me,' or whatever you think it was."

She continues, "But what the white male has done is gone around and talked to everybody who is going to be in that meeting, in advance, and understood where there are going to be pitfalls, [asking] 'what problems do you have with it?' 'can you support it?' 'if you can't support it in its current format, what do I need to do to get you to support it?' So, they already sort of know, before they go into that meeting, how the chips are going to fall. And it's not the first time that anybody in that room has heard it—or anybody who matters in the room," she finishes, adding, "Often, we don't understand how that part of the game works, because it's not anything that's written down; it's not anything that's public. But everybody in the room, you've had a conversation with. And I mean, I've seen people that I would also consider to be mentors and sponsors who are—most of them are majority [men]—absolute masters at that."

Isolation

Isolation can be another challenge for senior women of color. Although the number of women of color in senior roles is increasing, they still comprise a small percentage of senior executives. Because the typical senior management team is very small, when a woman of color reaches the senior levels there are only a handful of other people; the atmosphere is often clubby. At lower levels in the organization, a woman of color may have been one of several women of color. At the most senior levels, she is likely to be the only one.

In Their Own Words

Shannon Childress,* an energy executive, observes: "A challenge for professional women of color at senior levels is that they have virtually no peers.... Especially if they're just coming into [the] senior level of an organization, they don't have an ELC [an organization for senior African-American executives]...so there's nobody really there to help them through this new minefield that is [the] senior level."

The lack of women of color in senior leadership positions partially reflects stereotypes and perceptions that exist in corporate America—that women of color *cannot* hold such roles. As a result, a woman of color who does become a senior executive is often confronted with behavior from clients, colleagues, and others that fails to recognize her as a senior leader. Executive women of color often report being mistaken for secretaries or subordinates—when in fact, they are the boss.

In Their Own Words

Taylor Robinson* has experience with cases of "mistaken identity." A financial services executive with 25 years of experience, she notes that corporate America still has a long way to go in dealing with women of color. "The workplace is still not understanding of the 'deadly intersection' (I call

*Names have been fictionalized.

it), when gender and ethnicity and race collide for women of color.... I think it starts in many ways with stereotypes that find and seep into how women of color are dealt with, particularly as they move up the corporate ladder—the sense that they are not ever supposed to be in those kind of roles, and so [there's] this idea [of] 'why are you here?' and 'shouldn't you be in a lower level?'" She points to some of her personal experiences as examples: "I've been in many situations where I've been in meetings and I've been asked, you know, to serve a drink. There was a sense that I must have been the help there, as opposed to one of the executives there. I've been on business trips across the world with white colleagues who are subordinates to me (males)... there was always the assumption that they were the boss and not me. So these things still happen, and I think that it really points to the stereotypes that still exist."

Robinson's approach to handling these experiences is instructive—she refuses to bear the burden of other people's discrimination. "[M]y motto—in the words of Oprah Winfrey—is that the best deterrent for sexism and racism is excellence. And I have always felt like, if I was able to show my value and to show what I could bring to the table, then it was somebody else's problem to deal with if they did not think I should be there. And that has really guided my career and I think my success over the course of the 25 years that I've been in financial services. I have always put the problem on the shoulders of the person that had it, and not on my shoulders."

Managing Demands on Time

Time management is a major issue for executive women of color. Often, in addition to working long hours each day, their roles require them to attend social functions, leadership retreats, and other events outside of work. These events can take up considerable amounts of their personal time, leaving them with precious little time for significant others, friends, family, and other loved ones.

In addition to spending time on work-related activities, senior women of color are often approached to be involved in philanthropic endeavors, or to serve on prestigious corporate or nonprofit boards. These invitations stem from the women's extensive business expertise and corporate connections. They are also able to help companies and nonprofit organizations increase their board diversity with qualified professionals. Finally, in their respective communities, senior women of color are often sought after to provide sponsorship or mentoring to younger women, or to provide their insights on community projects. With so many people pulling them in different directions, it is no wonder that senior women of color have so little time for themselves.

In Their Own Words

Veronica Sims* knows just how valuable a commodity time is. "The additional social requirements of the job put additional demands on your time," she says. "At this level, if [a service provider] is having an event, we have to buy a table.... If our auditor is doing something...[or] if our customer is doing something...and there are certain positions that always have to be a part of [the event]," she continues. "So there are additional social requirements that are part of the job that require dinners, or whatever, or weekend events, or if you're in a sales or marketing area, perhaps entertaining, in addition to [the] long workdays and work on the weekend [that] also put demands on your time."

Greater industry and community demands become more frequent as women of color become more senior. "The pressure to be a role model requires multiple demands on your time," Sims observes. "There are so few of us at this level...you can get really caught up in all the different requests...to be on different boards...[to] be a spokesperson at different events; and while all of those things are personally fulfilling, and in some ways more personally fulfilling [than work], you can very easily get overextended. So balancing that is important, [as is] recognizing that my peers don't have those same pressures; they're not unique in their group. That's kind of a 'watch out.'"

*Name has been fictionalized.

The sheer volume of requests that senior women of color receive to be involved in projects or programs precludes them from being able to accept most of them. To accommodate so many different people, groups, and organizations, the women have to make tradeoffs. These tradeoffs are an important strategy senior women use to streamline their decision-making processes. By realizing that they cannot possibly do everything, they prioritize the events and programs that are important to them.

Self-Care

But some of their priorities are dictated to them by their status as senior executives. One such priority relates to their professional image and grooming. Women of color in senior roles are expected to "look the part," and often must spend considerable time on issues surrounding their personal grooming. Women usually spend more time on their grooming than men (with a few exceptions) because of the additional societal expectations placed on women regarding their hair, makeup, and wardrobe. In addition, women in "face" professions—such as marketing, communications, or community relations, or in industries such as fashion, retail, or cosmetics—are required to maintain a fashionable and consistently professional look.

In Their Own Words

Susan Davis* had an "aha!" moment at a panel she was moderating. One of the other panelists was describing her resentment about spending so much time on grooming issues. She begins the story: "One woman said on the panel—I'd never thought about it—she said 'I'm very resentful about how many hours I don't get to spend on things I want to do, 'cause I'm grooming,' she said. 'No, do you realize how much earlier we have to get up as women to get our hair done, to put on makeup?' Which I hadn't thought about; the time that I've got to get a manicure, get a pedicure, get my hair colored, I've got to get it straightened out. These are hours that I could use differently, but it's something that I need to do for my personal grooming for my position.... But that is part of the tradeoff that you make; the time that that you're working or you're traveling that you could be spending with friends

*(continued)**

*Name has been fictionalized.

(continued)

> or family. Now those are the tradeoffs, but those are decision points that you're going to have to make."

Business Travel

Senior women of color spend a lot of time traveling for business. They spend considerable time on the road visiting clients or customers, working in other company offices, or attending meetings or events in different locations. The frequency of business travel requires the women to be highly organized, and many of them have developed strategies to travel more efficiently. The more efficient their travel arrangements, the more time they will have to enjoy their lives outside of work.

In Their Own Words

Susan Davis,* a senior executive, spends a lot of time on the road for business; she has well-developed strategies to make her travel life easier. "I travel so much, so I have travel bags," she says. "All my makeup, all my personal items, they're in these bags. And once a month I replace and clean them out, straighten them out. So I don't have to think about it. When I'm packing, I just throw those in and I just have to put the clothes in, and it makes it easier for me to travel." She notes that women of color do not realize that these sorts of issues will crop up when they finally get a senior-level job. "But those are things that you don't think about when, you know, you're reaching for that brass ring.... You forget, there are going to be some tradeoffs."

Some of the other efficient travel strategies that executive women of color use are hilarious. Davis described how she takes care of her lingerie—she buys more. "I have enough lingerie to go for a month," she laughs. "I travel so much, it's like, I've got to have enough [lingerie]. And I want to wash my own lingerie...[so] I've got to have enough for a month, so that I can just keep on going until I have time to [wash] my own lingerie."

*Name has been fictionalized.

Business travel is just one of the tradeoffs that executive women of color are faced with in their careers. But business travel is short-term, and as women of color become more senior, they may be faced with the prospect of longer-term changes, such as relocation or temporary assignments. These roles may be in other U.S. locations, but at global corporations they may be asked to work abroad.

In Their Own Words

In describing the challenges senior women of color face, Wendy Pace,* an executive and popular public speaker, notes the lack of available time and the necessity of trade-offs. "You have less time. It sounds obvious, but you know, at some point you really think that you can do everything.... The truth of the matter is you've got to make choices. You're going to have less time for your family, you're going to have less personal time... You may have to relocate; you may love where you are, but you know the job is located in another state... [or] another country; if you really are interested in that particular role, then you're going to have to make those kinds of sacrifices."

Hypervisibility or Overexposure

But being a senior executive is not only business travel and sacri-fices. Women of color in senior roles receive considerable perks from their companies, as noted earlier. One perk they also receive is attention from local and national media, including newspapers and business, women's, and other magazines. The media is especially interested in senior women of color because they hold fewer high-level positions. Sims understands this firsthand. But she does not advocate stepping into the spotlight because of its potentially dam-aging effects on one's career *and* one's relationships with bosses, peers, and other influential people.

*Name has been fictionalized.

In Their Own Words

"The other thing that I've seen in a couple of different areas is that both peers and bosses can resent the extra attention [you receive]," Sims says. "There are times [when organizations have wanted to feature me in major publications], and I refused to participate, because I said, 'You know what? ...I've had enough attention.' [My company] may or may not have an issue with it, but at some point...you know, you have to be careful about [too much media attention]."

Sims learned the importance of discretion with some of her prior employers; she also learned that media attention can be viewed by colleagues as self-serving. "That [media attention] was a bigger sensitivity when I was at other companies, in terms of the level of attention that they liked their executives to have or not have, and sometimes it can be viewed as...'is this really for the company's benefit?' or 'is this for your own benefit!'. We are so good about championing people that within our community have attained a level of success, that sometimes it can create problems. I mean, the joke used to be...if one of us showed up on the cover of *BusinessWeek,* you know, you could almost count [on] the person a year from now—for whatever reason—that person is out of [a job].... Whatever level I achieve in corporate America, I will never be on the cover of *BusinessWeek!* You're [sure to] fall from there," she says ruefully. "That's something that...more recently I've kind of thought about and observed as a caution, and it's easy for me because I don't like a lot of attention anyway; I do what I do for my family."

The most successful senior women seem to take a tempered-visibility approach to dealing with the media. They carefully select which media appearances will be most beneficial to their careers and decline the other invitations. In doing so, they appear to best advantage in the media, while not appearing too often, and the media becomes an asset to their careers rather than a distraction. This strategy also defuses potential difficulties and jealousies with their companies and peers.

"Friendshifts"

As women of color become more senior, they often notice changes in their inner circle of friends. These relationship changes are known as "friendshifts." Friendshifts is a term coined by Dr. Jan Yager, an influential American sociologist. It describes how friendships change as people move through life stages, change jobs, or relocate.

This is highly relevant to women of color who become senior executives because most of their friends will not have reached their level. This often presents challenges for women who previously relied on a close circle of friends who were all peers, some of whom may have worked at the same company. Once a woman of color becomes senior, although she may see herself as the same person, her achievements can become grounds for jealousy and erode important support relationships at work.

In Their Own Words

Wendy Pace takes a pragmatic view of dealing with jealousy—understand it, and deal with it. "You've really got to understand that if you're going to start moving out of the pack, everybody is not going to be happy about it," she states. "And very often as you move up career-wise in your experience, you may actually have a shift in a lot of the people that, you know, you may have felt were your friends, who were really, in fact, just your acquaintances," she concludes. "So I think one of the things I would say, in terms of challenges, is that you've got to become very circumspect in who you bring into your inner circle. The other thing I think you've got to do, too, is you've got to understand that you've got to keep your own counsel.... You kind of get to a point where you can no longer just share all your life experiences with everyone."

These friendshifts often leave senior women of color looking for new, more fulfilling relationships at work, and leave them without a valuable source of support. How the women get this support and handle family and community relations is the subject of chapter 10, "Home Sweet Home? Issues in Relationships and Family." This chapter provides a more detailed discussion of the issues that women of color at all levels are facing at home and in their communities.

By the time women of color have reached the senior levels of corporate America, they are accustomed to performing well, debunking stereotypes, building cross-functional relationships, and having sponsors and mentors. These issues never completely go away, but to those challenges they add ambiguity, isolation, managing multiple demands on their time, and avoiding overexposure. These things, coupled with incessant travel, lack of personal time, and friendship loss or adjustments can make for a difficult transition into the senior ranks. That they are able to keep it all together is a testimony to their courage and strength as individuals.

These women of color are to be applauded for their great achievements and successes. Pace cites her divorce as an example of something that affects your entire life, but that is best kept out of the office. "I couldn't bring that [the divorce] into the workplace.... There's always a balance and an art with people understanding a little bit about you, and know a bit about your personal life. But at the same time too, you've...got to keep up a healthy amount of distance [between you and others], as you go further up the ladder."

PART 3 Fast-Forward

CHAPTER 7 Women of Color in the Management Pipeline

S uccession planning is crucial to the future success of any business, and a buzz always encircles those whom the company has tapped to lead the organization into the future. Such people are considered to be in the "pipeline" of leadership for the company. You don't have to want the CEO role to be in this pipeline; but you do need to be in the pipeline to advance your career.

This chapter addresses the behind-the-scenes activities that surround the "pipeline." It discusses how to get into the pipeline and the "power signals" that peers and management will send to you when you're in it. Other topics addressed include learning to "read the tea leaves" (understanding delicately crafted signals from the company culture) and "playing nice" (or at least appearing to) with pipeline peers.

If you've been in business for a while, you have probably heard of the "fast track," which is virtually synonymous with the "pipeline." Both enable the employees involved to move quickly up the ranks in an organization. And the similarities don't end there: Employees often gain access to them in similar fashion—through highly regarded organizational rotational programs or important company task forces.

Because of the manner in which the employees gain access, they are often highly visible in their organizations, in a positive way. They are usually regarded as future leaders at the divisional or corporate levels. Although the fast track still exists in many organizations, it is slowly being folded into the notion of a pipeline. The pipeline seems to be a more deliberate strategy employed by organizations to undergird their succession-planning process, which is critical to the continued success of an organization.

When an organization develops its succession plan, it wants to make the best use of its internal talent; either to fill employment gaps in business-critical divisions or to develop trusted future leaders for the company. Because of this strategic focus, an employee's movement into an organization's pipeline differs somewhat from an employee's movement onto the fast track. An employee can gain access to the fast track because he or she is well-liked by one or more key people in an organization. But the strategic nature of succession planning requires that employees tapped for the pipeline demonstrate the potential to perform at levels that benefit the organization. Moreover, these employees must have a leadership style congruent with the corporate culture.

The other distinction of the pipeline selection process is that it generally involves more people than an employee's colleagues and manager. It often involves strategic planning from the human resources and diversity divisions and input from one to three levels above the employee. Because of this, an employee is viewed in light of his or her contribution to the overall organization. A broader range of agreement as to the employee's abilities usually has to occur before she moves into the pipeline.

Becoming "High-Potential"

Companies generally select high-potential employees and develop succession plans at higher-level meetings, behind closed doors. These meetings are not heavily publicized, and the decisions as to which employees are high-potentials may or may not be made public. It sometimes happens that only the high-potentials and the decision-makers (including human resources) know the status of high-potential employees.

Because the process of selecting high-potential employees is lower-profile, it can be difficult to ascertain which ones are. Getting tapped as high-potential is not an exact science, but rather depends on a combination of factors. The factors include much of what conventional wisdom says is necessary for women of color to get ahead in corporate America:

- Excellent performance
- A professional image
- Sponsors, mentors, and solid informal networks—in other words exposure (the P.I.E. formula)

If you believe that you are doing all these things, but are still not on in the pipeline at your company, you may want to double-check with a trusted friend or advisor. Some questions you can ask are the following:

- What do you see as developmental opportunities for me?
- How do you think I am perceived in the organization?
- What behaviors do you think it takes to be successful at this company?

TIP: Pay attention to what your enemies say about you. There is no need to go looking for negative feedback; just think back on things they've said about you. But sometimes enemies are more adept at spotting our flaws, and they are likely to be more direct with us than friends.

Women of color who have everything together are often prevented from becoming high-potential by a lack of exposure to potential sponsors, mentors, and colleagues. One counterintuitive way to gain sponsors and mentors is by appearing not to need them. This does not mean that you should act blasé or defensively, as if you are super independent and don't need others. What it means is that stepping up to the plate, performing well, and acting professionally allows others to see potential in you. Once they see that potential, they are more likely to help you succeed in your career.

Even though a sponsor or mentor relationship may seem one-sided, it often has mutually beneficial elements to it. When a sponsor or mentor has a protégé who is very highly regarded at a company, the sponsor or mentor becomes known for their ability to spot talent and to develop talented employees. So sponsoring and mentoring can be a real win-win situation, *if* you are ready to move forward. By having your act together, you are more likely to attract an influential sponsor or mentor.

Another way that talented women of color miss out on being high-potential is their failure to read the "tea leaves" and interpret signals from their companies. Even where the selection of high-potentials is a secretive process, companies have ways of indicating that you (or another person) are being groomed for future leadership. The signals will vary somewhat across industries, but there are some commonalities. Following are some key signals:

- **Being invited to work on special projects or task forces that report their findings to senior management:** These projects allow you to demonstrate your abilities to others in the group and to senior management, providing you with much-needed exposure. The company benefits by testing how the high-potentials work together and by helping them to build solid support networks. These networks ensure their future success at the company. Be on the lookout for invitation-only in-house leadership development programs sponsored by your company; if you are invited to such an event, you are receiving a signal that the company supports your professional development.

- **Increased attention from senior managers and colleagues:** This can range from casual inquiries into your current projects, or more frequent invitations for lunch or coffee to "talk shop." This attention indicates that people like being around you and value your opinion. Conversely, a lack of interest from your colleagues is also telling and indicates that you are probably not on your way up the corporate ladder.

- **A company's financial investment in you:** This is one of the more important signals of approval that you can receive from a company. When a company pays for you to attend external leadership retreats or invests in an executive coach for you, the company is helping you to better develop your abilities. This means that it considers you an asset worth investing in.

Life on the Fast Track

The pipelines of organizations are where many corporate careers are made and lost for women of color. By employing smart strategies and being judicious about power, visibility, and competition, you can position yourself to move to higher levels at your company.

Once you find yourself in the pipeline for leadership, the next step is to begin preparing for the inevitable changes that you will soon begin to encounter.

In Their Own Words

Elise Hewett* became a director at her former employer, a financial services company, through a leadership development program. The president of the company had gone through the same program, so it was a recognized way to move quickly through the ranks. Elise used the program to expand her network and build her credibility in the organization: "It was a leadership development program that was pretty widely recognized by senior leadership, [and] supported, and therefore it was easy to get an audience with a lot of the senior management, to be invited to lunches, to be on task forces...because you were seen as high-potential."

Watch for the Signals

One decisive signal of career success involves you having solid relationships with your colleagues at work. Isolation is not a good sign of your future success. To gauge your relationships, Hewett believes that you should ask yourself whether anyone knows you "besides your boss and close circle of co-workers." Some signs of good relationships include being selected for cross-functional initiatives or for high-quality or important assignments. Another signal of success is the presence of a sponsor—someone senior in the organization who is also concerned about your career.

In Their Own Words

Once a woman of color has received the signals that the company views her as a potential leader, Hewett advises taking action, such as "being proactive. Knowing that you are in control of your career...you'd be amazed at how many people are just lackadaisical when it comes to scheduling meetings and talking to people and creating that circle.... You talk to a lot of individuals in corporations, but everyone you talk to who is more senior than you is not necessarily mentor material for you, or sponsor material for you...and that [knowledge] really comes from having those conversations and developing relationships." Hewett observes, "I think the difference in being on the fast track and [those who] pace themselves through the organization are that the people who move on are the go-getters."

*Name has been fictionalized.

Get the Right Sponsors and Mentors

Hewett cautions women of color against common mistakes, such as having only one mentor or sponsor, or believing that sponsors and mentors have to share your gender or ethnicity. Another crucial mistake that she believes women of color make is that they befriend the wrong people and assume that similarity is a proxy for an advocate. It is a mistake to believe that someone who shares your ethnicity is necessarily your ally. Hewett suggests that women of color be open and flexible to mentors and sponsors who do not resemble them.

She also notes that sometimes mentors who share our ethnicity and gender have a "medical school mentality"—meaning that because they went through difficulties, everyone else should too. Partially for this reason, Hewett suggests that women of color have a diversity of relationships at work. She likens different professional relationships to different friends; in the same way that you have different friends who meet different needs in your personal life, you should have different professional relationships that meet your different professional needs.

In Their Own Words

Hewett remembers, "I had a great contact in HR, [who] helped me with all of my negotiations; if I had employee issues, I would go to that person. But I would not necessarily go to her for career advice...and then I had someone else I would go to...to talk about my next steps." She also relied on company insiders, such as administrative assistants and other employees who had an insider's view of work situations. This helped her to gain perspective on the problems she was facing.

Having a diversity of relationships helped Hewett when one of her key mentors left the organization during her career. This mentor helped Hewett get introduced to key people in the organization and gave her a thorough understanding of the office politics. Partially because of her mentor's assistance, Hewett was able to develop enough of her own relationships to continue her ascent in the organization, even after her mentor's departure.

Have a Written Plan

Hewett advises women of color to come up with a written plan detailing their goals and objectives in the organization. This plan is for your own use only—not for sharing with colleagues.

The nature of Hewett's rotational program required her to think about her next functional role, around every 12 to 24 months. But she continued to develop her own personal plan because one of her mantras is to "*always* have a written plan." Hewett pursued the rotational program as part of a larger goal for herself: "I was pretty clear that I wanted to be a general manager; in order to do that, you need a diverse array of skills, so I wanted to be able to have exposure to finance, to marketing, to our service area.... Being in this kind of program...opened the doors for [me] to be able to get some of those additional skills across a wide variety of areas."

A bonus benefit of having a plan is that it prevents women of color from being sidetracked into roles with low career trajectories. Hewett observes that sometimes roles or functions that sound good will not ultimately move you ahead in the organization. She insists that you need to take control of your own career, and that although nothing is guaranteed, you are likely to fare much better with a plan.

Find Support and Balance

Finally, Hewett advocates finding balance and getting support with in and outside of the organization. Hewett's husband works in the corporate sector, so he understood the challenges she was facing at work. But she also had confidantes at work to ensure that she heard from those with an internal perspective on her work environment.

Once you have support, Hewett advises you to pursue some measure of balance in your life. She described a period during her life where she was totally out of balance. She worked more than was healthy or necessary, and lost touch with her friends. This imbalance impacted her career and close relationships. So she advises women of color to seek balance, because when you are balanced, you are healthy and happy. This leads to a better quality of life. An additional benefit of balance is that healthy, happy people are much more enjoyable for colleagues to be around. Because likeability is an important factor in building relationships at work, balance is also beneficial to your career.

Manage Hypervisibility

It goes without saying that women of color experience high levels of visibility on the fast track, sometimes due to visible distinctions such as skin color or hair texture; other times due to cultural differences such as language and religious issues. But once a woman of color's high-potential status becomes known throughout the organization, she may become hypervisible. This hypervisibility is not always a choice; it often happens naturally. But whether she receives hypervisibility or whether she seeks it out (an ill-advised strategy), it has serious implications for her professional future and should be given thoughtful consideration.

Drs. Stacey Blake-Beard and Laura Morgan Roberts, of the Center for Gender in Organizations at Simmons' School of Management in Boston, examined what they call the "double bind of visibility" for minorities at work.[1] Blake-Beard and Roberts note that reactions to visible minority professionals vary from excessive scrutiny to evaluating their performance more closely and critiquing it more forcefully than is done for others. As a result, when a minority makes a minor mistake, it is treated as convincing evidence of the minority leader's inability, rather than as a developmental opportunity.[2]

Hypervisibility also shines a light on the different expectations placed on white and minority leaders. Corporate America has a developed notion of leadership, and it is white and male. Leadership that occurs outside of this context, as when a woman of color leads, poses a threat to the "cultural stereotypes that ascribe leadership to white males. [Women of color's] white and male counterparts are often put off by their displays of traditional leadership traits, and as a result their behavior is interpreted through a different lens: Confidence is seen as arrogance, sharing accomplishments is deemed bragging, and seeking opportunities for advancement risks drawing accusations of not knowing their place."[3]

Women of color need to exercise caution in addressing this hypervisibility. One reaction internalizes the criticism and begins to self-doubt; another externalizes the criticism, blaming it on others, and becomes insensible to deficiencies.[4] In either case, the reaction of women of color to hypervisibility often deteriorates into self-destructive patterns and distances them further from colleagues. Blake-Beard and Roberts suggest avoiding hypervisibility altogether by adopting a more subtle approach: "tempered visibility."[5]

Tempered visibility is a proactive, more measured approach to handling heightened visibility, and focuses on three aspects of visibility:

- Exposure
- Timing
- Content

A tempered exposure approach allows you to determine in advance the length of time you will spend in the spotlight, on the fringes, or behind the scenes. This prevents you from always being the focal point of a conversation or meeting. Tempered timing is about selectively using visibility—choosing to be more visible in settings where you are best able to make valuable contributions.

Hewett mentions using this strategy by choosing to observe at several meetings prior to speaking up. In so doing, she was able to gauge the flow of the meeting and understand when to be quiet and when to speak. Women of color using the tempered timing approach do not seek to be visible for their ego, or for visibility's sake. Rather, they use visibility strategically—appearing and fading into the background as the situation requires.

The final aspect of tempered visibility involves tempered content, or as political consultants refer to it, staying "on message." This refers to strategically determining what "packet" of information you want others to have about you. This information is predominantly career related, such as a personal value proposition—the value you add to the company or relevant professional experience. It is also wise to include some personal information in your information packet, such as favorite sporting teams, exercise programs, but certainly nothing controversial. Once the message is developed, be on the lookout for opportunities to present the message to senior managers and colleagues, as appropriate.

Power @ Work

One potential landmine on the fast track for women of color is the burgeoning power that occurs in their professional lives as they begin to move up through the ranks of the organization. Although suggestions persist that women are uncomfortable with power, research indicates that women are very comfortable with power—but they may use it differently and for different purposes than their male counterparts.[6] Power is a key component of organizational dynamics, and it plays a solid behind-the-scenes role in the challenges women of color face.

Getting to the heart of power in organizations is a complex undertaking, because power relates to relationships between multiple parties. It cannot be understood in a vacuum; numerous social and economic strata underlie its exercise. Moreover, although power is most often exercised through individuals, systemic aspects of power do exist, once enough individuals explicitly or implicitly subordinate themselves to a particular system.

What Is Power, and Do Women Want It?

At its most fundamental level, power is the ability to get something done. At an individual level, it generally involves one individual getting another person "to do something that they otherwise would not do,"[7] in order to achieve a particular goal. A more elevated notion of power involves the exertion of control over decisions—which decisions are up for discussion, and which issues are relevant to that discussion. An even higher level of power involves the ability to shape others' perceptions, thereby limiting their grievances and indirectly determining their preferences—in other words, this power shapes what is considered normal.

It is evident from the definition of power that it is very broad and can have far-reaching consequences in the organization, so it is not surprising that women want it. Or do they? Drs. Deborah Merrill-Sands, Jill Kickul, and Cynthia Ingols, also of the Simmons School of Management, researched the "opt-out revolution"—a theory which asserted that more women were not at the tops of organizations because they did not want to be there. Underlying this revolution was the notion that women eschewed leadership and power. But the researchers found that 80 percent of their respondents (all women) enjoyed and were comfortable with power. Their research also found that women aspired to the highest leadership roles; 53 percent of women of color felt this way, as did 45 percent of white women. In terms of leadership influence, 85 percent of women of color had aspirations to be influential leaders, as did 70 percent of white women.[8] Yes, women do want to be powerful and influential in their organizations.

Women generally have myriad reasons for wanting power in their organizations. Many women want to use it in order to rise to higher organizational levels (45 percent), and even more want to make changes in their organizations (70 percent). Ultimately, the women surveyed were interested in power to change and influence organizational priorities, or wanted to use power to secure their organization's commitments to socially responsible business and to the community.[9] Women also believe that power is an "important" component of leadership (65 percent), although only 32 percent of women "actively" compete for power[10]—which is surprising, considering the larger percentage of women who find power desirable.

How Do Women Acquire and Use Power?

Generally, women believe that men and women use power differently. Both powerful men and women are believed to "make things happen" and "achieve results," but women viewed powerful men as using power over others. In contrast, they viewed powerful women as being more collaborative. This leads researchers to believe that men are more apt to use power in the traditional way (over others), whereas women tend to be more comfortable using power *through* others.[11]

But to exercise power, women must first acquire it, and women tend to acquire power in ways that reflect their usage of it: through relationship building and achieving results. This strategy makes sense for women (who use power through others) because the relationships that they build become the means through which they achieve their results. Women of color tend not to acquire power in this way; they are likely to focus more on achieving results than on relationship building. Ultimately, this lessens their power base because such a strategy often results in poor relationships and therefore the inability to achieve results through others. For women of color to use power, they must take the time to build relationships and alliances that will allow them to retain and use power.

Once power has been acquired, many pitfalls exist. One such pitfall is the abuse of power. Although abuses of power happen regularly, they are not a helpful business practice. And because power is important, women of color who wield it can expect their actions to be more heavily scrutinized. And, as with other corporate behaviors, abuses of power perpetrated by women of color are viewed differently than those done by their peers.

Part of the reason for this is that others are uncomfortable with women of color having significant power to begin with; any abuse of it will result in a lessening of that power. A white male who yells at a subordinate may be viewed as tough, angry, or prone to outbursts. But his yelling is tolerated by the organization. It is not a proxy for his character, and it does not preclude him from rising in the organization. A woman of color yelling at a subordinate is simply not tolerated by the organization. Why? Because a woman of color is not allowed to exercise her power at someone else's expense in an open, straightforward, manner.

This is partially because of her social status. In society, she is considered to have less power; thus, people are unwilling to accord it to her in a corporate context. They will allow her to accumulate power up to a certain point; after that, the company will take definitive steps to curtail any further open displays of power on her part. The only people who can act simply on the basis of authority are white men and occasionally white women.

Managing Others

The most readily available platform for the exercise of power at work occurs in the interactions between managers and their subordinates. One of the most important facets of organizational life that women of color must learn to master relates to managing others. This ability to manage others, and to elicit the best performance from them, is one of the hallmarks of a leader, and such a reputation will serve you well for your entire career. Good managers engender loyalty from their staff and respect from their peers. For those who seek to rise higher in their organizations, it is a core competency that they can't avoid learning. Good managerial skills are also a starting point for broader managerial skills, so every management situation or opportunity is useful in helping women of color to develop professionally.

If you are seeking a higher managerial role, it is worth taking the time to read about management. Make the most of every opportunity to take a course or receive training on the subject. Because the issue of managing others is fairly involved and somewhat complicated, to examine this issue more in-depth goes beyond the scope of this book.

> **TIP:** Get subscriptions to business magazines such as *BusinessWeek* and *Fortune* to keep up with the latest in management techniques.

Dealing with Competitive Behavior

Competition in corporate America is a fact of life. Part of this competition is the result of the pyramid structure of companies, in which numerous people are employed in the lower ranks, with only one (the CEO) at the top. As you rise through the ranks, the competition becomes more pronounced and often more subtle. Although much of the competition occurs among peers, those who sponsor or mentor those peers are also competing—to see whose protégés will rise through the ranks, or for a higher-level position themselves.

As such, people at the highest levels of corporate America tend to be aligned by quasi-visible teams: You may know which groups are aligned, but there are often other players involved who are more active behind the scenes. Very few corporate employees play the game like Colin Powell, who was highly regarded by two very different political administrations (Democratic and Republican). Most employees openly align themselves with a team. But it is important to realize that although sometimes team members may be good colleagues, these team relationships are often little more than loosely knit alliances. Because such alliances are formed in furtherance of a particular goal or agenda, enter into such relationships carefully.

The Rules

For anyone, competition at work needs to be dealt with very carefully due to a broad backdrop of "unspoken rules" that exist in corporate culture. Because women of color are already operating with heightened visibility, you might want to take additional care when competing for higher-level positions or increased influence. One of the first unspoken rules that you will encounter involves the nature of the rules themselves. Understand: The rules that govern corporate America were not originally intended for people of color, or women, and as such, they are best followed and accepted by white men (the original architects). Having said that, women of color can use the same rules, but need to adjust them in order to make effective use of them. Think of it as rules with a twist.

Consider the following hypothetical scenario: In a meeting of vice presidents at Company X's headquarters in New York City, a white male making an important point might pound his hand on the table for emphasis. The room's likely response to his table banging? Nothing. Consider whether the room would have the same reaction to a white woman banging her hand on the table to make a point. You might already picture a few people looking askance at each other and maybe even a raised eyebrow. Now consider what the response of this same room would be if an African-American woman banged her hand on the table to make a point. Or an Asian-American woman. Just reading this, you already get a sense that this behavior would not be viewed the same as it would be for the white male (assuming that they all hold the same title and have similar work experience). Much of the human response to these actions has to do with the tinting of the evaluative lens that occurs when the actions of women, people of color, and especially women of color are being analyzed.

Model Behavior

One of the wisest steps you might take at your company is to find a well-liked (by the company), competitive person, and to begin to develop a modified competitive model based on that person's behavior. As noted above, it is a risky strategy for you to precisely mirror the behavior of others who do not share your race and gender. This is because of the presence of stereotypes and biases that make it impossible for the woman of color's behavior to be perceived in the same way as her counterparts. But you can develop a way to compete that stays within the cultural bounds, but that allows you some freedom to adjust to circumstances.

Mentors familiar with company culture can also assist you and help you to act in company-friendly ways that will still move you toward your goals. In *The 48 Laws of Power,* Robert F. Greene cites one of the few universal rules regarding competition: Keep a civil appearance, and never actually seem to undercut your competition. He cautions that other people do not like to see competitors work against one another, even though they know it happens. People like for others to "appear" to get along, even when everyone knows that the competitors intensely dislike each other.[12]

Professional Image

Women of color need to be thoughtful about conspicuously showing the fruits of their success. Of course, to reach midlevel management, you had to understand the importance of a business-appropriate wardrobe. Maintaining a professional appearance is certainly valued in the corporate sector, and many women of color have and can develop an authentic style that works for them and fits in with the corporate culture. Conventional wisdom suggests that professionals "dress for the job they want, not the job they have." But that advice is best applied in a general sense.

In some industries, imitating executive behavior—including styles of dress—might be acceptable, but there are some limits. It is unwise to act too much like an executive before you become one. If your career is fast-tracked and you want to be a division president, you might want to hold off on purchasing and wearing a $2,000 custom-made suit like the division president might wear.

The reason? More than likely, your action will elicit more curiosity than admiration. Colleagues will be more interested in how you can afford the suit than in your ambitions at the company. You might find yourself faced with questions about your compensation, and will probably draw more attention to yourself. Worse yet, your colleagues might say nothing and be silently resentful.

Finally, you may be misunderstood. You might be viewed as thinking that you are on par with the senior executive you admire, when in reality you are imitating her because you *want* to reach her level—not because you think that you already have.

Of course, you can't spend all of your time worrying about what your colleagues think of your clothes. One good rule of thumb in developing your style is to select one that is congruent with your industry, company, and division. Take your cues from others, especially your manager; you should look like you are part of the team. If your team wears suits, so should you; if they are business casual, it is probably best not to dress up. You can still retain your individuality, but stay within the context of your corporate culture.

As a woman of color, you want to be careful not to add difficulties to what will undoubtedly be a challenging career path. It is important to take the time to develop a professional, appropriate style that includes your individuality. This is one of the few things in your career that you can control, so it is a good idea to make wise decisions, but also decisions that you can live with.

Publicity Stunts

Many women of color view publicity as an asset to their career, and they are partly right. Publicity can provide numerous career benefits. Internal publicity, like a company newsletter or intranet, can be useful in publicizing your professional expertise or accomplishments to senior managers and colleagues. External publicity, such as profiles in business magazines or newspapers, will provide you with even broader exposure within your company and outside of it.

But there is a downside to publicity, and women of color need to be particularly careful in their use of it. Their heightened visibility, coupled with a company's desire to tout their diversity, serve to make women of color a hot commodity for young leader and future executive lists. Many of these lists, such as *Crain's* "Forty Under 40," are multicultural and feature prominent young professionals in a variety of industries. In recent years, similar listings specific to people of color have increased. Spots on these lists are coveted, and provide positive exposure for rising professionals (as well as a credible third-party reference). But you should recognize that being on such lists does not always lead to positive results for your career.

Jealousy from Peers and Superiors

One common danger for women of color who gain media exposure is that it can engender quiet jealousy from peers and colleagues. This jealousy might not even appear on the surface, although it may manifest itself in snide comments or overly enthusiastic congratulations you receive. This is not to say that none of your colleagues will be genuinely happy for you; some certainly will, but it would be naïve to think that all of them will celebrate your success. Worse yet, media exposure in highly influential business publications can sometimes cause jealousy among your superiors.

Although this may seem counterintuitive—why would a senior executive be envious of a more junior one?—it does happen, and for a variety of reasons. Perhaps the senior executive has not appeared in the media (many have not). Or it could be that the senior executive was not as far along in her career as the junior executive at the same age. Although neither of these explanations makes a lot of sense, jealousy can be illogical. People do not necessarily need a good reason to be jealous of others. Thus, women of color with media exposure should also consider Greene's first rule, which is directly applicable to them: "Never outshine the master."[13]

Effect on Perceived Performance

Another pitfall of publicity concerns the effect that it can have on perceived work performance. Positive publicity (internal or external) can boost perceptions about your abilities and career potential. But excessive publicity, or extremely high-profile publicity, can overshadow your abilities by changing the focus from your capabilities to whether you deserved the publicity. Or colleagues may begin asking why another employee wasn't included on the list, or whether you have become proud or arrogant as a result of the exposure.

Then, of course, there is also the notion that once you become newsworthy, *everything* you do is newsworthy. Bad performance, or an ouster, can also lead to media attention. This is not to say that you should shun the media spotlight, but it is a good idea to be judicious about appearing in publications. Take care that you do not allow media hype to obscure your performance at work or to turn potential allies into enemies.

There are peaks and pitfalls to being in your company's pipeline. At its peaks, you will benefit from access to senior managers and gain entrance into important networks. You will also learn more about the broader vision of the company and get a better sense of how it functions. But the pitfalls of the pipeline can do serious damage to your career. Being aware of how you are perceived, forming relationships with key players, and understanding potential jealousy triggers are good ways to avoid potential traps. Add to that performing above expectations, and you are well on your way to career success.

Notes

[1] Blake-Beard, Stacey, and Laura Morgan Roberts. "Releasing the Double Bind of Visibility for Minorities in the Workplace." *CGO Commentaries*, No. 4 (September 2004), 2.

[2] Ibid., 2.

[3] Livers, A.B., and K.A. Caver. *Leading in Black and White: Working Across the Racial Divide in Corporate America* (San Francisco, CA: Jossey-Bass and the Center for Creative Leadership, 2003).

[4] See "Double Bind," note 1, 2.

[5] Ibid., 4.

[6] Merrill-Sands, Deborah, Jill Kickul, and Cynthia Ingols. "Women Pursuing Leadership and Power: Challenging the Myth of the 'Opt Out Revolution.'" *CGO Insights* (February 2005), 2–3.

[7] Fletcher, Joyce K. "A Radical Perspective on Power, Gender, and Organizational Change." *CGO Insights* (August 1999), 1.

[8] See "Opt Out," note 6, 2.

[9] Ibid., 2–3.

[10] Ibid., 2.

[11] Ibid.

[12] Greene, Robert F. *48 Laws of Power.* (New York: Penguin, 1998), xvii.

[13] Ibid., 1.

CHAPTER 8 The Last Ceiling: Corporate Boards

The business world is familiar with the metaphor of the "glass ceiling." In it, women aim for the top slots at companies, but the higher they rise, the more they find invisible obstacles that prevent them from moving up any further. Recent research on women of color has coined the term "concrete ceiling," which refers to the virtual impasse that women of color encounter as they rise through the ranks of corporate America.

But the "last ceiling" for women of color to reach involves the highest level of responsibility and power within any organization—its board of directors. A company's board is invisible to many employees of a company. But this invisible group exerts considerable influence over the company. They hire and fire the CEO, president, and other senior-level executives, and they sometimes vote to approve important company initiatives. Boards of directors wield broad power within organizations, and this power can take many different forms.

To the owners of the company—its shareholders—the board of directors is made up of those who are ultimately accountable to the owners for the welfare of the company. Part of the board's accountability to shareholders includes legal, financial, and sometimes other industry-related obligations. Diversity is also a part of a board's responsibilities to its shareholders.

One reason that diversity plays a role on corporate boards relates to the ethnic and gender makeup of shareholders. Today, shareholders are more diverse than ever because of individual retirement and pension plans, and other financial products. To properly represent all interests, boards should have some measure of diversity. Among institutional investors and other board governance organizations, diversity is considered to be a "highly desired" facet of governance policies. Thus, large-scale investors also find diversity to be a valued facet of the companies in which they invest. But little evidence exists of racial and gender diversity among the boards of major corporations in the U.S. and abroad.[1]

The ranks of shareholders are not the only people with a vested interest in the success of a particular company. A solid corporate governance strategy involves more than shareholders; it involves employees, customers, suppliers, and communities—the stakeholders of the organization.[2] Each of these groups is affected by the company's performance, so board diversity makes sense.

Obstacles Keeping Women of Color Off Corporate Boards

Traditionally, the ideal corporate board candidate is or has been a chief executive officer, usually of a major corporation. Outside of the CEO circle, companies typically seek people with functional experience that is similar to that of a CEO. This experience includes P&L oversight, financial experience, or proficiency in other areas critical to the core competencies of the organization. In addition to the functional requirements, most corporate boards are looking for candidates who "fit" with the board and organization. This basically refers to a person's professional style and manner of interaction. Because boards of directors operate by consensus, it is essential to have members who operate by similar professional protocols. Finally, with the recent corporate scandals related to boards of directors (for example, Hewlett-Packard and Enron), companies are looking for professionals with excellent reputations for integrity.[3]

Familiar Obstacles

Functionally, it is not difficult to see why women of color have made little progress at the corporate board level. Women, especially women of color, continue to lag behind other minorities with respect to their representation in the senior ranks of organizations, which serve as feeders to corporate boards. In addition, they hold considerably fewer line positions than other groups in corporate America. Because of this, women of color sometimes lack the necessary credentials to sit on boards. But these obstacles are "baked in" to the overall corporate structure; as more women of color reach the senior levels of organizations, we can expect to see some changes in board composition.

But other challenges persist. Women of color eligible to sit on corporate boards may find themselves faced with some of the same challenges they have faced previously, such as exclusion from informal networks. Irene Natividad, co-chair of Corporate Women Directors International, and an experienced corporate director, observes that "despite nominations committees and executive search firms, board recruitment is still a very informal process." Senior women of color who lack access to influential networks may not be considered for corporate boards—even if they have all the requisite credentials.

TIP: Junior or midlevel women of color who are interested in board service may consider serving on the board of a nonprofit organization. This will allow you to help out an arts or community organization, make further use of your professional expertise, and gain valuable experience with board service.

Lack of P&L Responsibility

Lack of profit-and-loss (P&L) responsibility or financial know how is a detriment to a senior woman's board application.[4] One of the reasons that boards seek candidates with P&L responsibility and financial savvy is that addressing financial issues is a critical aspect of board service. Staff roles generally don't require such expertise, rendering women of color in staff roles as less marketable for corporate boards. Although women of color in staff roles sit on influential nonprofit boards, many of which operate on a similar level to corporate boards (for example, United Way), these women are still likely to find some barriers if they want to move over to corporate boards because of their (lack of) functional expertise.

Visibility, Marginalization, and Stereotyping Issues

Other obstacles women of color face relate to a lack of visibility in their industries and across organizations, along with marginalization and stereotyping.[5] Visibility can be a challenge for women of color because the women who have reached senior levels in organizations are already visible within their organizations, and may not realize that companies and boards are struggling to locate them. By using a certain amount of strategic networking, they can make their qualifications and board interest known to a wider and more influential audience.

The perceptions of older white male and female directors also play a role in women of color's recruitment for board service. Many older executives remember racial segregation in the United States, and many have not had significant experience interacting with women of color. As a result, they may hold stereotypes that could play a substantial role in their understanding of and interaction with women of color who do hold board seats.[6] These stereotypes, as well as other factors, sometimes lead to the marginalization of women of color seeking board seats; the women are not taken seriously. Thus, women of color interested in sitting on corporate boards should consider getting an independent assessment of their viability as a board candidate before getting involved in the board recruitment process. This third-party validation could take several forms. It could be a director training seminar offered by the National Association of Corporate Directors, an executive education program at a top business school, or a nonprofit organization training program.

> **TIP:** Many nonprofit board training programs exist for midlevel and junior women of color. Organizations such as the United Way offer comprehensive training and sometimes provide board service opportunities to graduates of the program.

Changing Notions of the Ideal Director

Fortunately, in recent times, the notion of the ideal candidate for corporate boards has begun to change. The enactment of Sarbanes-Oxley in response to corporate scandals has caused a flurry of activity in the governance arena across industries, requiring a renewed focus on independence and fiduciary obligations. Companies that previously sought only CEOs suddenly found that their prize candidates were allowed to serve on only a couple of outside boards simultaneously. At the same time, companies were confronted with a new requirement for independent directors (those from outside the organization). In addition to regulatory forces, companies were also faced with departures from senior board members. Current estimates state that roughly 10 percent of the corporate directors in the S&P 500 are over 70 years old.[7]

As a result of these factors, companies are expanding their notions of the ideal corporate director. But these new ideal candidates are still required to have a high level of experience in whatever arena they are employed. Spencer Stuart has placed close to 300 women on corporate boards since 2000, and 70 percent of them were C-level officers—although not all were CEOs. Around 15 percent of the women Spencer Stuart placed on boards were SVPs or EVPs; another 8 percent came from the ranks of managing directors or partners, and 6 percent hailed from academic or not-for-profit organizations.[8]

Where Do Directors Come From?

In its *2006 Board Diversity Report*, Spencer Stuart examined the functional roles from which Fortune 200 boards are selecting directors (approximately 2,300 seats). The top three sources for male and female directors is shown in table 8.1.[9]

Table 8.1: The Top Three Sources for Male and Female Directors

Male Directors	Female Directors
Active chairmen, presidents, or CEOs (41%)	Academic or nonprofit community (23%)
Retired chairmen, presidents, or CEOs (22%)	Active chairmen, presidents, or CEOs (22%)
Other corporate executives (9%)	Other corporate executives (22%)

These findings indicate that the top three sources of male directors are the ranks of active or retired corporate executives. The top three sources for female directors are the academic/nonprofit community, and corporate executives. The major distinction between male and female sourcing is the proportion of men and women that become directors from corporate America. The percentage of men is higher because more men hold senior-level roles at companies. As more women reach the senior levels of corporate America, corporations will produce more women directors. Until then, boards of directors are reaching into other arenas, such as academia or nonprofits, to find women directors who have the required experience (23 percent). Although women of color are not specifically included in these statistics, it is likely that their top sources are similar to those of women, with smaller percentages from corporate America.

Looking at the functional roles from an ethnic diversity perspective, Spencer Stuart compared the functional roles of minority and non-minority male directors. The top three sources for minority and non-minority directors are shown in table 8.2.[10]

Table 8.2: The Top Three Sources for Minority and Non-minority Directors

Non-minority Male Directors	Minority Directors
Active chairmen, presidents, or CEOs (38%)	Active chairmen, presidents, or CEOs (36%)
Retired chairmen, presidents, or CEOs (21%)	Academic or nonprofit community (17%)
Other corporate executives (9%)	Other corporate executives (15%)

Although these statistics do not specifically focus on women of color directors, they do provide some idea of the board sourcing trends from an ethnic perspective. Virtually the same percentage of minority male and non-minority male directors come from the ranks of active chairmen, presidents, and CEOs. But, as with women, a larger percentage of minority directors comes from the academic or nonprofit community (17 percent) than from non-minority directors (9 percent). The trends indicate that boards of directors are looking in nontraditional arenas to recruit minority candidates.

Women of Color Directors

The Alliance for Board Diversity (ABD)[11] is a partnership among Catalyst, the Executive Leadership Council (ELC), and the Hispanic Association of Corporate Responsibility (HACR). ABD performed a study in 2004, which surveyed the composition of board seats at Fortune 100 companies (1,195 seats). ABD found that although women and minorities collectively accounted for approximately

28.8 percent of board seats, women of color held only 3 percent of those seats. All women accounted for 16.9 percent of seats, and men of color held 11.88 percent.[12]

In terms of board seats, men of color fared considerably better than women of color across ethnic subgroups:

- **African-Americans.** African-Americans hold the highest percentage of all board seats at 10.04 percent (120 seats); 93 of those seats are held by men (78 percent); African-American women hold 27 seats (22 percent).

- **Latinos/Latinas.** Latinos have the second-highest percentage of board seats, at 3.85 percent (46 seats); Latino males hold 40 of the 46 seats (87 percent), while Latinas hold 6 seats (13 percent).

- **Asian-Americans.** Asian-Americans are the least represented of all minority groups on Fortune 100 boards at 1 percent (12 seats); Asian-American men held 9 of those seats (75 percent); Asian-American women held 3 seats (25 percent).[13]

ABD's examination of individual companies found that on every Fortune 100 board a woman or minority held at least one seat. Ninety-nine boards had at least one woman; 92 boards had at least one minority board member. Fourteen boards had no African-American members, 63 boards had no Latinos or Latinas, and 88 boards had no Asian-American members.[14]

Part of ELC's separate study on *African-Americans on Boards of Directors Part II* also included statistics related to people of color on Fortune 100 boards. ELC found a small number of corporate boards with broad ethnic and gender diversity, and having representation from African-Americans, Asian-Americans, Latinos/Latinas, and women. The companies are Dupont, General Electric, PepsiCo, and Walt Disney. In addition to having each ethnicity represented, all of these organizations, except Dupont, have women of color on their boards, as well.

ELC also found other companies that have greater than 50 percent of board seats held by diverse individuals: Alcoa (60 percent); IBM (58.33 percent); HP and WellPoint Health Networks (55.56 percent); and Albertson's, Dupont, Target, and UPS (50 percent). Other Fortune 100 companies have improved or are improving the diversity of their boards; 38 companies have reported that at least 31 percent of their board seats are held by diverse candidates.[15]

International Corporate Boards

Corporate Women Directors International (CWDI) studies women's representation on international corporate boards. In their research of the Fortune Global 200, they found that women hold only 10.4 percent of board seats. They also found that U.S.-headquartered companies have the best representation of women on their boards for any country (17.5 percent). The U.S. also boasts the company with the highest percentage of women on its board (50 percent)[16]—meaning that the board representation of women is lower internationally; women of color's representation is probably even lower.

European companies in the Fortune Global 200 have women directors on their boards, but in lower percentages than the United States. Just over 12 percent of board seats in the United Kingdom are held by women, whereas women in Germany hold just over 10 percent of the seats. One European country, Norway, has the second-highest-ranked company on Fortune's Global 200 in terms of women's representation on board seats (44 percent),[17] although Norway is likely to have many more women directors in the future. Recently, Norway passed legislation requiring the demographic makeup of corporate boards to reflect that of society—of which women are 40 percent.

Among Asian countries, Japan has the fewest number of women directors; women hold only three board seats of the 431 available seats—less than 1 percent all seats.[18] In Latin America, the largest companies are found in the Latin Trade 100; CWDI found that only 36 percent of the companies have at least one woman director. In addition, close to two-thirds (64 percent) of Latin Trade 100 companies do not have any women on their boards of directors. Among the few seats that women directors hold in Latin America (5 percent), many are held by members of the founder's family, echoing a cultural pattern of ownership in that part of the world.[19]

Challenges in the Boardroom

As boards become more diverse, additional challenges for women and minority directors surface. One of these challenges is holding seats on multiple boards, sometimes referred to as "recycling" of board members. This phenomenon is partially due to the lack of available diverse candidates for board seats; companies often compete to recruit the same candidates for their boards. At some level, holding multiple board seats poses regulatory and fiduciary concerns because boards are expected to use a high standard of care in their oversight functions. When a director holds multiple seats, it can become difficult to be present at all meetings, and to properly attend to the company's business. Nonetheless, this practice of "recycling" the same board members continues. Recent studies found that diversity board members hold a higher average number of seats than their non-diverse counterparts.[20] As companies begin to develop their nontraditional sources for board candidates, this trend of "recycling" may decline.

Once women (including women of color) become directors, they encounter issues that are largely different than those they face in the trenches of corporate America. Much of this difference in issues stems from the confluence of power at the boardroom table. This is because a board meeting consists of approximately 10 to 20 high-powered executives from sectors interacting with each other. A newer board member may not be accustomed to this sort of experience.

To make an impact on boards, women directors initially seek to establish their credibility early among the group, to learn to discern when individual or group action is more appropriate, and to demonstrably add value to the board. To accomplish these goals, women directors focus on being thoroughly prepared for committee and board meetings, and on listening intently in plenary and individual meetings with their fellow board members. They also build up their confidence and develop relationships with board members outside of the board context.[21]

In Their Own Words

Natividad has learned a number of lessons from her board service: "You have to do politics with a small 'p,' and that means that you can't operate as a lone ranger. You must use the committee process...and if you're proposing an idea or an initiative, you must have allies...learn how to count how many other people are on your side." Her practical suggestions for boardroom interactions include learning that "there are conversations that can be conducted in between meetings," and in terms of board etiquette: "Never surprise the CEO...[or] go to a senior executive officer without alerting the CEO that you are going to do so." Of course, there are many other nuances and subtleties that women of color on boards will need to learn. Natividad advises women of color to seek the advice of those who are already on boards or have access to those who are on boards.

A recent Catalyst study found that women held 14.7 percent of Fortune 500 board seats (for which they had data), and they held 11.2 percent of the 1,307 committee chair seats. Among committee chair seats, the most powerful are those on the nominating/governance, audit, and compensation committees. The women's representation is shown in table 8.3.

Table 8.3: Women in Committee Chair Roles

Committee Name	% Women Chairs
Nominating or governance	14.2%
Audit	10.2%
Compensation	9.0%

The study did not include data for women of color in committee chair roles, but considering that women of color account for so few board seats, it is likely that they must hold even fewer committee chair posts. Women are underrepresented at the committee chair level of boards; women of color are likely to be even more so.[22]

The Leaderboard: Being an Influential Board Member

Getting a seat on a corporate board is the height of prestige in corporate America. But within the board structure, there are influential positions that wield even more clout, such as committee chairs. Because boards do much of their work through committees, and some committees are more powerful than others, the committee on which a director sits or chairs can influence the amount of power she wields.

When Irene Natividad was first involved with corporate boards, she asked one of her mentors, a pioneer of women on boards, about which committee to seek out. The advice she received from her mentor was hilarious (but true): "Honey, follow the money—compensation, finance, [and] audit." Those three committees, along with nomination and governance, are involved in transacting critical business for the board. The compensation committee is responsible for reviewing the compensation of the CEO and other senior-level executives, and the finance and audit committees have oversight of corporate assets. The nominating committee is responsible for recruiting board members and the governance committee has oversight of issues related to corporate actions. Because of the importance of these committees to the functioning of the company, those chairing these committees have more power than some of the other board members. These dynamics are also subject to other types of power as well, such as personal or family power.

Women's participation on boards is good for business and results in better decision-making and a broader representation of stakeholders. It is also critical in supporting the participation of other women in board work. Recent studies suggest that having a critical mass of women on corporate boards is essential if boards are to benefit from gender diversity, and that the presence of one woman may be viewed as tokenism, and her contribution will be marginalized.[23]

In Their Own Words

The comfort level for women on corporate boards can be related to the number of women holding seats. Natividad makes the following candid observation about women on boards: "One…is a token; two, they tend to avoid each other because they don't want to be considered a female cabal, three is [comfortable]…then people forget that it's a woman presenting an idea."

On almost half of the Fortune 500 boards that were surveyed, the composition of women directors was as follows:

- 53 companies (11 percent) have no women directors at all.
- 182 companies (36 percent) have only one woman on their boards.
- 189 have two women directors (38 percent).
- 76 have three or more women directors (15 percent).[24]

Besides tokenism, women directors operating alone may face other issues like marginalization of their contributions, exclusion from all-male socializing, and heightened scrutiny of their actions. If women do not handle these challenges well, their effectiveness as directors might be compromised; this would perpetuate the notion that women are ill-suited for directorship.[25] Again, such challenges exist for women of color, as well. Boards that are serious about gender diversity must make sure that sufficient women directors exist to ensure that their contributions are more than illusory.

Getting "On Board"

This section details strategies for getting on corporate boards, broken into two categories: junior and midlevel women of color, and senior women of color.

Junior and Midlevel Women of Color

For junior and midlevel women of color who are interested in serving on boards, you have several options on how to get started on the process:

- **Get training.** Several nonprofit organizations have board training programs to provide you with a broad overview of board service. These programs also provide instruction on board member responsibilities, including legal, financial, and operational. The United Way has such programs in many cities; if there's not one in your city, they can usually direct you to an agency with such a program.

- **Know your interests.** Determine what focus your target nonprofit organization will have: arts, education, community, health, children, or something else. This will help you narrow down your list of potential boards once you have completed your training. It will also help you refine your knowledge during board training because different types of nonprofits usually face different sets of issues, although some overlap exists.

TIP: Before you join any board, check with your company to be sure your board service does not present any conflicts of interest or other difficulties.

- **Get into a database.** Web sites such as www.boardnetusa.org link nonprofit boards seeking members with potential board candidates. You can search the database of nonprofits by geographic location, area of focus, or amount of required contribution. You can also post a profile, and boards that are interested in you can contact you directly.

TIP: It is a good idea to visit a board meeting before officially joining a board (some boards will require this). It allows you to get a sense of how the board members interact with each other and whether you are a "fit" with the group.

Senior Women of Color

The process of getting on corporate boards is more difficult for senior women of color. To be eligible for corporate boards, you must have achieved a high level of success, and must have expertise and experience at the most senior corporate levels.

In Their Own Words

Excellence in your field is a prerequisite for corporate board service. Irene Natividad notes that "you have to have arrived and excelled in your field before you can be tapped for board service." She also comments on the lack of net-working among successful women interested in boards. "There's an assumption on the part of women who have achieved that somehow people will find them" she says, but remarks that such assumptions must be overcome, because outside of a particular industry or geographic region, peo-ple may not know of your achievements. Instead, she believes you should articulate your interest in board service "to people who are influential, who are already on boards, or who have access to boards...seek their advice." Again, before you do this, you really need to be at the most senior level within your company.

For women of color who are eligible for corporate board service, a number of programs exist with targeted recruiting efforts aimed at getting women and minorities:

- **The Alliance for Board Diversity:** The Alliance for Board Diversity is comprised of Catalyst, the Executive Leadership Council, and the Hispanic Association for Corporate Responsibility. ABD serves as an informal referral service for member companies seeking diverse candidates for their boards. Carl Brooks, president of ELC, says that ABD is "available as a resource," and advocates "to be supportive of [companies]...filling board seats."

- **Catalyst's Corporate Board Services program:** This program is specifically tailored to senior executive women from Catalyst member companies. It includes, as appropriate, discussions with a senior woman's CEO or president, and the internal leadership development divisions at her company. Additional services that Catalyst provides are an overview of corporate boards, an individual assessment, networking assistance, and resources for board-related educational programs. Catalyst began Corporate Board Services in the 1970s, and has a database with more than 2,500 women.

- **The Executive Leadership Council:** The ELC offers certification programs to its members through the National Association of Corporate Directors, and through Northwestern's Kellogg School of Business. The certification programs provide ELC members with additional information on skills-building, board structures and committees, board financials, and strategic relationships. According to Carl Brooks, "about 200 [ELC] members have gone through an additional level of certification and validation for board participation."

- **The Committee of 200 (C200):** C200 is a high-powered businesswomen's organization in Chicago. Its members hold some of the most influential positions in corporate America, and are entrepreneurs of multimillion-dollar companies. Although its Web site does not provide information about a board referral service, it is certainly an organization with access to many women who are eligible for board service.

- **Search firms:** Executive search firms, such as Spencer Stuart or Heidrick & Struggles, have well-developed board search capabilities and can help senior women of color start discussions with companies, and provide information on corporate board service.

- **Business schools:** Some U.S. business schools offer board-related services, as well. The University of California–Los Angeles (UCLA) offers a Director Training & Certification Program through its Anderson School of Management. This program is a three-day seminar that provides information on corporate governance, regulations, and other relevant information. Institutional Shareholder Services has accredited UCLA's program as a Preferred Boardroom Education Program. Participants must successfully complete the program and pass a written exam. The program targets new directors, directors of private companies going public, or prospective directors. UCLA also offers a Director Match program for alumni of its program; Director Match maintains a database of certified directors (those who have completed their program). Senior women of color can enhance their board service credentials by completing this program.

- **OnBoard Bootcamp:** This nascent entrant to the arena of corporate board training offers a two-day seminar targeting professionals seeking to become directors, as well as more experienced directors. OnBoard Bootcamp provides participants with a thorough overview of corporate boards, including information about different types of boards, fiduciary obligations, board structure, and tips on securing a board seat and developing a board network.

- **Regional resources:** Regional resources also exist for experienced professional women interested in serving on corporate or nonprofit boards. The InterOrganizational Network (ION) is a group of several regional organizations that are advocates for the advancement of women to senior organizational levels, and for their participation on corporate boards. Each organization reports on the status of senior women at local companies, and on corporate boards. The organizations include the Board of Directors Network in Atlanta, The Boston Club in Boston, The Chicago Network in Chicago, the Forum of Executive Women in Philadelphia; Inforum in Detroit; Milwaukee Women Inc., in Milwaukee, and Women's Executive Leadership in Fort Lauderdale.

Senior women of color with the right blend of functional experience, industry expertise, personality, and organizational savvy can anticipate being tapped for corporate board seats; but it is not necessary for them to wait for the companies to find them—they can jump-start the process whenever they are ready.

In Their Own Words

Irene Natividad explains, "Understand that you have to be visible, you have to have excelled in your field, and you have to be tied to the networks where people will see your achievements; and lastly you must tell people that you are interested in board service, and that you have the skills to [serve]." By using available resources, women of color can find corporate board seats that will provide them with rewarding, insightful experiences and allow them to add value to corporate America as a whole, one (or two) companies at a time.

Notes

[1] Alliance for Board Diversity. *Women and Minorities on Fortune 100 Boards* (2005), 2.

[2] Ibid.

[3] Catalyst Corporate Board Services Web site, available at www.catalyst.org.

[4] Catalyst. *2005 Catalyst Census of Women Board Directors of the Fortune 500* (2005), 25.

[5] Ibid.

[6] Alliance for Board *Diversity*. *Women and Minorities on Fortune 100 Boards* (2005), 15.

[7] *Harvard Business School Alumni Bulletin Online* (June 2006), available at www.alumni.hbs.edu/bulletin/2006/june/.

[8] Warner, Joan. "Women Do Make a Difference." *Directorship* (June 1, 2006), 3.

[9] Spencer Stuart. *2006 Board Diversity Report*, 11–12.

[10] Ibid.

[11] The Alliance for Board Diversity also received input from the Committee of 100, an advocacy organization for Asian-Americans.

[12] Alliance for Board Diversity. *Women and Minorities on Fortune 100 Boards* (2004), 4.

[13] Ibid.

[14] Ibid., 6.

[15] Ibid.

[16] Corporate Women Directors International. *Women Board Directors of the Fortune Global 200 Companies* (2004).

[17] Ibid.

[18] Ibid.

[19] Corporate Women Directors International. *Latin Trade 100: Key Findings—Women Board Directors of the Latin Trade 100 Companies* (2005).

[20]Spencer Stuart. *2006 Board Diversity Report,* 13; Alliance for Board Diversity. *Women and Minorities on Fortune 100 Boards* (2005), 5–6.

[21]Catalyst. *2005 Catalyst Census of Women Board Directors of the Fortune 500* (2005), 26–27.

[22]Ibid., 11–12.

[23]Kramer, V.W., A.M. Konrad, and Sumru Erkut. *Critical Mass on Corporate Boards: Why Three or More Women Enhance Governance* (Executive Summary, 2006), 3.

[24]Catalyst. *2005 Catalyst Census of Women Board Directors of the Fortune 500* (2005).

[25]Ibid.

CHAPTER 9

Culture Shock: Women of Color and International Business

Over the past 10 to 15 years, globalization has permanently changed the way business is conducted in the United States and abroad. One of the effects of globalization has been the international expansion of U.S.-headquartered companies. This expansion has changed many companies' processes for developing aspiring leaders within their organizations. The change in these processes makes sense when you consider that the process of professional development at domestically focused companies should differ from those of multinational organizations. Although there will probably be some overlap in strategies that the two types of companies employ, one key difference is that multinational organizations are preparing employees to face cultural and operational issues that will differ considerably from those faced by employees in the United States.

One of the challenges surrounding international professional development for employees is the lack of international work experience among U.S. employees. Many U.S. corporations do not have a deep roster of talented employees with international experience. So companies who need such employees are beginning to provide international roles or assignments for employees to help them develop their competencies in international settings. If you are employed at an international company and hope to advance, opportunities abroad can be very helpful for your career. With just over one-third of the Fortune Global 500 headquartered in the U.S., it is becoming increasingly likely that employees will be called on to serve in an international capacity. For women of color at such companies, international rotations are a crucial aspect of career development.

The Challenges of Working Abroad

Despite its benefits, working internationally can prove challenging for women of color, who may find themselves marginalized as "foreigners," possibly due to their race and gender. This alienation may be exacerbated because in many countries, behavior deemed racist or sexist in the U.S. is not considered as such. It is quite likely that you will find yourself in the uncomfortable position of dealing with off-color jokes—or worse—from colleagues or clients. And your distance from home may only make dealing with these problems more difficult. But the reality is that you will probably not have to deal with new issues of racism, sexism, or colorism while abroad; it will just be a different (and sometimes more blatant) manifestation of these issues. So be prepared. You will also be pleasantly surprised to find that some of the issues you encounter in the U.S. are notably absent abroad.

The obstacles that you will encounter internationally will, in many ways, mirror those faced by women working abroad generally. The additive factor you may face has to do with your ethnicity which may raise additional considerations for you; or it may provide a welcome boost to your credibility. Employees going abroad—even in multinational corporations—often face career risks because of their distance from headquarters. This distance can prevent them from having access to critical information, and significantly limits their "face time" with higher-ups. Even something like time-zone differences can make all the difference in the communication between the employee who is abroad and her network back in the office. Employees accepting international assignments are rightly concerned that being "off the radar" can be detrimental to their careers. Women of color who are already working against invisibility at work may find that working abroad exacerbates this problem, at least until they return stateside.

> **TIP:** Getting an office clock (or a watch) with multiple time zones enables you to easily keep track of the time in your home zone. This makes it easier for you to catch up with colleagues back at headquarters.

You should also expect to have your managerial abilities tested when working internationally. Since you are likely to be viewed as a "foreigner," you will need to build credibility to make an immediate impact in your new role. Otherwise, you may find others initially resistant to your input. A resistant reaction from your new colleagues may have nothing to do with your gender or race, but might be due to your status as an "outsider." This problem may be rectified over time, depending on the culture in which you find yourself. Local reactions to you will also vary depending on your command of the local language. Employees who are semifluent or fluent in the local language will often gain quicker acceptance and be more effective in their roles because they can communicate with others in ways that make them comfortable. Women of color who speak a language that is helpful in their rotational program (for example, a Latina on an international rotation in Chile) may find themselves with enhanced credibility because of their language skills, and in many cases, familiarity with the general culture of the country or region.

Knock for Opportunity: Getting International Assignments

Getting selected for an international role is where the difficulty begins. Organizations often assume that women are not interested in such roles, whereas men are generally assumed to be interested.[1] Such assumptions on the part of the organization probably stem from concerns about women's family commitments, ambitions, or how they will be received internationally. As this is the case with women generally, it is highly likely these obstacles are greater for women of color, except where the women provide an immediate advantage for the company. Where women of color belong to a culture that presents a viable business opportunity for a company, she may be selected for an overseas assignment because of her familiarity with the language and cultural considerations.

> **TIP:** If you are considering leaving an international assignment, be sure to groom others to be your successor in the international role. Then, if another opportunity arises, you can move out of the international role without it being problematic for your company.

In situations where you do not share language or culture with your new country of residence, you may face additional hurdles to receiving an international assignment. One of the most common barriers women experience is that they are perceived to be unwelcome to do business in other countries. In certain contexts, this is undoubtedly true. But in the vast majority of countries, international businesspeople understand that both American men and women conduct business, and they will be prepared to interact with you as a business colleague. It is more likely that you will have to fend off unwanted sexual advances abroad than that you will not be taken seriously as a professional. One study found that women report successful relationships with clients outside of the U.S., without regard to the geographic location of their workplace.[2]

Companies often perceive women to be less internationally mobile than men because of family considerations, and may not even consider women for such roles, or will consider them less often. Some of the factors that weigh into this perception are women's expected responsibility for child care or because her spouse works full-time. But if a woman is qualified for an international role, and she is willing to go, then the decision whether to go abroad is best left to her to make with her family. This is not to say that every woman will respond positively to an international assignment. Depending on what's at stake, the woman may accept, refuse, or delay. But whatever her answer, companies should be sure that she is given a chance to consider the opportunity, particularly since studies have shown that both men and women have difficulty balancing work-life issues when working abroad.[3] The challenges that U.S. employees face abroad are not unique to women; men also experience them.

> **TIP:** Be vocal about expressing your interest in working abroad, because your company may have the impression that you are less interested in a global assignment because you are a woman.

Going International

Once you have made the decision to go "global" and have gotten an assignment, there are many preparations to make before going. This section discusses some of the professional and personal matters that you will probably need to address.

Taking Care of Family Concerns

Taking care of family concerns and issues prior to going abroad is critical to your success, because their resolution will determine, in large part, whether your global transition is smooth or choppy. Because virtually all women with international roles have working spouses (91 percent),[4] it is important that you help them find a role; your company may be able to provide you with some assistance. Of course, your spouse does not necessarily have to work at the same company as you do, but your company may be able to leverage its connections to help your spouse make connections at another nearby company. This is a common perk that corporations offer their employees, even for domestic relocations; it is worth checking your expatriate paperwork to see whether such benefits exist. If your company does not provide such services, you should ask whether other help is available.

Other considerations, such as living arrangements, school information, childcare, and the like are often provided by a relocation service, so there should be less legwork and more decision-making on your part when addressing these issues. If you care for extended family members, you may need to make arrangements for them, as well. Also, do not forget to stock up on personal items for yourself (for example, hair products or makeup) that may not be available internationally in the concentrations and colors that you need.

> **TIP:** Arrange to have a friend send a "care package" to you every few months with your favorite products from home.

Taking Care of Career Concerns

Career-wise, you will have a lot of work to do prior to leaving on your international assignment. Much of the work involves building relationships, but you will also need to work on developing cultural competency in your soon-to-be new home. Here are some things for you to take into consideration.

Establish Contacts

One of your first steps will be to establish contacts with your new colleagues. You may have already met with or interviewed with people who work in your new city; it makes sense to keep in touch with them by checking in periodically. Also, new colleagues will often prove to be a valuable resource for information on the corporate culture, and can help you avoid costly gaffes and mistakes. They are also likely to give you experienced advice about life in their country or city, although you should be somewhat cautious about what you can ask. Questions that do not require your new colleagues to do research on your behalf are generally best—inquiries about neighborhoods and school districts are good places to start.

> **TIP:** Get a street-level map of your new city, and several tourist books, so that you can plan outings for your family before you arrive. Sharing your new information with them is a good way to get everyone excited about the move.

Talk to Those Who Have Gone Before

If your assignment is part of a rotational program, or if other employees have previously worked in your new location, be sure to talk with those employees before you leave. Even if you already talked with them prior to accepting the assignment, they will still prove to be among your best resources for getting the "inside scoop" on office politics. And because they have already lived where you are moving, their practical advice can be invaluable.

> **TIP:** Don't just read the paperwork about handling taxes in your new country; ask employees who have worked there. Taxes are tricky in every country, and you don't want to run afoul of tax laws while abroad.

Get Introduced

Touch base with your mentors and sponsors at your company, to find out whether they can liaise with or facilitate introductions to their global counterparts on your behalf. Even when you are abroad, mentors and sponsors can provide valuable guidance, or can keep your name on the radar while you are away. They also can help you develop a timeline for an open-ended international role, although in some cases the time frame may be predetermined. They may even be able to help you chart your post-international career steps.

Prepare a Career Plan

Preparing a career plan is another critical issue that you should address before starting your global role. Really, you should do it prior to accepting the position, although circumstances do not always allow for such extensive advance planning. You should have a general sense of what you want the role after your international assignment to look like, although it may change once you move abroad. You might also look two steps ahead to be sure that the experience that you gain internationally will be of use to you (and the company) in future roles.

Familiarize Yourself with the Culture

Adjusting to the cultural aspects of business is a huge part of your transition abroad. If time and finances permit, you might consider making an extra visit or two to your new location to experience more of the country's culture. Learning the language and reading books on the country are essential components of your planning process. Finally, because many global companies do business across borders, you will need to be prepared to do business not just in your new location, but also in the surrounding countries—books on doing business in many countries will prove useful as you begin making your adjustment.

> **TIP:** Take time to visit travel Web sites, which often provide excellent cultural information and insights into life in a particular city or country.

Google, Google, Google!

Do you want a business perspective on working abroad, but from outside of your company? Try visiting Web sites for businesspeople working abroad, such as www.expatfocus.com or www.escape artist.com. These sites contain articles about countries, forums where you can post questions, and even online groups that you can join. Although the Web sites are sometimes not the most visually friendly, they do have a wealth of information.

International Challenges

The challenges of women of color working internationally are not well-understood because there has been very little research on the subject. By looking at the research that we do have, we can understand the issues that women face generally, and recognize that women of color will encounter these same issues and more.

As it happens, the challenges women face on global assignments do not appear to differ significantly from those who work in the United States. Certainly the view of ethnic diversity and gender differs in other countries, but stereotyping, invisibility, and favoritism are not unique to American culture. In a study comparing women executives in Europe and in the U.S., Catalyst found that the women had similar ambitions, success strategies, and barriers to advancement. But European women also felt differently about issues that are critical to American women's notion of career success.

One such issue is mentoring. Sixty-one percent of European women viewed a lack of mentoring as a barrier to advancement, but only 40 percent of European women have ever had a mentor.[5] While the majority European women view mentoring as important, it appears that companies in Europe have not made the development of mentoring programs a priority. In the U.S., the vast majority of companies have mentoring programs, and 77 percent of U.S. women have had a mentor in their career.[6]

If you are working abroad in Europe (or any other country), you should be aware that mentoring for women may be less common than in the U.S. This means that you need to be prepared to develop mentoring relationships on your own. If you have a U.S.-based mentor or sponsor, consider asking them to assist you in the process of finding mentors who can help you during your time abroad.

Informal networks are another major area where the viewpoints of European and American women diverged. In the U.S., 77 percent of women viewed exclusion from informal networks as a key barrier to their corporate success. In Europe, only 29 percent of women held a similar view.[7] The reason for this disparity is unclear; it could be that European women believe that they are part of informal networks. Or it could be that in their view of European culture, informal networking is not crucial to advancement, although such a scenario hardly seems likely.

Again, it is a good idea to keep in mind that informal networking may be perceived differently than in the U.S. It will be up to you to find out what the key success factors are in the culture of your new assignment.

Different Perceptions of Barriers

Overall, European women had different perceptions of the barriers to advancement than U.S. women. Their top three barriers to advancement were the following:[8]

- Stereotyping
- Lack of women role models
- Lack of general management or line experience

The two barriers they considered least problematic?

- Senior leadership's failure to be accountable for women's advancement
- Exclusion from informal networks

The barriers that European women considered the least problematic are viewed by U.S. women as highly problematic. U.S. women listed their barriers to success in this order:[9]

1. Lack of general management or line experience
2. Senior leadership's failure to be accountable for women's advancement
3. Stereotyping
4. Exclusion from informal networks

European and U.S. women agree that stereotyping and a lack of general management or line experience are hindrances to their career success. But they disagree noticeably concerning the other barriers. This difference in viewpoint also extends to the women's views regarding success strategies.

Different Views of Success Strategies

Between European and American women, there is no overlap in their views of what it takes to be successful in business. European women's list of top success strategies looks like this:[10]

1. International experiences
2. Cross-functional experience
3. Developing and adhering to career goals

Women in the U.S. held the following as their top strategies:[11]

1. Personal style
2. Exceeding performance expectations
3. Networking

European and American women have very different notions of what it takes to be successful in one's career. This makes it difficult to draw any solid conclusions as to how a woman, or a woman of color, might be successful in an international context.

Initially, it may be best to observe successful women in your new environment and to make adjustments to your behavior as you gain insights and confidence in your new setting. If there are no women whose behavior it is appropriate to model, do your homework on the culture, observe, and seek advice from people familiar with the culture, as appropriate.

If you are at a satellite office of your company, you might notice that the culture in the office is similar to what you are used to. But beware: Every organization takes on a different version of the headquarters culture when in a new location. Be mindful that behaviors accepted at home may not be viewed favorably in a new cultural context—even within the same company.

Global Minority Experiences

Catalyst found that European and American women have different views of professional women's challenges and which success strategies will overcome those challenges. But other studies have found that minority professionals generally have the same experiences at home and abroad.

The Center for Work-Life Policy (CWLP) researched executives in the United Kingdom, India, and South Africa to get their views on corporate culture. The U.K. executives were white men and women; the minority executives were from India and South Africa. The results of the study found that minority executives generally perceived hidden bias in their work environments. And much like minority professionals in the United States, they also felt that colleagues whose external appearance and style was congruent with senior management were "unfairly favored" in their receipt of advancement opportunities. These international minority professionals were also faced with some of the same responsibilities as those in the U.S., including extended care responsibilities. They were also active in their religious lives and communities.[12]

These similarities point to the possibility that certain of your professional experiences as a woman of color may not differ significantly from those you have in the U.S. One difference between these results and those found by Catalyst could be that gender issues play out differently in Europe, but racial and ethnic concerns are similar globally.

> **TIP:** Be aware of how people of your ethnicity are viewed in a particular culture; it might be more beneficial for you to seek out an international position in a culture that is friendly to your race or ethnicity.

CWLP found that global minority executives also viewed diversity initiatives similarly to minority professionals in the U.S. In the study, global minority executives supported the idea of cultural sensitivity training for employees to address stereotypes, as well as the development of mentoring relationships. CWLP's study of U.S. minority professionals found that such programs also receive broad support from them.[13]

Global minority executives also supported "safe harbors" for employees to anonymously address private issues; they also believed that a manager's performance should be partially evaluated in terms of their development of diverse employees, and that this evaluation should be based on input from their direct reports.[14]

Thus, in terms of solutions, global minority executives hold views very similar to those of minority executives in the U.S. It stands to reason that the keys to success are also similar, but there is insufficient research available to make this determination. The bottom line: Be prepared to face the same challenges that you face in the U.S., but with cultural twists.

Summary

Working internationally can be a challenging and rewarding experience, and often provides valuable skills for career advancement. If you are considering a global assignment, take care to remember that such roles often function best as part of an overall career plan, that planning your exit and re-entry into the company must be done carefully, and that you should remain engaged with colleagues back at headquarters so that you do not work "off the grid" and your efforts and accomplishments continue to be discussed even in your absence. This will also help facilitate your re-entry into headquarters, as will grooming successors for your global role because if you are doing well, your company may be reluctant to bring you home. Finally, keep your options open. Working abroad is a terrific way to get exposed to new ways of working and new companies. You may find that your global assignment moves you away from your current role but into a new role with exciting possibilities on the horizon.

Notes

[1] Catalyst. *Passport to Opportunity: U.S. Women in Global Business* (2000), Executive Summary, 5.

[2] Ibid., 6.

[3] Ibid.

[4] Ibid., 7.

[5] Catalyst. *Women in Leadership: Comparing European and U.S. Women Executives* (2002), 4.

[6] Ibid.

[7] Ibid.

[8] Ibid.

[9] Ibid.

[10] Ibid.

[11] Ibid.

[12] Hewlett, Sylvia Ann, Carolyn Buck Luce, and Cornel West. "Leadership in Your Midst: Tapping the Hidden Strengths of Minority Executives." *Harvard Business Review* (November 2005).

[13] Ibid.

[14] Ibid.

PART 4 Behind Closed Doors

CHAPTER 10 Home Sweet Home? Issues in Relationships and Family

After a long, exhausting day at work, you finally arrive home to your family. You've been anticipating spending some quality time with your loved ones, and the last thing you expect is to find yourself fighting with them about your career. But for many professional women of color, this scenario has happened more than once. Unfortunately, success in their careers often brings about challenges in their home lives.

The challenges women of color face in their personal relationships generally involve three key groups of people:

- A spouse or significant other
- Family members
- Friends

The specific challenges that women of color face in these relationships run the gamut, ranging from unsupportive spouses to jealous friends and needy relatives. This means that sometimes the relationships with friends and family that should strengthen and nurture these women, instead become burdens that these women struggle to carry throughout their careers. Certainly all of the relationships that women of color have outside of work are not negative, but some outside relationships may present difficulties for these women. Often these difficulties arise because the women are challenging cultural norms, a practice that tends to make others uncomfortable.

Relationships with Significant Others

Of all the relationships that women of color have outside of the office, the one they share with their significant others wields the most influence over their lives and careers. The power of this influence has led to numerous debates on the relationships of professional women of color. Some argue that women of color do not receive enough support at home; others argue that they receive more than enough help. In reality, the behavior of the partners of professional women of color runs the gamut: Some partners are supportive, others are less helpful, some are neutral, and others are opposed to their careers. But whatever their behavior, a woman of color's partner impacts her career in immeasurable ways.

In Their Own Words

Veronica Sims* views supportive relationships as integral to her career success. "Having a supportive spouse and supportive family in general, but in particular [a] supportive spouse and supportive relationships are very important...there's always balance with a significant other in your life, whether it is a spouse or a male friend or whatever. If they feel threatened by you, or [feel that] you're not paying them enough attention or [that] you're more successful than them or [that] you make more money than them... that is [agitation] that we [women of color] don't need. We've got enough to deal with battling during the day, trying to battle [those] that are trying to stab [us] in the back, let alone going home listening to [all these issues], [which] can create far more stress than we need. I'm fortunate...to have supportive relationships. I couldn't do what I do if I didn't, especially with two kids.... I really admire others that have gotten divorced...and they either have a family member that has stepped in to help or [something else]. But [the relationships] are important."

Emotional and Other Support

The main benefit that significant others provide to women of color is emotional support. This support is crucial for the women because

*Name has been fictionalized.

of the many difficulties that they encounter daily at work. Furthermore, because the corporate environment lends itself to unpredictability in alliances, women of color often cannot trust their colleagues with sensitive, work-related concerns. Instead, the women generally share their work-related issues with their spouses or significant others. These partners know the women well enough to validate their concerns about the workplace, including those related to race and gender—and the women don't have to worry about their concerns being repeated.

In Their Own Words

Taylor Matthews* is an executive woman of color whose husband is one of her biggest supporters. "I have one of the most supportive spouses on earth," she says. "My husband is my greatest advocate and he was actually an early mentor to me when I took on my first P&L role some 20 years ago, and I had no expertise in the particular area that I was asked to manage...and I got a tutorial from him every night; it helped me immensely. But he has always been a tremendous supporter of my career, my ambitions. He has not been jealous of my career; he has not been threatened by my success." She also adds that their children have greatly benefited from the positive relationship she shares with her husband. "...For our children to see [this] kind of harmony from a career point of view I think has been a great model for them, particularly my daughter...who can see what a mother and professional can do with a supportive spouse, so that has been outstanding. I'm doubly blessed to have someone who is such a great friend, supporter, and we just have a wonderful marriage of [over 20 years].

But work is not the only area in which significant others are helpful to women of color. Some women consider their partners as integral to their success because of their willingness to contribute to household chores and picking up their children from activities.

*Name has been fictionalized.

When Significant Others Are Not Supportive

For many women of color, a supportive spouse has much to do with the success of their marriage, but for others, such as Lydia Perez, a spouse who appears to be supportive might actually be a man who is averse to working—in disguise.

In Their Own Words

Lydia Perez's second marriage was to a man who preferred not to work, which caused some problems in their marriage. "My second marriage was to a South American man and lasted [over 15 years]. I had two kids. He was very supportive of my career. Unfortunately, so much so, that he chose to stay at home. I never asked him to be a Mr. Mom; in fact, he was too "macho" to even assume that role. The marriage ended in divorce [a short while ago]."

Although this husband was accepting of Perez's career and stayed at home, it seems that he was less than fully supportive of her, evidenced by his decision not to work (and contribute to the family income), and by not helping with their children. Such a scenario would overburden even the most dedicated career mom. In this case, a stay-at-home dad does not necessarily equal career support for mom.

Difficulties in relationships involving a working mom and stay-at-home dad are becoming increasingly common as women of color move up through the ranks of corporations; there are no easy solutions to these challenges. One way to begin to address such issues is to do some background reading on changing family dynamics, or on the challenges women face in families when they become the breadwinner. Once you have learned more about the issue, you may want to set aside some time with your spouse to discuss your feelings and concerns. Seeking out marital counseling from a trusted professional is another possible solution.

> **TIP:** If you don't have time to read a book on relationships, you may want to visit some Web sites, such as www.workingmother.com or www.ivillage.com, for articles and advice.

Another reason that women of color may find their partners to be unsupportive is that the partners have a notion of women's roles that is rooted in a particular cultural norm—such as women staying at home and caring for the children. Others may feel emasculated upon learning that their wives earn as much or more money than they do, or they may feel intimidated by the difference between their wives' corporate persona and the woman they first met. Lydia Perez also encountered a situation much like this one.

In Their Own Words

Perez's first marriage was to a man of a different ethnic heritage who was jealous of her success. "[He] was very intimidated by the fact that I was making more money than he was. That marriage ended because of his insecurities. If I was a...secretary, he would have been happy and [we] probably would still be married.... I was a manager of a division in [South America] and he could not handle it. He had major debt due to schooling and while he benefited from my paycheck, he resented it." Perez aptly observed that some men view women in lower-status corporate jobs as less of a threat to them than women occupying higher-status roles.

Another common issue surfaces when a woman of color's partner is initially supportive of her career, but becomes less supportive or resentful once her career rises to a higher level. Often as her career rises, she receives an increase in her compensation, she spends more time at the office, and she spends more time with other people. Early in Perez's corporate life, her career did not seem to have any noticeable impact on her relationships with her husband and immediate family. But as her career blossomed, she noticed some changes in those relationships. "[A]s I became more successful, I would say that it [my success] did in fact make [family life] more stressful. Increased travel and work demands led to less time with the family and lots of explanations as to why Mommy needed to be away."

> **TIP:** One way to balance career and family is to choose your company wisely. *Working Mother's* annual listing of the 100 Best Companies for Working Mothers is a great way to find companies with family-friendly policies.

The reasons why a woman of color's partner does not provide her with emotional support vary widely across cultures and people. While some significant others prefer that their wives not work professionally on cultural grounds, there is also the possibility that a woman's partner is just unsupportive generally, and that there is no gender-specific or cultural reason for his lack of support. But whatever the reason, the results of a partner's withdrawal of support can cause difficulty for professional women of color—mostly because a partner's lack of support deprives her of a confidant, a confidence booster, and a valued person in her support system. Lydia Perez's first marriage illustrates this scenario.

In Their Own Words

Perez's first marriage became troubled as she ascended the corporate ladder. "[My first husband] resented my career. My being bilingual became an asset at [my former employer] and naturally led me to their Latin American and Spain divisions. [My husband] could not handle my traveling throughout Latin America and became obsessed with what I was doing. I always felt that he did not think I was smart enough to manage people, let alone a division. He became verbally abusive, always attempting to bring me down, making me feel stupid."

Unfortunately, for many women of color, their career development will result in similar power struggles with their partners. When these struggles result in verbal attacks or other destructive and unhealthy behaviors, it is time to seek outside help in order to properly assess and resolve the issues you are having with your partner.

Friendships Inside and Outside the Workplace

Having a close group of friends is another important source of professional, personal, and social support for women of color. Friends will listen to your challenges, give helpful advice on work-related issues, celebrate your successes, and comfort you during difficult times. Your friends can also provide a "sanity check" when you encounter a situation and are unsure whether your perspective is accurate or overly defensive.

Generally, friendships arise in a variety of contexts, and for professional women that context is often work-related. Whether you've made friends at work-related events, in business organizations, or in graduate or professional school, these friendships can take on a character and tenor that differs significantly from friendships formed outside of work. Although these friendships themselves are not necessarily different than others, their impact on your career will probably differ.

Women of color who have recently risen to senior levels in their organizations may find that their new status presents challenges to their previously held friendships. They may find themselves isolated or misunderstood by their friends, or because of their new role, unable to confide in those friends about their new challenges.

In Their Own Words

Shannon Childress* tries to find mutually beneficial ways to move past unhealthy friendships. "Another challenge is that—and it's not just as you reach the senior levels, but as you're growing, period—some of your friends that you've had may not be able to keep up with you, and the challenge is, how do you shed out-of-date or no-longer-viable relationships for you, and do it in a way that leaves them and you undamaged? I think…it can be very difficult, but you've got to make sure that you are surrounding yourself with positive people; not necessarily people who are just helping you, because they [relationships] have a two-way street, but you don't have time for negativity in your life—that is optional."

*Name has been fictionalized.

Trust Issues

One of the main differences between a work-related friendship and one formed elsewhere has to do with the trust factor. Trust is hugely important in any friendship, but is even more important in corporate environments, which lend themselves to frequent allegiance changes. In such settings, a person who is a "career ally" can later become a "career adversary" because of changing circumstances in the workplace.

So it is important for you to distinguish between work or industry allies and true friends, in order to handle each of the relationships in a way that is appropriate to its character. But even if you have a true friend at work, there is wisdom in withholding some of your thoughts about work-related situations, because if your friend inadvertently exposes a confidence, it could have a disastrous effect on your career.

Jealousy

Putting aside changing loyalties for the moment, women of color who manage to find true friends at work will still face a number of challenges in those relationships. One of those challenges is jealousy, because of the competitive nature of corporate America. You may find yourself on the receiving end of resentment for earning a promotion—or you may find yourself resenting someone else because of their promotion.

The presence of jealousy in a true friendship leaves you with two potential issues: how to deal with your friend's jealousy or how to deal with your own. Dealing with your own envy is not as difficult as you might think; it requires you to take stock of your own life and to make some adjustments. In fact, understanding your own feelings of jealousy is crucial to eradicating them, because jealousy reveals your own unfulfilled desires or goals. Rather than stewing in envy, use your feelings of jealousy to spur you on to develop a plan to accomplish your goals and achieve your desires. This is the most straightforward way to deal with feelings of jealousy you may have toward a friend.

When a friend is jealous of you, you have two alternatives: Move on with your life (without the friend), or attempt to salvage the relationship. The first option is no-frills and easy, but the second requires a good bit more work, along with some sensitivity and compassion on your part. One way to handle a jealous friend is to reverse the strategy used in dealing with your own jealousy: Get a sense of your friend's aspirations and desires, and try to support her as she reaches for those goals and her own fulfillment. Keep in mind that while she is making efforts, you may want to downplay the fact that you have achieved some of her goals—although this is not always possible. Or you may opt to discuss aspects of your life with your friend that do not bring attention to what she sees as her own deficiencies. Although this means that you won't be able to share certain areas of your life with her, it will allow you to preserve the friendship, at least for a time.

Competitiveness

Competitiveness, a close compatriot of jealousy, also causes work-related friendships to suffer, especially if friends work in the same department or company. Generally, being competitive is little more than being ambitious, working hard, and doing your best work in an attempt to get promoted—this does not have to be problematic in and of itself. But some people hold beliefs about competitive behavior that includes beating out the competition at any cost. Such thoughts can lead a competitive person into destructive behaviors, such as undermining and manipulating others or sabotaging others' efforts. When competitive behavior takes the latter form, it will erode a friendship.

Dealing with competitive behavior requires different strategies than you would use when dealing with a jealous friend, although you are still faced with the same options concerning the friendship—move on (without the friend) or try to maintain the relationship. Trying to maintain the relationship will probably involve sitting down with your competitive friend and explaining how her behavior is affecting the friendship. If she does not listen to you or adjust her behavior, the friendship cannot continue. If she is willing to make some adjustments, have a frank and open discussion about what behaviors work in your friendship and which ones are detrimental.

Friend or "Frenemy"?

Having a friend who is jealous or competitive is one thing, but the combination of a friend who is jealous and competitive may require a reclassification of this friend—into a "frenemy." The term was originally coined in the television series *Sex in the City*, and is a combination of a friend and an enemy. It refers to a friend who wishes you ill or wants to sabotage you. You could even describe a "frenemy" as an enemy who is posing as a friend. But however you describe them, frenemies are not people who have your best interests at heart.

It is somewhat difficult to pinpoint exactly how we become "friends" with people who we know do not like us or have our best interests at heart. It seems to start with two people who have some things in common and develop the beginnings of a friendship. At some point during the friendship, they realize that they would not make very good friends, but continue to pretend that they are, when in fact they are indifferent to, or in some cases secretly dislike each other.

As long as you are friendly with a frenemy from a distance, there really isn't much of a problem. But if you pretend to be very close friends with them, this could pose some serious difficulties for you. Remaining friends with a person who has insecurities and issues like competitiveness or jealousy is not really good for you. But it is extremely unwise to become entangled with a person who is really your enemy, even under the guise of friendship. Just let the relationship go.

Cultural Clashes

Women of color's work-related friendships may also suffer from cultural clashes. It is natural for professional women of color to form cross-cultural relationships because of their small representation among corporate employees. Also, their home culture generally differs considerably from corporate culture. So many acquaintances and friendships they develop at work are likely to be with people who do not share their ethnicity and culture.

Once a colleague becomes a friend, the tenor of the relationship changes. When the work friendship is cross-cultural, the friendship is already influenced by corporate culture, with additional influences from each friend's culture; this can complicate the friendship. Some women of color choose to be close friends with others who share their ethnicity just to minimize the complications in the friendship.

Women of color in intra-ethnic friendships may revert to shared cultural norms in their informal interactions. Such norms may or may not transfer well to cross-cultural friendships. One of the easiest ways to handle potential cultural differences is to go into the friendship recognizing that differences exist. It is also important to be sensitive to the concerns and needs of the other person in your friendship. You may want to have a discussion to lay down some cultural ground rules such that if concerns do arise, they can be discussed in a healthy, non-confrontational manner.

Another challenge that cross-cultural friendships present for women of color is the discomfort that such relationships may cause for each woman's family or friends. Let's face it: Many people of color in the U.S. live more insular existences, and it often happens that their friends and (of course) family share their culture. This lack of exposure (or sometimes negative exposure) to people of other cultures can lead ethnic groups to remain wary of outsiders—or to discriminate against those who are unlike them. So it is not surprising that the discomfort between the new friend, family, and other friends may become more pronounced as the cross-cultural friendship deepens.

> **TIP:** Be aware that cross-cultural friendships at work may cause some dissension among family members and sometimes other friends, who are used to a more monocultural existence.

Family Matters

Family relationships play a significant role in the lives and careers of women of color. The immediate family of a woman of color, including her spouse and children, is an ever-present reminder that there is more to life than the office. Her extended family provides a link to her heritage and keeps her grounded in the values of her family's culture. Women of color's families are generally very important to them, including extended family members.

A woman of color has to work hard to maintain her family relationships. Her relationships with her spouse or significant other may become strained if she begins to out-earn him, if she does not feel supported by him, or if her significant other feels that he no longer holds an important position in her life.

In Their Own Words

One of the ways that Susan Davis* handles her relationship with her husband is that they are "partners." She says, "We are really a partnership with shared goals, supporting one another, and so communication is really important. But I know that [success] is a struggle, and I hear this from women, particularly when there's…a significant gap in income, and things like that. But people can feel valued and it's not just what the paycheck says, it's how you honor and respect your family members, and include them and love them."

When significant others do not feel valued, or if children feel neglected, it can lessen the sweetness of a woman of color's career successes. Women such as Wendy Pace have seen this phenomenon happen, and she suggests that a life with some balance can help prevent these difficult situations from arising. "The road to the top has been, I know, littered with broken relationships… [people] I know [whose]…marriages were lost along the way, kids [who]…never saw their parents when they were growing up…and things like that. You've got to really work towards bringing some kind of balance in a situation that just invites the opposite."

Supportive Family Members

When a woman of color's family is strong, both her immediate and extended family can serve as valuable support mechanisms in her career, although they are certainly more to her than just support. One way that a woman of color's family supports her career aspirations is through practical help; extended family members may provide trustworthy child care for her children or take them on various errands, such as to the doctor or to sporting events. Other times a woman of color's family supports her by reminding her that she can be accepted as a full human being and not just as a corporate version of herself. Family support can provide a refreshing alternative to the stereotypes that women of color encounter regularly at work.

*Name has been fictionalized.

Unsupportive Behaviors

But although a woman of color's entire family may love her and genuinely try to support her personally, they sometimes engage in behaviors that do not support her professional career. For instance, a relative may chide a woman of color about missing a school event or remind her repeatedly that she should be at home looking after her children. In the relative's view, this is the proper role of a woman from their culture. But this woman of color has chosen to make a different life for herself. Relatives constantly jabbing at her for not measuring up to their ideals may not realize the degree to which they impact her sense of self-esteem. While the relatives do not view their behavior as problematic, a woman of color may find it frustrating to constantly have to defend her life choices—especially when she takes full responsibility for those choices and is able to support herself and her family.

It can also be problematic for women of color to discuss work-related issues with their families, especially if the family has not been sufficiently acculturated to the United States to have an understanding of what her work experiences might be like. Sometimes families will not understand business trips where both genders are present, or the need to work late at the office during quarter- or year-end, and they may harbor suspicions about colleagues who are involved in such practices. Also, families may sometimes try to insist that women of color act in accordance with their cultural norms at their workplaces, which would bring about misunderstandings and difficulties for the women.

Dealing with Family Objections

Some strategies for handling home life are not often seen in communities of color, such as getting a nanny or a cleaning service. Because of this, women of color adopting such strategies may experience resentment among extended family members, who may not understand what challenges the women are facing or their new professional image. Family members may also be jealous of the women's success or their ability to get outside help. Being aware of these potential challenges is the first step in handling them.

In Their Own Words

Shannon Childress* observes that families can feel left out or resentful as a woman of color reaches the senior executive level. "How you have to carry yourself as a senior-level, as an executive, [as] opposed to a midlevel or even kind of upper-level manager...depending on whether you're the first generation to reach that kind of level, there may be some real resentment within your family, within your community, because you dress differently, you have to talk differently, your activities may be different, because there are different demands on your time," she says knowingly. "You know, you may have to be on a symphony board, or the board of a hospital, or whatever, and it's not just a matter of being part of your church.... So some of the things you did before, you may or may not have time to do. [It] doesn't mean that you're any less committed to them...."

She continues, "The other thing it may mean is that instead of actually doing something, you may pay to have it done, and that can be interpreted as 'showing off.' You know, sometimes you need to spend money to solve a problem. But what we [people of color] have done, generally, is...we figured out ways around a lot of problems that don't take money, because we haven't had it."

To manage family dynamics and to deflect jealousy, Childress advocates that women of color who are reaching senior levels at their companies communicate openly with their families: "Being open with your family, in particular, about what the change is, what you think it's going to mean, lets them know some of your discomfort and your insecurities, so that they don't automatically think that you've got it all together and they're being left behind."

She also observes that some of the challenges women of color face from their families and communities stem from people's new view of the woman of color as an insider. "In their [women of color's] extended families and in their communities, the challenge may be of all of a sudden being seen as part of the establishment, and there may be some feelings of resentment about 'you've got it made and what about us?' et cetera."

*Name has been fictionalized.

Another challenge that executive women of color face is in not being understood. Because there are so few women of color in senior roles, it is rare that they have family members that have already held senior roles. As a result, they may need to spend more time educating family or friends about their role (what they do each day), their experiences, and the impact it will have on their relationships.

In Their Own Words

Veronica Sims* has had to bring her family up to speed on her senior-level role, and why she has to work so many hours. "You may have a bit less understanding because, you know, it's not like other members of the family, in many instances, depending on how senior you are other members of the community, really can appreciate what your role really is, and what you do. My daughter asked me last evening, 'Mommy, first of all why do you have to work?... why do you have to work the hours that you work?'.... My mother asked the same thing, and my husband asked the same thing.... They don't have an appreciation for...at this level, what you have to do. Again, going above and beyond, when everybody at this level, if they're working 12 hours, then you're working [more]."

The relationships that women of color enjoy provide a backdrop for the way they approach their careers. A solid, healthy family life can help them reach new career heights, while difficult, tumultuous relationships can undermine their self-confidence and distract them from excellent performance. Although there is no hard-and-fast rule to use in managing home relationships (or any relationships outside of work), it is generally a good idea to take the following steps:

- **Take an honest look at the challenges you (or others) are facing.** Rather than automatically attribute your challenges to others, look at your own behavior and how you might be contributing to the problem.

- **"Get smart" about the issues you are encountering by reading some background information.** There are plenty of books about women, success, and life. Take advantage of other people's experiences and use some of the advice that is relevant to your situation.

*Name has been fictionalized.

- **Use cultural networking organizations for culturally specific answers to questions about family and relationships.** All cultures handle family concerns differently; talking to others who share your ethnicity will help you craft solutions to your challenges that can work for everyone.

- **If necessary, be willing to consult other professionals to help you build bridges to keep the harmony functioning in the various aspects of your life.** You may need outside help to deal with a particularly difficult family member. Don't be afraid to ask for help if you need it.

Striking a Balance

Ultimately, family relationships are one of the most important aspects of a woman of color's life. As such, it is critical that you find a way to balance your concerns with those of your family, and work at building understanding relationships with them. One of the ways that you can achieve a balance is by managing everyone's expectations. This is a strategy that Nancy Hess employs, so that her colleagues and her family understand her limits and what commitments she is able to make.

In Their Own Words

Nancy Hess,* a senior executive, suggests that one way to manage work and family is by "[providing] clarity in terms of expectations on what you are going to deliver, what you are not going to deliver, how it will be delivered.... I'm a mom," she says. "I have two young [children], I have a husband, I have a very full life outside of [my company], I have a very rich life inside [my company], but I'm very clear with 'I'm going to do this, this, and this, and I'm not going to do that, that, and that'—so [there is] real clarity around expectations," she finishes.

Hess also values the ability to juggle competing priorities. "I think you really have got to develop good time-management skills, I mean, that's what's critical. If you have poor time-management skills, it's going to bite you every time. The ability to multitask...and generally I find women are pretty

*Name has been fictionalized.

> good at this...if you can't really hone those multitasking skills, it's problematic because a lot of stuff is going to be thrown to you...both in the work arena and outside of the work arena."

Besides managing expectations and multitasking, women of color can take other steps to balance their home and family life. Joining a group of professional women who share your culture is one option. Groups such as the South Asian Women's Leadership Forum, the Asian Women Leadership Network, or Madrinas have access to resources specific to your culture that can help you deal with the challenges you are facing.

One of the areas where professional women of color often need help is with child care or other household affairs, such as paying bills or cleaning. Shannon Childress observes that "[for] women of color in particular, at home, our home life still tends to be fairly unequal.... [Men of color] tend to be more chauvinistic than some, and so it's a matter of making sure that you are not trying to do it all. One strategy...is to hire help in the home."

But even if you cannot afford to hire a nanny or cleaning service, you can still get help around the house. You might enlist neighborhood kids to rake the lawn or to take out your garbage, at a much lower cost to you. Or you may get your spouse and children to have a pizza/cleaning party, to help with some of the lighter cleaning. Or you may hire in a cleaning service once a month to help you deep clean your home. Madison Davies, a senior-level professional, sometimes uses outside help around the house, but does certain things herself.

In Their Own Words

Madison Davies* enjoys working from home as a way to retain her connection with her family and friends. "I am in my home office at least one or two days a week, which allows me to do things around the house that I know I need to do, allows me to add my touch to the home instead of having a lot of third parties [involved].... For instance, I don't have a cleaning service come in all the time; it's not a regular thing. There is someone who comes in twice a year—the rest of it is done by me. My gardening, I do. I choose not to outsource as much in order to create a better home life that shows my involvement in that home life, versus being completely detached with an outsourced environment."

One of Davies's strategies for managing her home life is quite funny: "I am a huge Internet shopper," she boasts, "I am such a huge Internet shopper that I will even clean my 'cookies' [from the computer] on a weekly basis, so that I can show up as a new consumer and receive all the new specials."

The Internet is a terrific way for busy women of color to order groceries, household medicines, and other items at home (or even at the office during a break). Many Internet shopping sites allow users to set up recurring shopping lists; this makes it even faster to shop online.

For other senior women of color, it is often simply not possible to balance their career and home-related responsibilities. Getting outside help just makes sense for them.

In Their Own Words

Taylor Matthews* has no problem with getting and using outside help in her home. "I think that for women of color, and specifically black women, we have had such a history of balancing work and family that these issues that have sprung up over the course of the last 15 years about the

*Names have been fictionalized.

demands of raising families and working are actually not new to us. Our mothers worked outside the home; our grandmothers worked outside the home and still took care of their children, and so I think that that has actually been a fairly good transition for me. Now I made a decision early in my career that when I decided to have children that I wanted to have care in the home, and I have had that over the course of the 20 years.... I've always had a nanny...that takes a tremendous amount of pressure off of the workplace, knowing that you have that and if I'm late, or if a child is sick I haven't had to deal with a lot of the issues that people that don't have child care have dealt with, so that has been a blessing."

For women of color, balancing the challenges at work and at home are numerous, but important if they are to develop a successful, happy life. Some balance can be achieved if the women manage the expectations of bosses, colleagues, friends, and family. They can also minimize difficulties at home by helping others to adjust to their new ways of life. But ultimately, women of color will be most successful when their friends and family become part of the solution—by supporting the women's efforts, helping them balance everything, celebrating their successes, and by simply loving them.

CHAPTER 11 Health and Wellness for Women of Color

The importance of a healthy lifestyle cannot be overestimated, and the notion of healthy living, including physical fitness, a healthy diet, adequate rest, and a healthy mental state, is crucial to your well-being in life. As a professional woman of color, a healthy lifestyle takes on additional importance to you because of the high level of energy that is required for you to sustain the heavy workloads and high stress levels that exist in corporate America.

But you need your health for more than just work. Current health research on women of color indicates that we have much to gain from living healthier lives, including enjoyment of life, good mental and physical health, and overall well-being.

Enjoying Physical Health

Generally, physical health includes physical fitness, a healthy diet, and proper rest. Dr. Gwendolyn Tabel,* an African-American physician, describes two components of healthy living: "a balanced, healthy, meal plan...[and] incorporating some activity into your life, a minimum of three times a week...[for a] minimum of 30 minutes."

Physical Fitness

The U.S. Department of Health and Human Services defines physical fitness as "a set of attributes that people have or achieve that relates to the ability to perform physical activity."[1] They define the five major components of physical fitness as the following:

*Name has been fictionalized.

1. **Cardiorespiratory endurance.** Cardiorespiratory endurance is "the ability of the body's circulatory and respiratory systems to supply fuel during sustained physical activity."[2] In short, this endurance is the length of time that your body can function when your heart operates at an elevated level for a specific time period, for example during aerobic activities like running or swimming.

2. **Muscular strength.** Muscular strength deals with a muscle's capacity to make use of force during an activity, such as lifting weight. This does not apply just to weightlifting, but also to the lifting of any household item, such as boxes or books. When this muscle force encounters resistance, it must then be exerted in greater quantities; the muscle's capacity to exert this force is muscular strength.

3. **Muscular endurance.** Muscular endurance relates to muscular strength, but centers on the capacity of the muscle to continue exerting force without becoming exhausted.[3]

4. **Body composition.** Body composition measures the quantity of bone, muscle, fat and other vital body parts in relation to each other, and can be used to determine susceptibility to a variety of illnesses.[4] One of the most common body composition measures is the body mass index (BMI), which measures the percentage of body fat based on an individual's height and weight. Individuals can calculate their BMI to determine whether they fall within ranges of the index that are considered underweight, overweight, or obese and may lead to health problems. BMI calculators are easy to use and are available on numerous Internet sites, including those of the National Institutes of Health (www.nih.gov) and the Department of Health and Human Services (www.hhs.gov).

5. **Flexibility.** The final component of physical fitness is flexibility, which relates to the "range of motion around a joint."[5] Flexibility is helpful in preventing bodily injuries that can result from stiff muscles.[6 7] Flexibility can be gained through stretching programs or exercises.

One of the best ways to develop a healthy lifestyle is to regularly engage in some form of physical exercise or activity. Physical exercise has numerous documented benefits, because it

- Reduces risk of contracting many illnesses
- Prevents of obesity or significant weight gain
- Lowers cholesterol
- Alleviates anxiety and depression
- Lowers premature death rates

In addition to its preventive benefits, exercise can improve muscular and skeletal strength, boost good feelings, and generally improve your overall lifestyle.[8] To receive these benefits, it is not necessary to engage in a full-scale exercise program—even walking briskly for 30 minutes five times a week (or more) can provide significant health benefits.

> **TIP:** Dr. Tabel recommends walking with a friend as a good way to exercise. "Walking…is a stress reliever as well as a way to exercise," she says. "Exercise doesn't have to create stress or anxiety."

Healthy Diet

Even the most physically active lifestyle will have limited benefits without being complemented by a proper nutritional diet. Many people focus on diet as a means to address weight-related issues, but diet plays a much more significant role in your overall well-being because it contributes to your body's functionality. This functionality can be enhanced or impaired by the quality, type, and amount of food that you consume daily, because of the nutrients that food provides. A lack of certain vitamins or minerals can impair or confuse bodily functions and lead to illness or disease, as well as to weight gain or obesity. Dr. Tabel believes that a healthy diet involves "making an assessment about your nutrition, and trying to eat healthy…and having some balance, some moderation, and some restraint with respect to your diet. You can have many of the things that you like to have, [but] you can't have them all at once."

After all, a well-balanced diet does not happen by accident; it requires considerable thought and attention. While many people associate a healthy diet with bland or uninteresting foods, one of the keys to a healthy diet is food variety—so you can enjoy different foods, but try to stay within certain categories. The *Foundations of Wellness* newsletter at the University of California, Berkeley, has some terrific ideas for developing a healthy diet. Among their suggestions are eating lots of high-fiber foods, including fruits and vegetables, as well as legumes (beans) and whole grains. These foods will help you meet the required amount of daily fiber, vitamins, and minerals, and help to slow down your carbohydrate absorption, which can be beneficial to your blood sugar.

> **TIP:** Making quick, healthy meals doesn't have to be a hassle. Select a meat (chicken), vegetable (green beans), and starch (potatoes) to keep your meal balanced (you can vary these every day; tomorrow might be fish, broccoli, and rice). Put the meat in the refrigerator so that it can thaw while you are at work. When you arrive home, prepare the meat first, and while it is cooking, prepare the vegetables and the starch, which will take less time than the meat. By the time the meat is finished cooking, everything else will be too. Dinner served!

Other foods that *Foundations of Wellness* suggests incorporating into a healthy diet are colorful (green, yellow, and orange) fruits and vegetables, which contain antioxidants and other vitamins and minerals that may help your body fight against developing some forms of cancer as well as other diseases. Other foods to consider adding to your diet are fish and nuts, which contain unsaturated fats (the healthy ones), and use olive or canola oil for cooking instead of butter, margarine, vegetable oils, or lard. Calcium is also important to a healthy diet, and helps to preserve strong bones and teeth and can help prevent osteoporosis. Of course, you should always check with your doctor before making changes to your diet.

> **TIP:** It is most effective to get your nutrients from food and not from vitamin supplements. Although supplements may help make up the difference on occasion, they should not be used as a substitute for eating properly.

Having a healthy diet also involves avoiding certain foods, including those containing animal and trans fats, which can contribute to high cholesterol and lead to other diseases. Cholesterol is not entirely bad, however, and since various meats, dairy, poultry, and eggs contain it, you won't be able to avoid it completely—but it is a good idea to limit your daily intake. Other foods to be avoided are those that are high in sugar, or high-fructose corn syrup such as soda, candy, cookies, and other sweets. Starches made with refined flour (white flour) have often had most of the original nutrients removed; healthier options are multigrain breads, rolls, and chips, which contain more of the original nutrients. Processed foods, such as frozen meals and lunchmeats, are not healthy at all, are often high in sodium, and are simply not as healthy as fresh foods.

Finally, the process of balancing your daily diet is something often forgotten, but is essential to your good health. Eating moderate portions, balancing your calorie intake with your burned calories, and limiting your intake of alcoholic beverages can also help you maintain a healthy diet.[9]

Sleeping

Sleep is foundational to a healthy lifestyle. It plays a vital role in physical health by providing a daily boost to your immune system, which equips your body to fight against illnesses. Sleep also aids in proper functionality of your nervous system, which helps to regulate muscle coordination, monitors organs, and deals with bodily senses and actions. It also helps the body deal with mental health issues, such as stress. Lack of sleep can lead to problems with memory, concentration, and physical performance.

> **TIP:** The National Sleep Foundation recommends that adults get eight hours of sleep each night. Getting significantly more or less sleep than the recommended amount can interfere with your body's functionality.

For many professional women of color, living with less sleep than physicians recommend is the norm. Some women of color juggle so many different responsibilities—between work, family, and community—that they have very little time for themselves or for rest. In addition, many companies have cultures that value ridiculously hard work, and women of color may feel compelled to adopt the corporate culture of around-the-clock workdays, resulting in very little sleep for themselves. In either case, women of color are often just not getting enough sleep to maintain good health.

The Mayo Clinic, a nonprofit medical diagnostic and treatment center, provides several strategies to help you sleep well at night. First on their list is setting specific sleep and waking times and adhering to those times daily (weekends included),[10] which benefits you by ensuring that you get sufficient sleep and allows your body to become accustomed to specific sleep patterns. Such a pattern is helpful for those who enjoy structure, with a bonus benefit of streamlining the time required to handle other areas of your life. If you know you must be in bed by 9 p.m., you may become more efficient with task performance or prioritization during the day so that you can be in bed on time each night.

Also recommended: unwinding after work. Even if you can squeeze in only 30 minutes of downtime, you can engage in one of these tried-and-true favorites: listening to your favorite music, reading an interesting book, taking a bath or shower, or even exercising. Exercise can be an excellent way to relax or clear one's head after a long day at work. Aerobic exercise is particularly helpful in promoting faster and more restful sleep. But to be most beneficial, exercise needs to occur consistently, and should not be done close to your designated sleep time or it may interfere with your ability to sleep.

> **TIP:** Remember your "after school" clothes? Getting some comfy "after work" clothes is a good way to draw the line between your day at work and your time at home. When you get home, before you dive into home chores, change into your relaxation duds.

Eating, drinking, and taking medication prior to your sleep time can also affect your ability to sleep—eating too much may trigger digestive issues, and drinking alcohol or products with caffeine (for example, coffee, energy drinks, or colas) can also prevent you from getting a full night's sleep. Medications require extra care because some will cause stomach issues if they are taken on an empty stomach, or they may contain ingredients that interfere with your rest. Sleeping pills must be used with extreme care, and you should talk to your physician before you begin taking them. If you are on other medications, you must consult with your physician before taking any sleep aids to ensure that the combination of medications will not harm you physically.

Finally, it is important to reserve your sleep space for sleeping and to keep it separate from work activities and other non-restful activities, such as television and radio. Designate another area of your house for work-at-home activities, such as a home office. To enjoy television or radio, you may consider setting up shop in your family room or living room. If you live in cramped quarters, work wherever you can—just not where you need to sleep. Keeping work and other distractions away from your sleep area allows you to focus on resting when it is time to rest. Although you have probably heard many of these sleep suggestions before, putting them into practice can make a difference in your rest, and as a result, in other areas of your life.

Physical Health Concerns

The physical health concerns women of color face vary depending on the women's race, ethnicity, education, and socioeconomic status. And many of these concerns have only recently begun to surface because of a lack of research on women of color's health issues. Moreover, current research on women of color's health issues is often incomplete, and even when it includes information on women of color, it contains broad generalizations (for example, Asian-American or Latina) that do not account for the unique statistics of particular subgroups or of multiethnic people.

Multicultural issues also play a role in the diagnosis and treatment of women's health conditions. For example, many African-Americans are multicultural, having European and Native American heritages as well as African. Such multiethnic heritages have implications for how disease affects their bodies and the manner in which they should be treated.

Women of color are also confronted with other barriers in their search for proper healthcare. Among these barriers are language or cultural differences, lack of insurance, culturally inexperienced healthcare providers, lack of understanding of the seriousness of certain diseases, and late-stage diagnosis of medical conditions. The final and most pernicious barrier is discrimination in diagnosis and treatment by healthcare providers. The U.S. Department of Health and Human Services (USDHHS) found that "substantial numbers of minority women experience racial, ethnic, gender, and other forms of discrimination, which can interfere with appropriate diagnosis and treatment."[11] These barriers contribute, in part, to the higher mortality rates that women of color have for some diseases— even when the women of color have considerably lower occurrences of the disease than their white counterparts.

For professional women of color, many of these barriers are less significant, but you still need to take them into consideration when seeking out healthcare for yourself or your family.

Following is an overview of the major health concerns facing each subgroup of women of color.

Health Concerns for African-American Women

More research has been done on the health of African-American women than on any other group among women of color. The health concerns of African-American women vary widely, but many of their major health concerns center around weight issues. Over 75 percent of African-American women are considered overweight, and 51 percent of such women met the classification for obese. Among all women in the United States over the same period, 62 percent were overweight, with 34 percent of such women being considered obese.[12] The results of being overweight are significant, according to the USDHHS, which notes that being overweight or obese can lead to increased risk for many major illnesses, including diabetes, high blood pressure (hypertension), certain forms of cancer, and osteoarthritis.[13]

Due to the prevalence of weight and obesity issues among African-American women, it is vital that they develop a healthy diet and physical fitness program under the supervision of a physician. Almost 60 percent of African-American women lead sedentary lifestyles that include no physical activity.[14]

So it comes as no surprise that diabetes, high blood pressure, and cancer are among the major health concerns for African-American women. But because each of these illnesses increases the risk of developing other diseases, African-American women also face elevated risks related to kidney disease (from diabetes), heart disease (from diabetes and hypertension), and stroke (from hypertension). Other health concerns for African-American women include breast cancer, lupus, and HIV. Also, African-American maternal mortality rates are five times the national average; infant mortality rates are 2.5 times the national average.[15]

Health Concerns for Asian-American Women

Asian-American health concerns begin with access to healthcare, as some Asian-American women face language or cultural barriers that prevent them from taking full advantage of available healthcare. This is evidenced, in part, by the screening rates for breast and cervical cancer among Asian-American women, which are considerably lower than the national average. Awareness of the need for testing may also be a factor in these rates.

The illnesses for which Asian-American women are more often at risk include tuberculosis (which is 13 times more common in Asian populaces than in others), Hepatitis B (which for some subgroups is between 25 and 75 times the national average), cervical cancer, osteoporosis, and suicide. One positive health factor for Asian-American women is that they have the lowest rates of obesity among women in the United States; however, 49 percent report not engaging in exercise.[16]

Health Concerns for Latinas

Latinas also face more significant challenges related to access to healthcare, and are the most uninsured group among women of color (30 percent), despite the fact that many are employed or reside with an employed person.[17] Certain Latina subgroups have high incidences of being overweight or obese—71.8 percent of Mexican-American women are overweight; 40.1 percent are obese, leading to health risks such as diabetes, heart disease, hypertension, and stroke. As with African-American women, research showed that 57 percent of Latina female immigrants live sedentary lifestyles,[18] which has other implications for their overall health. Other health concerns of Latinas include HIV and prenatal care, although Latinas generally have low infant mortality rates.

Health Concerns for Native American Women

Obesity is a challenge that Native American women also face: Sixty percent of Native American women living on reservations and in urban areas are obese.[19] As a result, they face an increased risk of heart disease, diabetes, hypertension, and stroke. Other health concerns for Native American women include accidental deaths (almost three times the national average), alcoholism, lung cancer, tuberculosis, gallstones, and suicide. The infant mortality rate for Native American women is 30 percent greater than the national average.[20]

Mental and Emotional Health

Mental health "refers to the successful performance of mental function, resulting in productive activities, fulfilling relationships with other people, and the ability to adapt to change and cope with adversity."[21] The U.S. Surgeon General also notes that mental health contributes in large part to an individual's well-being and interpersonal relationships, as well as to their functionality in community and society. Specifically, the Surgeon General states that "from early childhood until death, mental health is the springboard of thinking and communication skills, learning, emotional growth, resilience, and self-esteem."[22] The notion of mental health is also fluid, and may vary depending on an individual's culture. At its core, mental health is comprised of an individual's self-perception, their ability to form relationships, and how they handle issues of adversity or stress.

While the concept of mental health is more fluid, at the other end of the spectrum is mental illness. The National Alliance on Mental Illness defines mental illnesses as "medical conditions that disrupt a person's thinking, feeling, mood, ability to relate to others, and daily functioning...mental illnesses are medical conditions that often result in a diminished capacity for coping with the ordinary demands of life."[23] In the U.S. alone, mental illness accounts for more than 15 percent of all diseases from any causes.[24]

Although women of color generally experience the same mental disorders as white women, the types of conditions vary depending on the ethnicity of the women of color. For example, the USDHHS found that African-American women have lower incidences of depression than white women, but have more phobias. Also, Asian-American and Native American women experience depression more than white women.[25] Among the more common mental health issues women of color face are depression and dealing with stress.

Depression

Generally, depression is a mental disorder that is characterized by persistent thoughts of sadness, guilt, worthlessness, lack of interest in previously enjoyed activities, and decreased energy. Depression is much more serious than "having a bad day" or going through a challenging time. According to the National Institute of Mental Health, "A depressive disorder is an illness that involves the body, mood, and thoughts. It affects the way a person eats and sleeps, the way one feels about oneself, and the way one thinks about things."[26] Several types of depression exist, ranging from mild to severe, and depressive episodes can be triggered by stress, genetics, hormonal imbalances, or other physical body changes. Women generally experience depression at twice the rate of men.[27]

The best way to deal with depression is to get it diagnosed and treated by a mental health professional.

TIP: The Mayo Clinic notes that two of the most common symptoms of depression are feelings of sadness or hopelessness, and a loss of interest in activities that you normally enjoy. They also note other symptoms of depression such as difficulty thinking or concentrating, fatigue, low self-esteem, or difficulty sleeping. If you think you might be depressed, make an appointment to talk with a mental health professional.

Stress

Stress is essentially the human body's response to change, good or bad, and it may be the most uniform mental health concern among women of color. It is difficult to define stress beyond this point because the notion of stress varies considerably from person to person—what may be stressful for one person may be energizing for another. But bad or negative stress can reach a point where it is unhealthy, and at that point it needs to be addressed. Bad stress can stem from any type of adversity, including difficulties at work, in relationships, or from illness.

Because everyone experiences stress, many people underestimate its effect on physical and mental health. But stress can be very hazardous to your health. According to the American Psychological Association (APA), stress plays a role in the six leading causes of death in the United States: heart disease, cancer, lung ailments, accidents, cirrhosis of the liver, and suicide.[28] Furthermore, between 75 and 90 percent of visits to physician's offices are because of illnesses that are stress-related.[29]

For corporate women of color, stress is a major part of everyday life, and the workplace is often filled with circumstances that are adverse to them. In addition to the normal corporate stressors, women of color are often subject to heightened visibility at work, leading to additional stress. On top of their work-related stress, women of color often juggle home and family responsibilities (sometimes including extended family) with their daily work routine, increasing their stress levels even further. Thus, it is essential that women of color understand stress and become savvy at managing it.

The APA suggests a six-part solution for dealing with stress:

1. **Identify the origin of your stress.** The root cause of your stress may be obvious to you, such as work or a relationship; but if not, you may want to enlist the help of a psychologist to determine the cause of your stress.

2. **Monitor your moods throughout the day.** Write down the times when you feel more stress, as well as what you are thinking and feeling at that time.

3. **Relax.** Take time for yourself to relax two to three times each week with no distractions.

4. **Deal with anger.** Because anger can be a source of stress, mentally recuperate by counting to ten, or by engaging in exercise to clear your head.

5. **Eliminate and delegate.** Analyze your schedule and priorities and eliminate unnecessary tasks, and delegate where possible.

6. **Set reasonable expectations.** Be reasonable in terms of the standards that you set for yourself and for others. Being a perfectionist only causes more stress.[30]

Mental Health Concerns for Women of Color

Following are some of the mental health concerns and barriers to treatment for the various subgroups of women of color.

African-American Women

One of the most prevalent barriers to African-Americans receiving healthcare relates to mistrust of the U.S. healthcare system. This mistrust stems from historical events where sick African-Americans were used in experiments instead of being treated for diseases. Even if the experiments have now been discontinued, the USDHHS has found that women of color continue to experience discrimination in the diagnosis of health conditions.[31] In light of this, an African-American woman who decides to seek treatment for a mental health concern might feel most comfortable visiting with an African-American psychiatrist or psychologist. Unfortunately, only 2 percent of each category exists in the United States, so she may ultimately refuse to seek treatment for this reason.

African-American women's predominant mental health issue is depression. But although only 16 percent of African-American women have depression, of those with depression almost half (47 percent) have severe depression.[32] Often these mental health concerns go untreated because of cultural stigmas and distrust of healthcare providers,[33] including mental health practitioners. Thus, in order to deal with mental health issues, African-American women generally rely on religion, social networks, and family to resolve their issues, which may or may not help them, depending on the mental health concerns at issue. More recent studies have shown that African-American women suffer from eating disorders, as well as fasting and laxative or diuretic abuse.[34]

Asian-American Women

Asian-American culture contains several barriers that may prevent Asian-American women from seeking help for mental health issues. One such barrier may be rooted in the traditional notion of Asian healing, which links the mind and body together and involves alternative medicinal treatments. Asian culture often has the tendency to recognize physical symptoms before mental ones, thus Asian-American women may seek care for their physical symptoms without realizing that there are underlying mental health issues to consider.

Another cultural barrier relates to stigmas regarding mental illness, such that Asian-American women may consider seeking help for mental health concerns as an embarrassment to one's family or an individual sign of weakness. Or, since some Asian cultures have family-oriented healthcare, these same expectations may flow into mental health treatment. If Asian-Americans do decide to seek help for mental health issues, their communications with the mental health provider may be difficult, not because of language issues, but because of the way Asian and American cultures describe mental and physical conditions. Certain Asian cultures do not distinguish between mental and physical conditions; in several Asian languages, the same word is used to describe anxiety, pain, and insomnia.

Depression is a significant mental health issue among Asian-American women, and Asian-American women have the second highest rate of mortality from suicide. And among women of color over 65, Asian-American women have the highest mortality rate from suicide. Research has shown that social-related anxieties and phobias occur at high rates among Asian-Americans, as well as depression and trauma-related disorders.[35]

Latinas

Some of the barriers Latinas face when seeking help for mental health concerns are that they seek to resolve mental health issues by visiting clergy or medical practitioners instead of mental health professionals. Latinas seeking mental health treatment are also likely to face stigmas, and will probably meet with some reluctance in the community to address mental health issues—fewer than 1 in 11 Latinos with mental concerns contact mental health professionals. But even if Latinas were to seek out a mental health professional, in the American Psychological Association, only 1 percent of licensed psychologists with "active" practices self-identified as Latino.[36] So a Latina may decide to forego mental health treatment, rather than discuss her concerns with someone who may not understand her culture.

Mental health concerns for Latinas include depression and anxiety. There is also a difference in how mental illness affects Latino immigrants: U.S. born and long-term U.S. residents are affected by mental health issues more than Latino immigrants. One study found that among Latinos, "long-term residence in the United States significantly increased rates in mental disorders, with particularly dramatic increases in the rates of substance abuse."[37] Among women of color, Latinas have the highest rates of lifetime depression at 24 percent, but they have a low mortality rate from suicide.

Native American Women

One of the major difficulties in assessing the mental health of Native American or Alaska Native women is that no significant studies have been done on the subject.[38] As a result, the universe of mental health issues Native American women face is not clearly understood. As with Asian-Americans, Native Americans have cultural healing methods that they often use to treat physical and mental health conditions, which may prevent them from seeking care from a mental health professional. This is significant because depression is documented as a significant mental health concern among Native American women, as is suicide. One study in 2000 found that Native American and Alaska Native women up to age 65 had the highest mortality rate from suicide among women of color.[39] This points to the presence of mental health issues in the Native American community, but further research needs to be done to gain a clearer sense of the nature of the mental health issues such women face. Finally, Native American women may also face issues of mistrust of the U.S. medical system because of their sociopolitical history in the United States.

Getting Help

If you are struggling with depression or another mental condition, there are several ways you can get help. Step one is to discuss your concerns with your primary doctor, or to gather basic information about mental health and illnesses on the Internet. A number of Web sites provide background information on mental health issues, and many provide information on mental health providers. Once you are armed with information about your concerns, making an appointment with a licensed mental health practitioner is the next step toward starting the healing process.

> **TIP:** To find mental health professionals who share your ethnicity, visit www.ethniccounselors.org or www.nami.org.

If you want to live life to the fullest, good physical and mental health are key ingredients to developing that life. With a relatively small amount of time and effort, you can make lasting, healthy changes in your life and in the lives of your loved ones. You can start by taking it one day at a time and by meeting with your doctor to discuss your concerns. From there, develop an action plan to get your physical and mental health in top condition, and keep a journal to document any issues you encounter along the way. The process of getting healthy may take time, but your ultimate reward—a good life—is worth it.

For more information on physical and mental health, and advice on contacting healthcare professionals, see appendix D.

Notes

[1] Centers for Disease Control and Prevention. "Physical Activity for Everyone: Components of Physical Fitness," available at www.cdc.gov/nccdphp/dnpa/physical/components/index.htm.

[2] Ibid.

[3] Ibid.

[4] Ibid.

[5] Ibid.

[6] Ibid.

[7] U.S. Department of Health and Human Services. "Physical Activity and Health: A Report of the Surgeon General." Atlanta: U.S. Department of Health and Human Services, Centers for Disease Control and Prevention, National Center for Chronic Disease Prevention and Health Promotion; 1996.

[8] Centers for Disease Control and Prevention. "Physical Activity for Everyone: The Importance of Physical Activity," available at www.cdc.gov/nccdphp/dnpa/physical/importance/index.htm.

[9] University of California at Berkeley. *Foundations of Wellness.* "13 Keys to a Healthy Diet," available at www.wellnessletter.com/html/fw/fwNut01HealthyDiet.html.

[10] Mayo Clinic on the Internet, available at www.mayoclinic.com.

[11] Office on Women's Health/U.S. Department of Health and Human Services. *The Health of Minority Women* (July 2003), 4.

[12] Ibid., 9.

[13] Ibid.

[14] Ibid., 12.

[15] Aetna Intelihealth. "African-American Women's Health," available at www.intelihealth.com.

[16] Office on Women's Health/U.S. Department of Health and Human Services. *The Health of Minority Women* (July 2003), 12.
Aetna Intelihealth. "Asian-American and Pacific Islander Women's Health," available at www.intelihealth.com.

[17] Aetna Intelihealth. "Latina Women's Health," available at www.intelihealth.com.

[18] Office on Women's Health/U.S. Department of Health and Human Services. *The Health of Minority Women* (July 2003), 12.

[19] Ibid.

[20] Aetna Intelihealth. "Native American Women's Health," available at www.intelihealth.com.
National Alliance on Mental Illness/NAMI Multicultural Action Center. "American Indian and Alaska Native Communities Mental Health Facts" (2003).

[21] U.S. Surgeon General. "Mental Health: A Report of the Surgeon General" (Executive Summary).

[22] Ibid.

[23] National Alliance on Mental Illness, available at www.nami.org.

[24] American Psychological Association. "How Does Stress Affect Us?", available at www.apahelpcenter.org/articles/article.php?id=11.

[25] Office on Women's Health/U.S. Department of Health and Human Services, available at www.4women.gov.

[26] National Institute of Mental Health. "What Is a Depressive Disorder?", available at www.nimh.nih.gov.

[27] Ibid.

[28] American Psychological Association. "How Does Stress Affect Us?", available at www.apahelpcenter.org/articles/article.php?id=11.

[29] Ibid.

[30] American Psychological Association. "Mind/Body Health: Stress," available at www.apahelpcenter.org/articles/article.php?id=105.

[31] Office on Women's Health/U.S. Department of Health and Human Services. *The Health of Minority Women* (July 2003), 4.

[32] National Alliance on Mental Illness/NAMI Multicultural Action Center. "African-American Community Mental Health Fact Sheet" (2004). U.S. Department of Health and Human Services.

[33] Office on Women's Health/U.S. Department of Health and Human Services. *The Health of Minority Women* (July 2003), 4.

[34] Ibid.

[35] Ibid., 24.

[36] National Alliance on Mental Illness/NAMI Multicultural Action Center. "Asian-American Community Mental Health Fact Sheet" (2004).

[37] National Alliance on Mental Illness/NAMI Multicultural Action Center. "African American Community Mental Health Fact Sheet" (2004).

[38] National Alliance on Mental Illness/NAMI Multicultural Action Center. "Latino Community Mental Health Facts" (2003).

[39] Office on Women's Health/U.S. Department of Health and Human Services. *The Health of Minority Women* (July 2003), 24.

CHAPTER 12 Off-Track Betting: Careers Beyond the Fast Track

The past decade has seen huge growth in the number of businesses owned by women of color. During this period, the number of businesses owned by women of color increased by 54.6 percent. The number of their employees also increased, by 61.8 percent, and the revenue generated from their companies increased by 73.6 percent. Currently, women of color own 1.4 million businesses in the United States and employ roughly 1.3 million people, with sales revenues close to $147 billion.[1] If you decide to leave corporate America and start your own business, you are not alone.

> **NOTE:** From 1997 to 2004, women of color–owned businesses grew at six times the rate of all U.S. companies.[2]

When women of color decide to move away from the corporate arena, they have many different avenues through which they can pursue their passions: whether entrepreneurship, running a non-profit enterprise, becoming an author, or working as a consultant.

Women of color account for approximately 20 percent of majority women-owned businesses.[3] In their own communities, their progress has been even more significant—women of color now own 36 percent of all businesses owned by people of color. The sales breakdown is as follows:

- Asian-American and Pacific Islander women gross the highest sales at just under $70 billion.

- Latinas have the second-highest sales, with more than $44 billion.

- African-American women have the third-highest sales revenue, with over $19 billion.

- Native American and Alaska Native women have more than $12 billion in sales.[4]

Also, each of these groups of women of color has increased its sales over the past 10 years. In the past decade, Asian-American, Pacific Islander, Native American, and Alaska Native women have increased their sales by 83 percent. Latinas have increased their sales by 62.4 percent, and African-American women by 43.9 percent.[5] Not only are women of color starting businesses, they are starting *successful* businesses.

Why Women of Color Are Leaving Corporate America

A recent study on women (including women of color) entrepreneurs found that women starting companies in the past 10 years were more likely to have held professional or managerial roles than clerical roles before becoming entrepreneurs.[6] A significant number of entrepreneurs are former professionals who have left the ranks of corporate America, and one of the main reasons for their departures is frustration.

Considering the issues women typically face in corporate America generally, it is likely that some of this frustration resulted from "glass ceiling" issues. Of the women who cited the glass ceiling as a reason for their departure, almost half did not believe that their input was "recognized or valued."[7]

In Their Own Words

Aqualyn Laury, founder of AQUA-LYNK Marketing Agency LLC, and a former marketing professional, felt frustration from her career in corporate America, and also felt that her career did not move her any closer to her ultimate purpose in life. "I was not fulfilled by the work and was literally sick of the politics in the remote, renegade worksite (where I worked).... If you're going to endure something, it should return on what you value." Around the same time she found herself pressed for time, and had to make a decision to stay in corporate America or to launch out on her own. "After two and a half years in my position, it was time for my next assignment," she reflects. "My options were to transition to a struggling part of the company in an unhealthy political environment; to move to an undesirable location; or to leave the company. I decided to put my needs first—a rarity for me, and a large percentage of women— and leave the company in search of a better opportunity," she concluded.

Laury also realized that she had other interests that were going unfulfilled—along with 14 percent of other women entrepreneurs who started their business based on a personal interest.[8] "I knew that I was not doing what I was meant to do [in her corporate role]—to affect change in my world. My job wasn't my reason for being, and I would be wasting time to shift to a new workbox with different wrapping paper. Granted, so few of us have jobs that are aligned with our purpose, but the job must at least enable us to move closer to that purpose. It's quite difficult when your values do not reflect your management team's [values]."

In addition to the challenges she felt, Laury also felt the need for a more balanced life: "I desired the flexibility of choosing my work plan...[then] I was motivated to achieve both my professional and personal goals."

But not all women entrepreneurs leave their employers for the same reasons. Plenty of women leave for the same reason that other entrepreneurs do: opportunity, and the realization that they could make a living in their same professional industry—independent of their employers.

NOTE: Among women entrepreneurs with previous experience in the private sector, 51 percent of those starting a company wanted more flexibility in their careers.[9]

According to the survey, some of the women who desired flexibility could be lured back to corporate America by getting that flexibility (11 percent), but 24 percent of women would require additional salary to convince them to return to the corporate lifestyle. But the most telling statistic in the survey is that 58 percent of women who left corporate America to start their own companies said that "nothing" could entice them back to corporate work![10]

Advice for Starting Your Own Company

If you are considering leaving corporate America to start your own company, here are some things that you may want to consider before you begin your transition.

Are You in a Position to Start Your Own Company?

One of your first steps will be to figure out whether you are in a position to start your own company. This is an individual decision, based on your family dynamics and personal considerations. During this process, if you determine that you are well-positioned to start a business, a great first step is to set up a personal support network. You may also want to build additional networks to advise you with your business, but that will factor in a bit later. Initially, you need a handful of your friends, colleagues, and family members who are supportive of your efforts. You might consider sharing a few business matters sporadically with each of them—in this way, you will always have someone to talk to about the business—without the subject taking over every relationship you have.

What Are Your Goals for Your Company?

Once you have made the initial decision to start your own business, it is important to start thinking about your goals for the enterprise. Entrepreneur.com, the Web site for *Entrepreneur* magazine, suggests that new entrepreneurs develop two types of goals: internal and external. Internal goals are those that are specific to you and that you know well, such as financial independence, freedom to be your own boss, satisfaction of a creative streak, and the like. Although you will probably disclose your internal goals with only a few key people, such disclosure can generate interest and support for your company, or at least affect the way your new enterprise is viewed by those close to you.[11] Aqualyn Laury found that "sharing your vision with others inspires them to help you and to live vicariously through you."

External goals are those that affect your customers or consumers and that they should understand, such as the products or services offered by your company—that your company provides high-quality office furniture, for example.[12] Besides letting potential customers know what products and services your firm offers, such goal setting can provide valuable guidelines when you begin setting up your business. Knowing the goal of your enterprise will keep you from getting sidetracked into projects that do not directly impact your mission, and will help you refine your networking or contact list.

Your external goals will also impact the manner and venues in which you market your products or services. If your company plans to provide temporary employee services to law firms, for example, you would probably not advertise your services on the radio or in the newspaper. This is because professional firms tend to frown on publicity—they generally prefer word-of-mouth communication. Instead, you might consider taking out advertisements in legal periodicals or journals, and attending law conferences to advertise your services.

External goals can also impact a financial institution's decision to fund your idea. An amorphous or unclear idea, or one that banks have seen fail many times, can cut short your attempts to get funding. But being experienced in a particular industry can help. A recent study found that women who have recently become business owners, and those with higher sales, tended to have started businesses that were related to their previous occupation.[13] Also, one area that financial institutions consider in their analysis of your company is the management team and amount of experience they hold, individually and collectively, in the relevant industry. Thus, it generally makes sense to start a business in an area in which you (and your partners, if any) are experienced. But having experience in an industry is only part of the equation—an *interest* in the new enterprise is crucial because you will need to log a considerable number of hours to get your new business off the ground.

Get Input

Once you've decided on a business idea, an important next step is testing your idea with others. One way to do this is to get input from people whose opinions you value, and maybe even some people you don't know very well. Entrepreneur.com suggests that budding entrepreneurs set up a focus group to review their new business idea and to provide feedback on it.[14] This focus group could be made up of family, friends, and acquaintances whose judgment you trust, and who are willing to keep private the information that they learn in the focus group. Before convening the group, prepare yourself to accept positive, negative, and constructive feedback about your idea.

> **TIP:** If you are concerned about confidentiality, you can have the focus group members sign a nondisclosure agreement, which will prevent them from sharing any aspect of the focus group meeting (including your business idea) with others.

Another way to get input on your idea before you launch your business is to enlist an executive mentor from the Small Business Administration through their Service Corps of Retired Executives (SCORE) Program. SCORE mentors are retired business executives who can help you think through or make decisions regarding your business, free of charge. They can provide you with valuable advice via e-mail or telephone about your future company.

Depending on the feedback you receive from your focus group and SCORE mentor, you may need to go back and refine your business idea, or you may be ready to move ahead.

Put Together a Business Plan

Once you have received "go-ahead" feedback from your focus group, your next step is to get a sense of what decisions you will need to make to get your company started. Among the decisions are the following:

- The legal structure of your company
- Whether to go it alone or with a partner
- A generous calculation of start-up costs
- Financial projections for the next three to five years
- An approximate timeframe for launching the business
- Hiring employees
- Technology matters
- Space or real estate considerations

In short, you will need to develop a business plan.

Having a solid business plan is critical to the success of your business for a variety of reasons. A business plan requires you to think through the steps of forming and running a business, alerting you to potential difficulties in advance. It can help you clarify your company's mission and goals, and it gives you a format in which to present your idea to potential investors. It also acts as a roadmap once you start your business, providing guidelines, benchmarks, and goals for your operations.

The process of developing a business plan requires a considerable level of detail, which is too broad to include here. If you are considering starting your own business, the following tips may be useful to you.

> **TIP:** The specific regulations for starting a business in each state differ, so it is crucial that you consult with legal, financial, and tax advisors. These advisors should be licensed in your state.

Make Legal, Risk, and Regulatory Decisions

Many of the initial decisions that you make for your business will have legal and risk implications. These decisions range from the legal form you choose for your business, to the products and services that you offer through your company. Because of the importance of these decisions, it is crucial that you initially hire excellent legal counsel licensed in the state where you form your company.

The form of business that you choose for your company is one of the first legal matters that you will need to address. A variety of options exist, depending on the state in which you want to form your business. Some entrepreneurs do not see the need to form a separate business entity when they start out, choosing instead to have a sole proprietorship. In a sole proprietorship, you and your business are legally the same, and you are responsible for its debts and taxes. The biggest risk of using the sole proprietorship form is that any lawsuit filed against the company extends to your personal assets. Still, some entrepreneurs use a sole proprietorship form, preferring the relative ease of setting up the business.

A popular formation option offered by most states is the corporate form; some states offer different types of corporations that are dependent on the size of the business. Among the advantages of corporations are that they are well-established under most state laws, giving the business owner a strong idea of what protections they can expect if the company is sued.

Corporations are separate "legal persons" and provide business owners with protection, so that their assets are not available for payment of company debts, although circumstances do exist in which a business owner's assets may be attached. Investors also like corporations because of the availability of a market to transfer their shares of ownership. Finally, a corporation enjoys perpetual duration, so its existence is independent of the people involved in its formation.

Among the negatives of forming a corporation are the extensive amount of paperwork required to form it, recordkeeping requirements, periodic reporting to the state, and taxation issues, which are sometimes unfavorable (read: double taxation) for the business owner. Professionals, such as doctors, lawyers, and accountants, starting their own businesses often use the professional corporation (PC) form for their business enterprise.

> **TIP:** In addition to sharing the responsibilities of a new enterprise, partnerships receive favorable tax treatment in some states. If you are considering forming a partnership, be sure to consult an experienced tax advisor who is licensed in your state.

A general partnership is an enterprise formed by more than one person and usually governed by a partnership agreement, which specifies the details of the partnership arrangement. Such details include the amount contributed by each partner, management responsibilities, and administrative matters such as how the assets will be divided if the partnership ends.

In Their Own Words

When Aqualyn Laury started her agency, she did not take on a partner, a decision she occasionally revisits. Laury believes that partners can be helpful in shouldering the workload, in addition to sharing the financial burden of a new enterprise. She notes: "You should seek out partners prior to starting the [business] plan—you've never felt guilt like the guilt you feel when you're cheating yourself...when you're unable to deliver everything today because there aren't enough hours, nor is there enough energy no matter how passionate you are...."

One downside to general partnerships is that the partners share personal liability for the financial obligations of the company. To limit this liability between partners, the limited partnership (LP) form was developed, such that individual partners are usually responsible for only their own liabilities—up to the amount they contribute to the partnership. The typical form of a partnership involves a general partner, who runs the operations of the business (and carries the liability), and one or more limited partners, which act as passive investors and are not liable for the debts of the partnership. In cases where all of the partners want to be active in managing the partnership, such as at a law or consulting firm, a limited liability partnership (LLP) form is a good alternative. It allows all partners to participate in the management of the enterprise, while retaining their limited liability.

The limited liability limited partnership (LLLP) is a relatively new phenomenon that exists in several states. The LLLP has attributes of both the LP and the LLP—it has a structure with general and limited partners, and requires limited partners to be inactive with respect to the firm's management. One key difference between the LLLP and the LLP is that in the LLLP, both the general and the limited partners have limited liability with respect to the financial obligations of the enterprise. For more information, you should consult a legal professional regarding the treatment of partnership revenues.

A third option, the limited liability company (LLC) is among the more popular business forms, and is a blend between a corporation and a limited partnership. The LLC is designed to provide the same protection to its owners as a corporation while allowing for the beneficial tax treatment often afforded partnerships. It also has the advantage of being relatively easy to start, although the filing fees may be higher than those required to form a corporation.

In addition to selecting the form of your business, you are likely to need ongoing legal counsel to assist you in certain regulatory matters, such as your business license application, and for other contractual arrangements you may make with independent contractors, employees, or landlords. Legal counsel may also be able to assist you in addressing risk-related issues, such as insurance coverage for your business.

Financial Considerations

Some of the most important components of your business plan are your financial statements, projections, and cost analyses. If you are looking for outside investors, you can expect that banks and other financial institutions will base most of their funding decisions on the information contained in this section of your business plan. Most of your costs can be segmented to fit with the stages of your company's growth, including start-up and operating costs. You will also need to develop a forecast of your future earnings to identify how you expect to pay these business costs.

Start-Up Costs

Start-up costs generally take two forms: business and personal. Personal start-up costs will not be included in your business plan, but will need to be accounted for prior to launching your business. Such costs relate to what it will cost you personally to start the company, including expenses you will incur for the company until it is formed, your time, and the opportunity cost of leaving your current employer, including healthcare and retirement benefits.

Business start-up costs are fairly straightforward and include incorporation fees, legal fees, accounting fees, hardware or software purchases, rent and utilities (if applicable), salary, and administrative costs. One of the most important start-up costs is your personal financial contribution, which will be included in your company's initial financial structure.

> **TIP:** Keep in mind that investors and lenders will give considerable weight to the amount of your financial contribution to the company. After all, if you don't invest a significant amount of money in your own company, why should they?

Operating Costs

Once you have a sense of your personal and business start-up costs, it is time to do more in-depth research into the cost of operating your business over the next several years. This research will involve gathering detailed information on fixed and variable costs. Fixed costs are costs that remain the same no matter how much of the goods or services you provide, such as rent, salary, and administrative costs. Other costs are variable, and change depending on the amount of your output of goods or services, such as the cost of manufacturing or of product materials. Sample business plans can help you get a sense of the cost structure of your enterprise, but you will need to know your own costs first-hand, through research.

One important cost decision you must consider is your own salary. Do you plan to take a large salary and build it into your business plan? Or will you take a smaller salary until the business reaches a certain level of stability? This is an important decision, and whatever your choice, explain it fully in your business plan.

Other overlooked costs are the frequent small expenses that come along with starting a business. Expenses such as photocopying, faxing, and postage arise regularly in the course of business, and until the business gets off the ground, you will probably bear those expenses. Aqualyn Laury cautions entrepreneurs to be prepared to spend money, and to understand that "no matter how much money you have, it's never enough."

> **TIP:** In addition to your initial funding, you may want to set up a slush fund to use for the smaller expenses that occur in the early stages of your business.

Forecasts

After calculating your costs, the next step is to develop projections for your expected revenue, which ideally will exceed your costs. Your revenue calculation is made by multiplying your sales by the amount you charge for your goods or services. Your sales numbers are calculated by estimating the size of your market, and then by estimating the percentage of the market that you expect to purchase your goods or services.

The pricing structure is an important part of your business because it relates directly to your industry competition and places a value (and perception) on your goods or services. Developing a pricing structure requires you to perform considerable research on current market rates or prices for your goods or services. Pricing also involves revenue-generation strategies: Is your company low-cost/high volume (read: discount stores) or high-cost/low volume (read: luxury goods). These decisions will all factor into the price you set for your products or services.

But even the most carefully prepared revenue and expense projections will not necessarily prevent your business from experiencing a shortfall (when expenses exceed revenue) during its first few years of operations. In these cases, you may want to rely on a financing option (or provide your own money) to cover the discrepancy until your business can generate sufficient revenue to fund itself (the break-even point). After the break-even point, the revenue generated by your business will help to increase your profits.

Once you have a full understanding of your start-up and other initial costs, you can use this information to inform your other business decisions, such as whether to take on a partner, or determine the time frame in which to launch your business.

Marketing

Now that you have determined how to finance your company, how do you plan to market it? Successful entrepreneurs know that marketing is essential to the growth of their business—people cannot purchase goods or services of which they are unaware. Also, financial institutions will be very interested in this aspect of your business plan because it gives them an estimate of your potential customer base, and details how your company plans to reach those customers. Your target market and plan to market your company will also be a factor that banks and lenders consider in determining whether your business can earn sufficient income to repay any loans or credit extensions they offer you.

The marketing analysis starts with the smallest unit of a people group (an individual) and broadens to include the entire geographic region you are targeting (a nation). Because of the prevalence of business-to-business companies (firms that do business only with other businesses), our analysis will examine only customers that are individuals or organizations. If your company is targeting individual consumers, you will need to determine the gender, age range, geographic location, and (if relevant) ethnicity of your ideal customer. If your customer is an organization, a similar analysis is necessary, including the size, revenue, geographic location, and number of years of operation for your target organization. Once you know who your target customers are, you will need a sense of how many exist in your target geographic market. You can find these numbers through federal or state agencies such as the U.S. Census Bureau (www.census.gov).

Once you have an idea of the composition of your target market, determine what medium (for example, magazines, flyers, radio, direct mail, and so on) you will use to reach that market with your business information. This decision will be constrained somewhat by your target market and product or service offerings. If you are starting a company that makes hairclips for teenage girls, you might advertise your product through the Internet (for example, myspace.com or facebook.com), flyers around high schools or malls, and for a more visible (and more expensive) option, *Seventeen* magazine. But if your goal is to start an automotive-parts business targeting automobile enthusiasts, you might advertise your company's services through *Auto Trader* or by attending national or regional car shows.

> **TIP:** Publicity, or news stories about your product or service, is an excellent way to increase your visibility. Although publicity can be difficult to generate, it's much less expensive than advertising.

But determining the identity of your target customer and planning the best way to reach them is only half the battle. Your next step is to develop marketing materials to reach these potential customers. And unless you're a marketing expert, you will probably need some assistance. Get to know graphic designers, copywriters, and printing companies; they are important people to know when you are trying to market your business.

Technology

When starting any type of business, you will need to make some decisions about the technology you plan to use in your business operations. This technology may include computers, software, telephones, or audiovisual equipment. A large part of these decisions depends on the logistics of your company. But it is probably a good idea to develop a comprehensive technology plan; you can scale it back to suit your needs and budget. Among your considerations will be networking solutions (LAN or wireless), the number and style of computers (laptop or desktop), firewall and antivirus software, accounting or financial software, and e-mail and word-processing programs. You may also need to address wiring and related concerns, along with telephone and voice-mail issues.

If your business is home-based, you may be able to use your preexisting technology—assuming it is reasonably current and functional. Even so, you may still want to do some research on technological options and build them into your business plan in case you decide to upgrade later.

Office Space

The degree to which you need to address office space or real-estate issues depends in large part on the type of business you are starting. Technology companies, for example, are notorious for starting out in garages, a much lower-cost option. Freelance writers can probably set up shop at home. But if you are starting a business that needs customized space (for example, an automotive company or restaurant), you will need to pay careful attention to real-estate issues.

One way to start out is to talk with real-estate professionals to get a better sense of what your estimated expenses will be.

For many start-up companies, real estate is simply too expensive to be an option. But some useful alternatives to renting office space do exist in the form of virtual offices. A virtual office consists of a physical office space with a receptionist, conference rooms, voice-mail boxes, mail pickup, and related services. Individuals or companies pay a modest fee (around $99 to $299) to use the office services on a monthly basis. The virtual receptionist (a real person) will answer calls with your company name and can forward the calls to your telephone line (for an additional fee) or send them to a provided voice-mail box. For entrepreneurs starting a business that requires phone coverage, the virtual office option is an efficient and cost-effective way to establish a professional presence.

Starting a home-based business is undoubtedly the most cost-effective option, and if your business lends itself to such an arrangement, it can be very beneficial to your income statement as you start your business. Also, because some tax breaks exist for home-based businesses, you may want to consult with a tax professional to determine whether you can write off any of your home office expenses.

Minority and Women-Owned Certifications

Supplier diversity programs, which include minority and women business owners, have increased their budgets considerably over the past decade. Many major corporations routinely spend in excess of $700 million annually for goods and services from diverse suppliers. But to partner with a major corporation's supplier diversity program, your business must be formally recognized as a diverse supplier by a third-party certification as a minority or woman-owned business, or both.

The National Minority Supplier Development Council (NMSDC), through its regional council, certifies businesses that are majority-owned by a member of one of the following ethnic groups: African-American, Asian-American, Latino, or Native American. The NMSDC has certified more than 15,000 minority-owned businesses, and has also matched them with 3,500 corporations nationwide—including many well-known companies—through its regional meetings.

The Women's Business Enterprise National Council (WBE) certifies businesses that are majority-owned by women (51 percent or more) through its partner organizations in the United States. Currently, more than 700 companies accept the WBE certification, and many federal and state government agencies also accept them, giving an opportunity to certified entrepreneurs to provide services to the largest consumer in the United States: the federal government.

The good news for women of color: If you own 51 percent or more of your company, you can receive NMSDC *and* WBE certifications because you are both an ethnic minority and a woman. These certifications can greatly assist your business in getting on the radar of major companies and federal and state governments through their supplier diversity programs.

Your Action Plan

Once you have developed a complete business plan, you can use that plan as a basis to create your business action plan. A business action plan serves to make your business plan more of a working document, and keeps it updated with your progress, decisions, and achievements. This document will serve as a to-do list, a reminder of decisions made but not implemented, and will celebrate the successes you have achieved. Most importantly, your business action plan allows you to see the progress you are making on your business plan and to spot potential changes down the road, affording you the ability to adjust your plan accordingly.

After getting a handle on your business and action plans, a larger decision looms—whether you should leave your employer immediately to start your business, or whether you should begin to phase in your new idea by working full-time and starting your business on the side. If you decide to stay on with your employer while starting your business, it is important that you understand and comply with your company's policy on dual employment, and find out whether your business idea triggers that policy. Once you have the go-ahead to form your company, it is essential that you are well-organized to ensure that you do not allow the demands of either position to overlap with the other.

In Their Own Words

Before leaving her former employer, Aqualyn Laury did some diligence of her own—within her company. "I searched the job postings, including the headhunter's e-mails, and couldn't locate anything that I was truly passionate about. I knew that I was supposed to chart my own way—it's how I was wired. I took the opportunity to make a few major life decisions, including moving closer to my family to fulfill both my professional and personal aspirations."

But Laury also notes that all entrepreneurs do not have to take such a large risk early on, and that an entrepreneur who is "clear about her objectives and all of the [ways to reach them]...may not have to leave [her employer] to achieve [those] objectives."

If your company will be formed in your current industry, you may want to use your lunch or other breaks to build relationships with people who may have an interest in using your product or services after you leave. Laury advises women of color to "understand [their] company's hiring practices for contract work, and work those relationships." Although you might not divulge your future business plans, it might be a good idea to get a sense of your employer's interest level in your products or services—of course, that also means that you must leave your employer *on good terms* in order to benefit from that relationship.

If you decide to leave your employer and launch your business venture, be prepared to negotiate your severance package, benefits, and other related issues that may arise. "Negotiate everything," advises Laury, and because of the importance of access to healthcare, she notes that women of color should be sure to "find a healthcare solution prior to leaving or negotiate with [your] employer about extended health benefits." Of course, negotiating the financial terms of your departure is important to your life and future success as an entrepreneur; women of color who want to negotiate well should consider reading some of the business books on negotiation—especially those focused on negotiating strategies for women. This preparation will help women of color to negotiate well with their employers, while preserving a potential future client relationship.

> **TIP:** Women of color have heightened susceptibility to a number of diagnosable conditions. Having healthcare coverage provides a greater likelihood that a potentially fatal disease can be detected early. So don't be tempted to let your coverage lapse.

Resources for Entrepreneurs

If you are an aspiring entrepreneur, plenty of resources are available to help you start, build, and eventually grow your business. The good news is that one of the best resources for new entrepreneurs won't cost you much at all: people who have already started their own companies. If you are fortunate enough to have such people in your circle of friends or acquaintances, it's a good idea to take the time to meet with them, and to get their thoughts and insights on starting a new venture. The only cost to you would be a cup of coffee or the price of lunch.

In addition to other entrepreneurs, it is generally a good idea to build a network of professional colleagues and acquaintances in your industry. When starting her marketing agency, Aqualyn Laury found it helpful to join industry-related organizations and other groups for professional women. She also attended annual conferences where she could add people to her network. Other ways to build your network include the following:

- **Professors:** Get back in touch with your former professors from undergraduate, graduate, or professional school (whichever is most recent). Because of their expertise, professors are great resources for industry research. Professors often have broad networks, and may be able to connect you with other academics and industry professionals in your geographic area. They can also provide you with excellent advice as you work through the logistics of your business plan.

- **Alumni associations:** Joining your alumni organization is a good idea—especially if you went to business school for your undergraduate or graduate degree. Many influential business schools have clubs in major cities such as New York; Washington, D.C.; Chicago; and others. If you are an alumna of a school that has a city club, by all means take advantage of the opportunity to network with your former classmates and make the acquaintance of potential clients and colleagues.

- **Chambers of Commerce:** Another place to build your network is your local chamber of commerce. Chamber events are a good place to meet other entrepreneurs, who are an excellent source of wisdom for new business owners. Some cities also have ethnic-specific chambers of commerce, where you can network with more business owners and get additional exposure for your company.

While you are building your informal networks, you can also learn useful information to help your new business from business books and periodicals. Magazines such as *Inc.* and *Entrepreneur* are geared specifically toward budding entrepreneurs and small-business owners, whereas *BusinessWeek* and the *Wall Street Journal* help to inform your perspective on the business world generally. Many of the articles in *BusinessWeek* and the *Wall Street Journal* are informative, as well as good discussion topics for business-related events.

One of the chief benefits of starting your own company is the ability to be your own boss and to chart the course for your life. If you find a corporate career that allows you these same freedoms, you may very well want to continue your ascent up the corporate ladder. If you have decided that the corporate life is no longer for you, know that many other women of color have gone before you into the entrepreneurial unknown—and have been very successful. The choice is yours.

Notes

[1]Center for Women's Business Research. *Businesses Owned by Women of Color in the United States, 2004: A Fact Sheet* (2004), 1–2.

[2]Ibid.

[3]A majority women-owned business is one in which 51 percent or more of the company is owned by a woman.

[4]*Businesses Owned by Women of Color,* 4.

[5]Ibid.

[6]Committee of 200. Summary of "Paths to Entrepreneurship: New Directions for Women in Business," a study by the Center for Women's Business Research (February 24, 1998). Available at www.c200.org.

[7]Ibid.

[8]Ibid.

[9]Ibid.

[10]Ibid.

[11]Wolter, Romanus. "Countdown to Startup." Entrepreneur.com (June 22, 2005), available at www.entrepreneur.com.

[12]Ibid.

[13]"Paths to Entrepreneurship," see note 4.

[14]"Countdown to Startup," see note 11.

Appendices

Appendix A: Discussion Questions

Appendix B: Additional Reading on Professional Women of Color

Appendix C: Business, Professional, and Civic Organizations

Appendix D: Internet Resources

Appendix E: Diversity Resources for Companies

Appendix F: Selected Research, Books, and Papers on Women of Color in Business

Appendix G: Leadership Development Programs and Conferences

APPENDIX A   Discussion Questions

These discussion questions are intended to facilitate reflection on and discussion of the challenges faced by professional women of color. The questions can be used in group or individual settings, for book clubs, in classroom discussions, or just for personal reflection.

1. **Do you feel like a "double outsider" at work?** What specific interactions or experiences make you feel that way? Are there ever times at work when you feel like an "insider"?

2. **What stereotypes do you have about other women of color?** Did you realize that you were holding these biases? What steps can you take to overcome these feelings?

3. **What are some of the challenges you face at home and at work?** Are these challenges unique to women in your culture, or are they challenges that women face generally?

4. **What are some of the challenges that other women of color (outside your ethnicity) face at work?** Have you witnessed a situation where you thought another woman of color was being treated unfairly at work? What was your reaction?

5. **What kinds of relationships do you have with men of your ethnicity at work?** Are these relationships supportive of you, or do you find them to be burdensome?

6. **Do you feel like your colleagues notice "every little thing" that you do?** Do you sometimes feel "singled out," as if you are being treated differently than your coworkers?

7. **How do you avoid internalizing the challenges you face at work?** What are some of your confidence boosters? How do you work through difficult periods at the office?

8. **Does your culture or religion require you to wear certain attire at work?** Do colleagues seem understanding, or does it feel as if they resent you or are uncomfortable?

9. **Do you think your company's diversity initiatives adequately address issues that women of color face?** If not, what are some steps you can take at work to raise this awareness?

10. **Would you consider working with other women of color at your company to develop a women of color employee network?** Why or why not? What do you think are some of the challenges you might face?

APPENDIX B
Additional Reading on Professional Women of Color

Black Power Inc.: The New Voice of Success by Cora Daniels (John Wiley & Sons, Incorporated, 2004)

Book of Latina Women: 145 Vidas of Passion, Strength, and Success by Sylvia Mendoza (Adams Media Corporation, 2004)

Breaking the Bamboo Ceiling: Career Strategies for Asians by Jane Hyun (HarperCollins Publishers, 2005)

Cracking the Corporate Code: The Revealing Success Stories of 32 African-American Executives by Price M. Cobbs and Judith Turnock (AMACOM, 2003)

Dear Sisters, Dear Daughters: Words of Wisdom from Multicultural Women Attorneys Who've Been There and Done That by Karen Clanton (American Bar Association, 2000)

La Vida Rica: The Latina's Guide to Success by Yrma Rico and Nancy Garascia (McGraw-Hill, 2004)

Latina Power!: Using 7 Strengths You Already Have to Create the Success You Deserve by Ana Nogales and Laura Golden Bellotti (Fireside, 2003)

Leading in Black and White: Working Across the Racial Divide in Corporate America by Ancella B. Livers and Keith A. Caver (Jossey-Bass, 2002)

Minority Rules: Turn Your Ethnicity into a Competitive Edge by Kenneth Arroyo Roldan and Gary M. Stern (HarperCollins Publishers, 2006)

Our Separate Ways: Black and White Women and the Struggle for Professional Identity by Ella L. J. Edmondson Bell and Stella M. Nkomo (Harvard Business School Press, 2001)

Shifting: The Double Lives of Black Women in America by Charisse Jones and Kumea Shorter-Gooden (HarperCollins Publishers, 2004)

Vault Guide to Conquering Corporate America: For Women and Minorities by Patricia Kao and Susan Tien (Vault Inc., 2003)

APPENDIX C

Business, Professional, and Civic Organizations

This list is not exhaustive, but is intended to provide information on major national organizations and select local organizations. Please visit each organization's Web site for program and membership information.

Business Organizations for Women of Color

Asian Women Leadership
Network
www.awln.org

Indus Women Leaders
www.induswomenleaders.org

Las Madrinas (Latina)
www.madrinas.org

South Asian Women's Forum
www.sawf.org

South Asian Women's
Leadership Forum
www.southasianwomen.org

South Asian Women's NETwork
www.sawnet.org

Business-Related Organizations for Minority Professionals

Asian-American Journalists
Association
www.aaja.org

Executive Leadership Council
(African-American)
www.elcinfo.com

Hispanic Association on
Corporate Responsibility
www.hacr.org

Minority Corporate Counsel
Association
www.mcca.com

National Association of Asian American Professionals
www.naaap.org

National Association of Black Journalists
www.nabj.org

National Association of Hispanic Journalists
www.nahj.org

National Black MBA Association
www.nbmbaa.org

National Society of Hispanic MBAs
www.nshmba.org

Network of Indian Professionals of North America (South Asian)
www.netip.org

NextGen Network, Inc. (African-American)
www.nextgennetwork.com

Unity: Journalists of Color, Inc.
www.unityjournalists.org

Business-Related Organizations for Women

Athena International
www.athenafoundation.org

Board of Directors Network, Inc.
www.boarddirectorsnetwork.org

The Boston Club
www.thebostonclub.com

Business and Professional Women/USA
www.bpwusa.org

Catalyst
www.catalyst.org

The Chicago Network
www.thechicagonetwork.org

The Committee of 200
www.c200.org

The Commonwealth Institute
www.commonwealthinstitute.org

Financial Women's Association
www.fwa.org

The Forum of Executive Women
www.foew.com

Forum for Women Entrepreneurs & Executives
www.fwe.org

InFORUM
www.inforummichigan.org

Milwaukee Women inc.
www.milwaukeewomeninc.org

National Association for Female Executives
www.nafe.com

National Association of Women MBAs
www.mbawomen.org

Women Executive Leadership
www.womenexecutiveleadership.com

APPENDIX D

Internet Resources

Business-Related Resources

BusinessWeek
www.businessweek.com

DiversityInc Magazine Online
www.diversityinc.com

Fortune Magazine
www.fortune.com

HireDiversity.com
www.hirediversity.com

Hispanic Business Magazine
Online
www.hispanicbusiness.com

Hispanic Publishing Group
Online
www.hispaniconline.com

The Network Journal
www.tnj.com

Profiles in Diversity Journal
Online
www.diversityjournal.com

Culture and Heritage-Related Resources

African

American Legacy Magazine
www.americanlegacymag.com

Bahiya Magazine
http://bwmmag.com/magazine

Black Woman and Child
http://nubeing.com/bwac

Essence Magazine
www.essence.com

Heart & Soul
www.heartandsoul.com

Mocha Moms
www.mochamoms.org

Nia Online
www.niaonline.com

Onyx Woman
www.onyxwoman.com

Latina

Latina Magazine
www.latina.com

Latina Style
www.latinastyle.com

The Latina Voz
www.thelatinavoz.com

Asian

Asian Woman Magazine
www.asianwomanmag.com

Asiance Magazine
www.asiancemagazine.com

Audrey Magazine
www.audreymagazine.com

Hyphen Magazine
www.hyphenmagazine.com

Jade Magazine
www.jademagazine.com

Native American

Indians.org
www.indians.org/articles/
native-american-women.html

Indigenous Women's Network
www.indigenouswomen.org

Institute for the Advancement
of Aboriginal Women
www.iaaw.ca

Native American Rhymes
http://nativeamericanrhymes
.com/women/index.htm

Native Culture Links
www.nativeculturelinks.com/
indians.html

Native Web
www.nativeweb.org

South Asian

Divanee Magazine
www.divanee.com

iStyle Magazine
www.istylemagazine.com

Monsoon Magazine
www.monsoonmag.com

Nirali Magazine
http://niralimagazine.com

South Asian Life
www.southasianlife.com

Middle Eastern

Arab Women's Court
www.arabwomencourt.org

Araboo
www.araboo.com/dir/
arabic-women

Avaye Zan (Iranian Women's
Voice)
http://tvs.se/womensvoice

Center for Arab Women
Training and Research
www.cawtar.org

Middle East Online
www.middle-east-online.com

Persian Mirror
www.persianmirror.com

Multicultural

MAVIN Foundation
www.mavinfoundation.org

Métisse
www.metisse.com

The Multiracial Activist
www.multiracial.com

National Advocacy for the
Multi-Ethnic
www.namecentral.org

Swirl
www.swirlinc.org

All
OneWorld.Net
http://us.oneworld.net

WomenOne
www.womenone.org

Health and Wellness Resources

American Diabetes Association
www.diabetes.org

American Dietetic Association
www.eatright.org

American Heart Association
www.americanheart.org

Ethnic Counselors
www.ethniccounselors.com

National Alliance on Mental
Illness
www.nami.org

U.S. Department of Health and
Human Services—Office on
Women's Health
www.4woman.gov/minority

U.S. Federal Government
Nutrition
www.nutrition.gov

APPENDIX E

Diversity Resources for Companies

Books

Building on the Promise of Diversity: How We Can Move to the Next Level in Our Workplaces, Our Communities, and Our Society by R. Roosevelt Thomas. AMACOM, 2005.

Creating the Multicultural Organization: A Strategy for Capturing the Power of Diversity by Taylor Cox, Jr. Jossey-Bass, 2001.

Harvard Business Review on Managing Diversity, by R. Roosevelt Thomas, David A. Thomas, Robin J. Ely, and Debra Meyerson. Harvard Business School Press, 2002.

The Inclusion Breakthrough by Frederick A. Miller and Judith H. Katz. Berrett-Koehler, 2002.

Leading in Black and White: Working Across the Racial Divide in Corporate America by Ancella B. Livers and Keith A. Caver. Jossey-Bass, 2002.

Micromessaging: Why Great Leadership Is Beyond Words by Stephen Young. McGraw-Hill, 2006.

Motivating Hispanic Employees: A Practical Guide to Understanding and Managing Hispanic Employees by Carlos A. Conejo. Multicultural Press, 2001.

Periodicals/Web Sites

Diversity Inc.
www.diversityinc.com

The Multicultural Advantage
www.multiculturaladvantage.com

Profiles in Diversity Journal
www.diversityjournal.com

Conferences and Institutes

The Johnetta B. Cole Global Diversity and Inclusion Institute
at Spelman College
www.jbcinstitute.org

Society for Human Resource Management (SHRM) Workplace
Diversity Conference & Exposition
www.shrm.org/conferences/diversity/

Spelman College Women of Color Conference
www.spelmanwomenofcolorconf.com

Working Mother Best Companies for Women of Color
Multicultural Conference
www.workingmothermediainc.com

APPENDIX F

Selected Research, Books, and Papers on Women of Color in Business

Academy of Management Perspectives

http://journals.aomonline.org/amp/

"The Pipeline to the Top: Women and Men in the Top Executive Ranks of U.S. Corporations"

Catalyst

www.catalyst.org

2005 Catalyst Census of Women Board Directors of the Fortune 500

2005 Catalyst Census of Women Corporate Officers and Top Earners of the Fortune 500

Advancing African-American Women in the Workplace: What Managers Need to Know

Advancing Asian Women in the Workplace: What Managers Need to Know

Advancing Latinas in the Workplace: What Managers Need to Know

Connections that Count: The Informal Networks of Women of Color in the United States

Different Cultures, Similar Perceptions: Stereotyping of Western European Business Leaders

Leaders in a Global Economy: A Study of Executive Women and Men

Passport to Opportunity: U.S. Women in Global Business

Women of Color Executives: Their Voices, Their Journeys

Women of Color in Corporate Management: Three Years Later

Women "Take Care," Men "Take Charge": Stereotyping of U.S. Business Leaders Exposed

Center for Women's Business Research
www.cfwbr.org

Businesses Owned by Women of Color in the United States

The Spirit of Enterprise: Latina Entrepreneurs in the U.S.

Women Business Owners of Color: New Accomplishments; Continuing Challenges

Center for Gender in Organizations at the Simmons School of Management
www.simmons.edu/som/centers/cgo

"Complicating Gender: The Simultaneity of Race, Gender, and Class in Organization Change"

"Disappearing Acts: Gender, Power, and Relational Practice at Work"

"How Do I Talk to You, My White Sister?"

"Reader in Gender, Work, and Organization"

"Releasing the Double Bind of Visibility for Minorities in the Workplace"

"Simultaneity and the Limits of Sisterhood in One Women's Membership Organization"

"Tempered Radicalism Revisited: Black and White Women Making Sense of Black Women's Enactments and White Women's Silences"

"'Tired of Choosing': Working with the Simultaneity of Race, Gender, and Class in Organizations"

"Women in Organizations: Why Our Differences Matter and What to Do About It"

"Working with Diversity: A Focus on Global Organizations"

Center for Women Policy Studies
www.centerwomenpolicy.org

Defining Work and Family Issues: Listening to the Voices of Women of Color

Making the Case for Affirmative Action: Women of Color in Corporate America

No More "Business as Usual": Women of Color in Corporate America—Report of the National Women of Color Work/Life Survey

Center for Work-Life Policy
www.worklifepolicy.org

"Executive Women and the Myth of Having It All"

Global Multicultural Executives and the Talent Pipeline

The Hidden Brain Drain: Off-Ramps and On-Ramps in Women's Careers

Invisible Lives: Celebrating and Leveraging Diversity in the Executive Suite

"Leadership in Your Midst: Tapping the Hidden Strengths of Minority Executives"

"Off-Ramps and On-Ramps: Keeping Talented Women on the Road to Success"

Corporate Women Directors International
www.globewomen.com/cwdi/colloquium03.asp

Latin Trade 100: Key Findings; Women Board Directors of the Latin Trade 100 Companies

Women Board Directors of the Fortune Global 200 Companies

Women Board Directors of the Largest Global and U.S. Banks

Women Board Directors of the Largest Healthcare and Pharmaceutical Companies

Women Board Directors of California's Fortune 1000 Companies and Financial Institutions

Women Board Directors of South Africa's Top Companies

Women Board Directors of Spain's Top Companies

Women Board Directors of Texas' Fortune 1000 Companies and Financial Institutions

Network of Executive Women

www.newonline.org

Women of Color: The Challenge and Opportunity Ahead

APPENDIX G Leadership Development Programs and Conferences

Leadership Development Programs

Center for Creative Leadership (www.ccl.org)

- Leadership Development Program
- The Women's Leadership Program
- The Looking Glass Experience

Leader's Edge: Leading Up for Women of Color
(www.the-leaders-edge.com)

UCLA Anderson School of Management (www.uclaexeced.com)

- African-American Leadership Institute
- Latino Leadership Institute
- Women's Leadership Institute

Conferences for Women of Color

Essence Magazine's Women Who Are Shaping the World:
www.essence.com/essence/summit

Spelman College's Women of Color Conference:
www.spelmanwomenofcolorconf.com

National Women of Color Technology Awards Conference:
www.womenofcolor.net/v2/index.php

Working Mother Media's Best Companies for Women of Color
Multicultural Conference:
http://events.workingmother.com/wocreg/conference.html **265**

Other Conferences for Minority Professionals

National Association of Asian American Professionals National Convention: www.naaap.org/NAT/convention.asp

National Black MBA Association Annual Conference: www.nbmbaa.org/annual_conference.cfm

National Society of Hispanic MBAs Annual Conference: www.nshmba.org/conference2007/

Network of Arab-American Professionals Annual Conference: www.naaponline.org

Network of South Asian Professionals: www.netip.org

INDEX